To Anne
With all
[signature]

May 2019

Breaking the Mould of Christendom

Kingdom Community, Diaconal Church and the Liberation of the Laity

Second Edition

An environmentally friendly book printed and bound in England by
www.printondemand-worldwide.com

Mixed Sources
Product group from well-managed
forests, and other controlled sources
www.fsc.org Cert no. TT-COC-002641
© 1996 Forest Stewardship Council
FSC

PEFC
PEFC/16-33-415

PEFC Certified
This product is
from sustainably
managed forests
and controlled
sources
www.pefc.org

This book is made entirely of chain-of-custody materials

Second edition

This second edition of *Breaking the Mould of Christendom* is being published because the first edition continues to sell well. As the Epworth Press, the original publisher, has now closed, it is being printed by FastPrint Publishing, Peterborough. The book now takes its place as a companion volume to *The Kingdom at Work Project* (2014), also printed by FastPrint Publishing.

David Clark
Bakewell, Derbyshire
December 2014

Commendations

In times of crisis, prophets appear in the church. David Clark is such a prophet. His book brilliantly analyses the mission of the church in contemporary life presenting a vision of a church for the world which is full of the spirit of Jesus Christ. The contrast Clark draws between the Christendom church and the diaconal church is highly significant for the British churches just now, and presents a vision of renewal and hope not only for the church but for a suffering world.

John Hull - Emeritus Professor of Religious Education at the University of Birmingham and Honorary Professor of Practical Theology in the Queen's Foundation for Ecumenical Theological Education, Birmingham

-----

David Clark offers an arresting portrayal of 'the diaconal church' that deserves to become a key text for those who are concerned about issues around faith and life ministries in the world. His thoughtful and perceptive insights, born out of hands-on experience of facilitating the engagement of church and world over many years, lifts the debate about 'the liberation of the laity' to a new level. His unique vision of the church as the servant of 'the kingdom community' is of immense importance to those on this side of the Atlantic who are seeking to discern the future for the church.

Sally Simmel - Former Director of 'Ministry in Daily Life' for the Evangelical Lutheran Church in America for seventeen years and former President of the Coalition for Ministry in Daily Life in the USA

In this ground-breaking text, David Clark provides a comprehensive vision of church and ministry from a diaconal perspective. He challenges Christians to convert their institutions and practices to support a diaconal vision of the church as the servant of 'the kingdom community'. A fundamental theological insight and ideal, so old and yet so new, so familiar yet so radical, is here given new life and grip.

Stephen Pattison - Professor of Religion, Ethics and Practice at the University of Birmingham

-----

David Clark challenges all Christians, and not least deacons, to make a Copernican shift in their understanding of diaconal mission. Too frequently the discussion leaps from the servant church to the diaconate as exemplifying it. David Clark argues that it is first and foremost the laity, not deacons, who are called to represent the servant church in the world. The deacon's all-important task is to raise the awareness of lay people to that calling and help them fulfil it. The book addresses urgent questions about the self-understanding, practice and formation of the diaconate. It is a must-read for deacons worldwide.

Sue Jackson - Formerly Warden of the Methodist Diaconal Order in the UK

Breaking the Mould
of Christendom

Second Edition

Kingdom Community, Diaconal Church
and the Liberation of the Laity

David Clark

www.fast-print.net/store.php

BREAKING THE MOULD OF CHRISTENDOM
Kingdom Community, Diaconal Church and the Liberation of the Laity

Second Edition
Copyright © David Clark 2015

A catalogue record for this book is available from the British Library

ISBN 978-178456-156-7

First Published 2005 by Epworth
This edition published 2015 by
Fastprint Publishing of Peterborough, England.

Contents

CONTENTS

To Sue, Peter and Kirsten,
very special fellow travellers

Foreword

It is unusual to be given the opportunity to look back over one's life's work and to try and bring together one's experiences, thinking and earlier writings into some kind of coherent whole. So I am very grateful to Natalie Watson, the Commissioning Editor of Epworth Press, for having had the courage to allow me to do just that.

This book describes a journey that began when I first thought that becoming a Methodist minister was where God wanted me to be. I was a Methodist because my parents had always been deeply involved in the life and work of the Methodist Church. But I entered the Methodist ministry in the 1960s with an awareness, even then, that we were on the threshold of an era of immense changes which would call in question much that as a young person I had taken for granted about the church. So it was perhaps not surprising that within a few years of being ordained, I found myself launched on a journey that, in a half-autobiographical book I wrote in 1987, I described as a search for 'the kingdom community'. I had by then come to recognize that the coming of the kingdom was what being a Christian was all about and that the church was thus a 'diaconal church', the servant of that kingdom or nothing.

My journey has taken me onto the edge of one city, Sheffield, and into the heart of another, London, out of the institutional church into teaching and lecturing, brought me into contact with a host of small and innovative Christian communities in Britain and the United States, involved me in getting several hundred people to write about their vision for the church's contribution to the public life of our society, and driven me to try and find ways of making one great city, Birmingham, a bit more human.

Throughout that journey my question has always been, what does the kingdom look like and how can the church serve it more faithfully? I have no fear for the future of the church, because the kingdom it serves is for ever and that is all that matters. But I am saddened that our preoccupation with the church, and not least the church that we have inherited from

Christendom, can often lead us to miss out on recognizing the gifts of the kingdom constantly on offer, celebrating these and sharing them with others.

This book is about a journey begun, not finished. If, as I believe, the kingdom is a learning community, then we who belong to the church are also learners. What divides us as Christians is not our denominational loyalties, but whether we see Christian faith as a journey of discovery or 'a closed book'. So for me the journey continues, out of the Methodist ministry as a presbyter into the Methodist Diaconal Order with 'L' plates on again. The great joy of such a journey is that it brings a new community and new friends.

I hope that the reflections in this book on my still continuing journey will not be seen as any attempt to lay down a blueprint for the future, but as a means of enabling others to share my search for the kingdom community and, through that, stimulating them to share their journey with others.

Sections of this book have gone out for comment to some of those with whom I have shared my search for the kingdom over many years. I am very grateful to Phil Aspinall, Martyn Atkins, Peter Challen, David Gardner, Sue Jackson, Chris Lawson, Stuart Murray, Sally Simmel, Maurice Staton and John Munsey Turner for their very thoughtful criticisms. However, I take personal responsibility for all that appears in the text.

One final word of thanks goes to Sue, my wife, who has read this book with great care and helped me to revise much of what would otherwise have been far less readable than hopefully is now the case.

David Clark
Bakewell, Derbyshire
July 2005

Introduction

This book is about how the church can fulfil its mission in a new era. The book has six main themes. First and foremost is our belief that in this new millennium our world faces a momentous choice: that of 'community or chaos'. Humankind has always faced this choice, but we have now acquired, as never before in human history, the means to destroy both ourselves and our planet. If we do not discover how to live together as a global community then the future looks bleak. However, ours is a time of 'crisis' in the Chinese sense of the word (*wei ji*). It is a time of potential calamity, yet also of great hope. If we choose community and commit ourselves to work together to build it, then humankind will not only survive but flourish.

The book's second theme is 'the kingdom community'. We believe that the image of 'the kingdom' refers not only to the sovereignty of God, but to all those living in accordance with his purposes. God's kingdom is a kingdom *community*. We see its gifts to humankind as *life, liberation, love* and *learning*. Thus, the kingdom community is a *learning* community, the zenith of all learning communities. The kingdom community is omnipresent throughout our world, though it is still to come in its fullness. We are called to seek it out, learn from it and use its gifts with thankfulness.

Our third theme is 'the diaconal church'. We believe that God is now calling his church, as he has always called it, to be the servant (*diakonos*) of the kingdom community. It is thus a *servant* church: 'a diaconal church'. As such, it is called to make manifest the gifts of the kingdom community within its own life. It is called to bring into being communities that, in their turn, manifest the gifts of the kingdom community. And it is called to enable humankind to discern, comprehend and receive those gifts.

Our fourth theme is 'breaking the mould of Christendom'. We believe that the diaconal church is unable to serve the kingdom community because it is held captive by a Christendom model of church that is now obsolete yet still all-pervasive. We are convinced that the mould of Christendom has to be broken if the diaconal church is to be able to offer the gifts of the kingdom community to a world facing a stark choice between community and chaos.

Our fifth theme is 'the liberation of the laity', those who make up the vast majority of the diaconal church. We believe that the calling of the laity is to be the servants of the kingdom community. In that capacity, their task is to be *community builders*, empowered by and offering to others the gifts of the kingdom community. But they too are held captive by the legacy of Christendom. Until they are liberated to fulfil their ministry as community builders, the diaconal church will not come into being and there will be little to offer to a world in crisis.

Our sixth theme is 'a renewed diaconate'. We believe that a renewed diaconate has a vital leadership role to play in the life of the diaconal church. A renewed diaconate's primary task is to be *community educators*, equipping the laity to fulfil their calling to build communities that manifest the gifts of the kingdom community. We believe that through the fulfilment of this task, the liberation of the laity and, thereby, the coming into being of the diaconal church will be accomplished.

How did this book come to be written?

This book comes out of my search, over many years, to learn about the nature of the kingdom community and how the church can serve it more faithfully. From 1962 to 1973 I worked as a Methodist minister, first in Woodhouse on the outskirts of Sheffield and then in West Greenwich, London. In 1973, as a 'sector minister', I took up the post of senior lecturer in community and youth work at Westhill College, Birmingham, a Free Church foundation and member of the Selly Oak Colleges' Federation. From the early 1980s until I retired from the staff of Westhill College in 1997, the focus of my work was the field of community education. I was Director of the Human City Institute from 1997 until 2000.

Throughout my ministry, I have been acutely aware that the church has been struggling to find its way amid a maelstrom of change. For me, the issue has never been how we can arrest the church's numerical decline (which is clearly not a problem outside western society), but what the church has to offer to a civilization that will eventually destroy itself if it fails to become a global community of communities. My way of addressing that issue has been through a series of action research projects (Part 3), some lasting a decade or more. I have documented many of these initiatives in books or articles (see Bibliography).

Over the course of my ministry, a number of things have become clear to me. I now believe that the church has no reason to stay in business unless it recognizes that it is called to be the servant of the kingdom community. I believe that the church cannot fulfil this calling until it assumes a radically different form (that of the diaconal church) from that which has dominated the scene over the many centuries of Christendom. I believe that putting the laity as community builders at the heart of the church's mission is crucial for the transformation of church and world alike. And I believe that a new understanding of the leadership of the church, in particular of the role of deacon, is imperative.

The role of deacon is one that I have increasingly felt that I have been fulfilling throughout most of my ministry, though I would not have described it in that way until now. In recent years, my growing awareness of the diaconal nature of my ministry, and the Methodist Church's developing understanding of the nature of the diaconate, have come very close together. This has led me, even if somewhat late in the day, to bring my time as a presbyter to a close and to offer for the Methodist Diaconal Order. I was inducted into that Order at the Methodist Conference in June 2005.

An outline of the book

Part 1 explores the nature of the kingdom community.

Chapter 1 examines why the quest for community is now urgent. We argue that because this quest has to be pursued in an ever-changing world, the communities we seek to build must be learning communities.

Chapter 2 discusses the meaning of community from a sociological and a theological point of view, using that analysis to develop the image of the kingdom community and to identify its Trinitarian gifts.

Chapter 3 looks at the meaning of learning from an educational and a theological perspective. We argue that the kingdom community is the epitome of all learning communities.

Chapter 4 explores the form of leadership needed to help build human communities that are transformed by the gifts of the kingdom community. We describe such leaders as community educators and identify a number of important facets of that role.

Part 2 sets out a model of the diaconal church.

Chapter 5 looks at the diaconal church from the perspective of its mission, of its culture, of its servant ministry and of the vocation of its laity.

Chapter 6 describes five types of social collective conducive to furthering the life and mission of the diaconal church.

Chapter 7 explores the forms of leadership needed to enable the diaconal church to break free from the mould of Christendom and fulfil its mission as the servant of the kingdom community.

Part 3 presents five case studies of the diaconal church in action.

The case studies focus on:

Chapter 8   The local church
Chapter 9   Groups and networks
Chapter 10   The laity
Chapter 11   Mission
Chapter 12   Leadership

All five case studies are about initiatives in which I took a leading role.

Part 4 is concerned with the emergence of the diaconal church.

Chapter 13 explores the potential of five Christian 'renewal' movements to bring the diaconal church into being. These movements are: Basic ecclesial communities; Pentecostalism; the Christian Right (USA); Evangelical workplace associations and agencies (UK); and the 'emerging church' (UK).

Chapter 14 explores how a renewed diaconate is in a key position to become the means of liberating the laity to fulfil their calling as servants of the kingdom community and thus the means of freeing the diaconal church from the mould of Christendom.

An Appendix sets out a course model for the education of a renewed diaconate.

Part 1

'The kingdom community'

1

Community or chaos?

'In retrospect the millennium marked only a moment in time. It was the events of 11 September that marked a turning point in history, where we confront the dangers of the future and assess the choices facing humankind.' Thus Tony Blair began his speech to the Labour Party Conference in Brighton in October 2001.

We begin this new millennium facing the age-old problems of poverty, homelessness and disease. It is a sobering thought, as Glover (1999) graphically reminds us, that the twentieth century was one which witnessed more people perish in wars than any other in human history. The new millennium, however, sees endemic problems assuming new forms, and fresh challenges to the sustainability of human civilization taking centre-stage.

Conventional wars have become ever more dangerous not least 'because technology makes them a threat to the survival of the whole species' (Glover, 1999, p. 41). Virulent diseases, such as HIV/AIDS and SARS, appear on the scene just as others are apparently vanquished. Our small and fragile planet is now faced with an exploding world population and the destruction of a life-sustaining environment, matters which caused previous generations little concern ('Two-thirds of world's resources "used up"', *Guardian*, 30 March 2005). And the emergence of international terrorism, allied to the proliferation of weapons of mass destruction, means that no corner of the globe can any longer regard itself as a safe haven.

Yet these self-evident threats to the survival of human civilization remain 'presenting problems'. Their resolution is possible only if we put at the top of our agenda the fundamental issue of how we can affirm the riches of our common humanity and work together in pursuit of the common good. It is not the dangers outlined above which threaten our world most profoundly, but the breakdown of community. As Tony Blair put it in his Brighton address in 2001: 'Today the threat is chaos. [Our response must be] the power of community.' But why is 'the power of community' so difficult to harness?

A civilization on the move

My grandfather worked as a booking clerk on the Great Western Railway. Though associated with transport all his life, he never left England, either for work or for pleasure. In a life of over 90 years, he lived entirely in middle England – Ludlow, Birmingham and Nottingham. My father, who was over 100 when he died, also lived in middle England. However, his work as the first personnel manager for a large pharmaceutical company often took him to the continent and occasionally, by sea, to the USA. As a boy, an army officer, a student, a Methodist minister, a college lecturer and now retired, I have already lived in 11 different locations from London to the Lake District and have travelled around four continents. Our son married a Swiss girl and now works for a multinational aircraft company in Seattle. His three children hold passports for several countries. The story of my own family, as well as that of many others, shows that over only a few generations 'mobility' has transformed human life in a quite dramatic way. If this were merely physical movement then perhaps the world would have changed more slowly. But alongside spatial mobility has gone cognitive, cultural and social mobility.

My mother was a remarkable correspondent, so much so that we always said that a logo of pen and paper should have appeared on her epitaph. I have produced many thousands of words, but it was only a few years ago that I replaced my battered typewriter with a lap-top. Our son lives by the computer. He accesses the web daily as a matter of course and his e-mails constantly traverse the globe. His three young children operate their home PC with total ease and competence. We have well and truly entered what Drucker calls 'the knowledge society' (1993, p. 2). This not only means that 'information is power' for each and every one of us, but that every person with a phone (fixed or mobile) or television, and now computer, is offered instant access to worldwide contacts and global experiences. Such 'cognitive mobility' has profound implications for the creation and sustaining of community at every level of human civilization from the local to the global.

Spatial and cognitive mobility bring with them 'cultural mobility'. It may not be entirely true that 'You can always tell a Brummie by the shamrock in his turban', but from my experience of living for many years in Birmingham I can empathize with that sentiment. Cultures are in transition more rapidly than ever before because people, spatially and

4

cognitively, are on the move. Mobility means the emergence of pluralism. Mobility and pluralism together are bringing into being a new era, call it 'postmodern' or what you will.

Spatial, cognitive and cultural mobility go hand in hand with 'social mobility'. The latter indicates the way in which the traditional class and caste structures of human society, though still tenacious, are being slowly eroded. Here education is playing a crucial role. Old hierarchies, secular and religious, are being challenged as the 'layman' becomes increasingly well informed, and knowledge and expertise are made available to all. Status and privilege founded on birth or tradition have by no means disappeared, but are giving way to a more open world in which 'equal opportunity' is regarded as an entitlement.

Centrifugal and centripetal forces

Mobility, in the forms we have described, gives impetus to two other powerful forces now impinging on every society worldwide. They have been present throughout human history, but where they were once limited or latent, they are now global and manifest. One such force is *centrifugal*. It dislodges people, their beliefs, values and relationships, from traditional foundations, and thrusts them outwards into a bewildering 'cosmopolitan' world (Merton, 1957, pp. 387–420). The other force, often arising as a reaction to it, is *centripetal*. Here people are impelled inwards in an attempt to retain or reclaim their physical and human roots, their common heritage and a distinctive identity.

Centrifugal and centripetal forces are essential for the future viability of human life on this planet. But they also have the potential to destroy it. Thus the most critical task facing humankind as it enters a new millennium is discovering forms of community that can enable these two forces to become complementary, not mutually destructive. It is a task that is a central concern of this book.

'Moving out'

Centrifugal forces at work in our world are shifting people around spatially, cognitively, culturally and socially and in unprecedented ways. There is no doubt that the resulting transformation of human relationships is hugely creative.

We are now aware, as never before, how the rest of the world lives. Many people will remember for years what they were doing when news of the 9/11 attacks on the World Trade Center in New York reached them, whether they be American or Arab, English or Indian, German or Japanese. Likewise news of the tsunami on Boxing Day 2004 spread across the world in a matter of hours. Knowledge of those who suffer through human violence or natural disaster is now an immediate and worldwide experience.

'Moving out' means that opportunities to share knowledge, skills, ideas, values and beliefs are now available, not just to the rich and powerful but to billions of people across the globe. Our generation has access to a storehouse of human resources past and present like no generation before it. From finance to films, from cooking to sport, from architecture to wildlife, from fashion to property, all now constitute a worldwide 'exchange and mart'.

These centrifugal forces currently at work also bring massively enhanced opportunities for scientific and technological innovation and change. Medical discoveries, commercial experience, engineering knowhow, information technology expertise, together with many other scientific and technical resources, can be passed around the globe at immense speed. The potential benefits from such advances promise a vastly enhanced quality of life for millions of people in every continent.

'Moving out' is also a phenomenon that offers the possibility of a more humane and responsible international ethic for economic and political affairs. Organizations such as the United Nations and the Commonwealth, however much they may fail in practice, symbolize a growing global commitment to human rights, social well-being and ecological stewardship. And alongside the international search for a just and sustainable world order, there now exists the myriad 'special issue' groups, from Amnesty International to Greenpeace, themselves networking widely.

'Moving out' brings immense enrichment to our quality of life worldwide. But it is about far more than 'enrichment'; it is about the preservation of life on earth. Economically, politically and ecologically, the centrifugal forces at work today offer us the means to make human interdependence a reality and to create a world working for the common good. Daunting as the challenge is, we now have the means to get our human act together for the sake of future generations.

However, there is a problem. The centrifugal forces at work on our civilization today also contain within them the seeds of disaster and chaos. The misuse or mishandling of nuclear power or biological expertise, and the ecological collapse of our planet through pollution or the wasteful use of finite resources, can only be overcome if we discover new forms of community that will enable us together to work for the common good. Yet the very mobility that brings us such benefits also disconnects people from their territorial, mental, cultural and social roots and profoundly weakens those human bonds that previously held life together (Bauman, 2001, pp. 39–49). Two words sum up the shaking of our communal foundations: *anonymity* and *amorality*.

Anonymity

Our cosmopolitan society is one in which we now relate to people through role rather than personal relationships. Typically, I do not want to know the life-history of the mechanic who services my car, of the assessor who deals with my insurance claim or even of my local newsagent. In a society of such immense numbers and variety, we cannot cope with more than a handful of intimate and ongoing relationships. This is why 'bureaucracy' is essential; effective organizations can no longer operate on the basis of interpersonal affinities that get in the way of the job to be done.

Such anonymity can be a liberating experience, as young people leaving home to study or work elsewhere know full well. Yet it can also be exploited in the quest for unaccountable power and material gain, a response which Bauman calls 'the secession of the successful' (2001, pp. 50–7). However, anonymity remains a high-risk gamble even for members of 'the globe-trotting elite' as Bauman acknowledges (p. 113), with loneliness, isolation and loss of identity also stalking them. 'The homeless mind', as Berger (1974) calls this loss of our moorings, or getting lost in 'the lonely crowd' as Riesman describes it (1950), can be a hugely destructive phenomenon. Such anonymity can bring an acute sense of alienation from the real world of people and increase the threat of communal chaos, individually and collectively.

Centrifugal forces foster anonymity, or what Beck (1992) calls 'individualization', at all societal levels. The demise of the extended family in the western world, the emergence of 'organization man' (Whyte, 1956) who must be trained in the art of constant uprooting, and the huge rise in the number of migrant workers across the world, are but indicators of forces steadily affecting us all and weakening sustainable personal relationships. 'Moving out' may bring us a great enhancement of choice, but increasing exposure to insecurity and isolation are also part of the package.

Amorality

Hand in hand with anonymity goes the problem of amorality. Mobility of mind and culture are key factors in the emergence of 'the vertigo of relativity', as Berger terms it (1980, p. 9). 'Never before', he states, 'has "the pluralization of meaning and values" [been] experienced as massively by as many people' (p. 58).

Among the first to have to come to terms with an increasingly relativistic and amoral world have been the great religious traditions. Their claims to embody codes of ethics based on ultimate values are now openly exposed to questioning and are often summarily dismissed. But into the vacuum come other mechanisms of social control, economic and political, that have little interest in the well-being of humanity.

Amorality has been given an immense boost by the emergence of 'the market' as a core ideology in the shaping of human affairs. The credibility of the market rests on the assumption that it is ethically neutral and that it lifts economics out of the realm of contested values onto firm and universally reliable ground. In reality, the market attempts to raise amorality to the status of a virtue. The problem is that amorality has a good deal in common with what Emile Durkheim (1951) calls 'anomie', a state of normlessness wherein the roles and rules sustaining human relationships and giving people a sense of identity and purpose collapse. Durkheim found that the consequences could be the destruction of our social moorings and, not infrequently, suicide. Today, amorality lies at the heart of the threat to identity and meaning experienced not only by individuals, but also by ethnic, religious and social groupings whose values have hitherto been rooted in a common heritage and cohesive cultural tradition.

The centrifugal forces now affecting our world have much to commend them: a new openness and enrichment of experience, greater choice, the chance to learn from one another and share resources, and the hope of tackling critical global problems with at least some chance of success. The wizardry of modern technology offers us a unique opportunity to build a new worldwide community and human civilization. 'Massification', the coming of a universal culture, it is argued, is not to be feared but welcomed as the harbinger of a new 'global embrace' which can overcome the barriers of 'both space and time' (Mcluhan, 1973, p. 11). And if such a global community is not yet in place, at least we seem to be well on the way to it, as seen

8

in the emergence of new identities that cross national boundaries and derive from shared interests rooted in our experience of being cosmopolitan citizens (Isin and Wood, 1999).

However, centrifugal forces have their dark side. They threaten to atomize relationships, create anonymity, promote amorality and destroy cultural identity and destroy those shared values that have previously given meaning and purpose to life. No wonder, therefore, that many people are now seeking to discover or rediscover forms of community that can hold together a world that seems to be rapidly fragmenting.

'Moving in'

It will come as no surprise, therefore, that opposing these centrifugal forces are centripetal forces resisting dispersal and disintegration. The quest for community is as much about depth as about breadth. It is an inward as well as an outward journey.

There are many signs of an ongoing search for human relationships that can give us a renewed sense of community. A vital aspect of this is an attempt to retrieve 'human scale' relationships. It is a quest seen in the explosion of communes in the 1960s on both sides of the Atlantic, the growth of the human potential movement and its many forms of group therapy, the vast expansion of 'special interest' associations and support groups, political, professional and leisure (Wuthnow, 1994), the emergence of what Drucker (1993, pp. 152–61) calls 'citizenship through the social sector' (the latter made up of 'autonomous community organizations'), as well as the 'escape' from cities in the West into towns and villages. All are indicators that we need the human group as an essential building block in any new world order.

However, the search for community also goes on at societal level. Many communities are born out of 'moving in' (or 'moving back') in order to recover a common heritage that has been latent or suppressed. So, following the collapse of colonialism, we have the attempted resurrection of historic cultures such as those of the Indians in North America, the Maoris in New Zealand, the Aborigines in Australia, as well as many tribal cultures in Africa. Cultural retrenchment in places such as Canada, Kurdistan and the old Russian states, which Ignatieff (1993) describes as the resurgence of 'blood and belonging', also features here. Renewing bonds of this kind can bring a powerful sense of community.

However, as with centrifugal forces, centripetal forces have their dark side. If fragmentation threatens to be the cost of 'moving out', fundamentalism and exclusivity can be the consequences of 'moving in'. The quest for community can become circumscribed by rigid boundaries that foster paranoia by persuading those engaged in such a quest that beyond their own group or clan lies a hostile world.

The destructiveness of 'moving in' is evident not only where there is poverty, marginalization or deprivation, but also wealth, privilege or good fortune. There is just as great a danger of élite and articulate groupings who have attained a 'culture of contentment' (Galbraith, 1992) carving out for themselves impenetrable niches in order to secure their status and ensure their influence, as there is of alienated and vulnerable groups becoming ghettos or sects. 'The "community" the former seek stands for a burglar-free and stranger-proof "safe-environment" . . . "Community" (in their case) stands for isolation, separation, protective walls and guarded gates,' states Bauman (2001, p. 114).

Even more destructive of our common humanity is the kind of 'moving in' which takes history with it and locks collectives into an anachronistic tribalism in the name of past glories or defeats. The Afrikaner in South Africa and the Jew in Palestine, for example, have frequently championed the concept of 'the chosen people' and 'the promised land' in a way that has brought bitter conflict and suffering to millions. Protestant and Catholic in Northern Ireland have for years entrenched themselves in a past as degrading as it was glorious. The horrors of the conflict between Serb, Croat and Muslim in the former Yugoslavia and acts of terrorism perpetrated by al-Qaida further underline the human cost of a quest for community that becomes culturally or historically myopic.

Most calamitous of all has been that 'moving in' which has led to a peculiarly twentieth-century form of communal incest, the totalitarian state. Such states are rooted in the power of 'community' which, when turned in on itself, has corrupted nations absolutely the more absolute it has become. Totalitarianism has taken a diversity of forms: imperialism, fascism, Stalinism, Maoism. All have proved how easy it is for genocide to triumph over humanity. More recently there are those, such as Philip Jenkins (2003), who are warning us that a confrontation between Islam and 'the coming of global Christianity' in the form of 'the next Christendom' may be the next threat to the future of human civilization. Centripetal as well as centrifugal forces can turn community into chaos.

The quest for community

Universalism is destroying the particularity needed to nourish it; particularity, especially in the political order, is threatening the universalism needed for human survival, not just for progress. Can the two be reconciled? (Davis, 1994, pp. 133–4)

Where, then, do we go from here in our search for forms of community that can prevent the annihilation of humankind? The challenge is by no means a new one, but, as recent events have shown, it is even more urgent than when George Simpson summed it up some 70 years ago (1937, p. 39):

The challenge facing humankind is that of communalizing those who are in conflict. That is a large problem. It is the problem of carrying over the ideal of the primary or face-to-face group which is most easily communalized, to the larger group, and ultimately to nations and international action. What is needed is a return to the ideals of the primary group in such a shape and so adjusted as to be capable of application to cosmopolitan conditions. Otherwise, a sort of return to the communal womb is being urged, a nostalgia for the infantile.

It is a sentiment echoed in more recent times by Vaclav Havel when he was President of Czechoslovakia (1990): 'We must not be ashamed that we are capable of love, friendship, solidarity, sympathy and tolerance but just the opposite,' he writes. 'We must set these fundamental dimensions of our humanity free from their "private exile" and accept them as the only genuine starting point of meaningful human community.'

'Community', writes Palmer (1987, p. 15), 'means more than the comfort of souls. It means, and has always meant, the survival of the species.' And the 'survival of the species' is now what we are about. 'At no other time has the keen search for common humanity, and a practice that follows ... been as imperative and urgent at it is now,' writes Bauman (2001, p. 140). The momentous choice before us is community or chaos

A global community

The survival and flourishing of human civilization in the millennium ahead requires a compelling vision of the power of community. 'Without a vision the people perish,' warns Proverbs 29.18, a word of wisdom as true today as it was when written.

The first task before us is a global commitment to share our visions. This means our being open to listen to and learn from one another. The kind of communities we now need are *learning communities*. They are communities that recognize and utilize the experience, insights and resources of each and every member, while being open to learn from and draw on the experience of other communities. 'The real community of man, in the midst of all the self-contradictory simulacra of community,' writes Bloom (1988, p. 381), in his attack on *The Closing of the American Mind*, 'is the community of those who seek the truth, of the potential knowers, that is, in principle, of all men to the extent they desire to know.' (And to the extent they desire to *learn*, we would add.)

If human civilization is to survive, the search for community is one in which all of us must be involved. Every social collective from the smallest group to the largest institution must play its part. Our attempts to create learning communities will have profound implications for the home and the neighbourhood, for the school and the hospital, for shops and offices, for the world of business and that of law and order, for local and national government and, not least, for religious institutions such as the church. In our case, however, there really is no alternative. To prevent the chaos that threatens us, our world has to become *a global community of learning communities*.

2

What is community?

We argued in the last chapter that the only hope of addressing the chaos that threatens human civilization as we enter a new millennium is to liberate the power of learning communities on a global scale. Groups, associations and institutions, neighbourhoods and cities, regions and nations have to become learning communities if our world is to survive. Thus the daunting yet exciting task facing us is to make the learning community the norm in every arena of social life.

Learning communities are a source of immense energy and a means of radical transformation. They are life-giving and liberating collectives that offer the exhilaration of a journey into the unknown, as well as the colleagueship to make it worth the risk. Learning communities have the potential to become sources of friendship and faith, of freedom and fulfilment. They are interdependent not incestuous, mutually supportive not sectarian.

However, the creation of learning communities is no quick fix. Staying with and strengthening interpersonal relationships is a long and demanding undertaking, however great the eventual rewards. Bringing into being and sustaining communally creative forms of social collectives requires not just commitment but experience, skill and wisdom. Community building is an art, and an art that has to be learnt (Bauman, 2001, p. 14).

How do we set about this large undertaking? Clearly, we will not even achieve lift-off if we remain oblivious to the fact that the choice facing our world is community or chaos. Thus an awareness that the stakes have never been higher and that the situation requires urgent action is a prerequisite for addressing the task before us. The creation of learning communities also requires ongoing commitment. This can only be sustained if the enterprise is a collective one, undertaken by all those with a vision of a new world order and with a will to work together with others to make that vision a reality.

Yet even awareness of the crisis and a commitment to overcoming it will not be enough if we have no clear understanding of the nature of community. In this chapter, therefore, we explore the concept of community on which so much depends. Our thesis is that *it is the image of 'the kingdom community' that offers the most profound and compelling vision of what community is all about.*

We begin our discussion from a sociological perspective. We then take a theological perspective, arguing that the image of the kingdom community gives a whole new meaning to a sociological understanding of community. Finally, we identify a number of social collectives that are particularly important for community building.

A sociological perspective

The choice facing us is between community and chaos. But a difficulty we face is that, though the threat of world chaos is not difficult to recognize, the concept of community, like a bar of soap in the shower, seems to slip from our grasp the harder we try to get hold of it. Why is this? Boswell (1990, p. 1) writes: 'In advanced western societies, our consciousness of community has become threadbare. There is an impoverishment in our sense of what it is to be social beings and members one of another, and builders of community.'

The problem is that the word 'community', like aerosol, has been sprayed onto so many human activities to give them a pleasant aroma – community development, community care, community health, community policing, community newspapers, community schools, community businesses, up to the European Economic Community (as it was) itself – that it has come to mean all things to all people and thus little to anyone.

This casual use of the concept of community, and neglect of its power to transform human relationships, Boswell calls 'a gigantic omission' (1990, p. 3). It is an omission of which we need to be acutely aware, and which we have to be wholeheartedly committed to remedying, if we are to bring any kind of order out of chaos. To appreciate the full implications of this 'omission' we must explore what lies at the heart of the concept of community by which we are laying so much store. We begin by looking at the current uses of the word 'community', all too many of which have reduced the term to a cliché (Clark, 1996, pp. 26–39).

Weak definitions of 'community'

The word 'community' is most frequently found accompanied by the definite article, in such sentences as: 'The community should have a say as to where the new road goes', or 'Representatives of the community were present at the meeting.' The problem in this context is that the term 'community' is so all-embracing that it becomes little more than a synonym for *people* in general as an ill-defined collective.

To address the problem of this kind of vagueness, and to show that community is also related to *place*, a definitive word is often added. Thus we get such sentences as 'We live in a pleasant suburban community,' or, sometimes more specifically, 'Notting Hill is an inner-city community.' Even here, however, the word community refers to little more than a loosely defined location where a very diverse collection of people might well reside.

Community is given a more precise meaning when it is used in connection with *interests* that draw people together. Thus we speak of 'a school community', 'the medical community' or 'the business community'. Yet, though this use of the term now distinguishes its members more clearly, it still reveals little about the style or quality of life characterizing such communities.

We get nearer to the heart of the matter when community is used to describe groups or associations in terms of *relationships*, usually assumed to be close-knit, such as 'a village community', 'an expatriate community' or 'the Muslim community'. Yet problems remain. We know only too well that these and similar relationships can at times be anything but communal. In 'the suburban village' of Woodhouse, where I worked as a Methodist minister, there were families that refused to speak to one another because of supposed indiscretions committed a generation or more ago.

If, therefore, the concept of community is of limited value when it refers to people in general, to place, to interests or even to those supposedly bound by close-knit relationships, where do we go from here? It is our contention that until we are prepared to bring *feelings* into the picture, to speak of '*a sense of community*', the concept will always promise more than it can deliver (Clark, 1996, pp. 40–53).

One criticism of an emphasis on feelings is that it reduces the concept of community to a purely psychological one. A sense of community might be important for individuals, but it cannot be applied to or have relevance for groups and associations. Yet it is clear that feelings are not simply experienced on an individual basis. We need only attend a football match to experience feelings of elation or frustration along with others, or to be present when there is a bomb alert to share feelings of fear and insecurity as a group. Many such emotions are as powerfully collective as personal experiences.

Another criticism is that if we move into the realm of feelings, community cannot be measured 'objectively'. It is, therefore, beyond the reach of a genuine sociological approach. We have two responses to this argument. First, that it remains professionally 'objective' to ask people whether or not they have a strong (or weak) sense of community. For what matters is how they assess their own well-being and not how the researcher assesses it for them. If I report that I get little sense of community where I live, then that is important 'objective' evidence for those who seek to regenerate neighbourhood life. Second, a number of indicators to assess the strength of community have been developed (Clark, 1996, pp. 62–80). These have their limitations, but they do indicate that we are dealing here with a phenomenon whose strength can be ascertained and enhanced.

The real issue is why we go on living with an ill-defined and trivialized understanding of community and so fail to do justice to community's immense human potential.

Community feeling: the three 'S's

What, then, are the feelings that typify this all-important sense of community?

Some years ago, MacIver and Page (1950, pp. 291–6), in their classic study, *Society*, pin-pointed three core components of what they termed 'community sentiment'. They called these 'we-feeling', 'role-feeling' and 'dependency-feeling'. We shall follow their approach, but describe the core components of community as 'a sense of solidarity', 'a sense of significance' and 'a sense of security' (our three 'S's).

A sense of solidarity is a sentiment closely akin to what MacIver and Page (p. 293) call 'we-feeling' and which they define as: 'The feeling that leads men to identify themselves with others so that when they say "we" there is no thought of distinction and when they say "ours" there is no thought of division.' Solidarity is by far the most commonly recognized sentiment associated with community. As Handy (1994, p. 248) puts it, 'We need to belong – to something or someone.' It is this feeling that most people have in mind when they refer to fraternity, fellowship, togetherness or belonging. Solidarity encompasses all those feelings that draw and hold people together – sympathy, loyalty, gratitude, trust and so on – a river into which many tributaries flow.

Unfortunately, preoccupation with solidarity has led to the neglect of the second core component of community as feeling: *a sense of significance*. This sentiment is that which MacIver and Page (1950, p. 293) term 'role-feeling', defined by them as: 'The sense of place or station [experienced by members of a group] so that each person feels he has a role to play, his own function to fulfil in the reciprocal exchanges of the social scene.' Like solidarity, significance is made up of a complex of related feelings, such as a sense of standing, dignity, worth or achievement.

MacIver and Page (p. 293) add a third communal component that they call 'dependency-feeling': 'This involves physical dependence, since man's material needs are satisfied within it [community], and a psychological dependence, since community is the greater "home" that sustains him, embodying all that is familiar at least, if not all that is congenial to his life.' From our perspective, 'psychological dependence' is already dealt with under the heading of solidarity, for where such dependence exists some sense of solidarity will always be evident, as with mother and child or adolescent and peer group. However, we shall retain *a sense of security* as a third core component of community. For if human beings are subject to distressing levels of physical or material insecurity, with more extreme cases being experiences such as starvation or homelessness, any existing sense of community will be greatly weakened or fail to survive at all.

To gain a deeper understanding of the nature of community, we believe it helps to reverse the order in which MacIver and Page present their core components. We see a sense of security, physical and material, as providing the soil within which the other two sentiments are able to grow and flourish, and thus place it first. Our thesis is that that *the strength of community within any human collective is revealed by the degree to which its members experience a sense of security, of significance and of solidarity within it*. This thesis might also be expressed in terms of people feeling they have 'a place to stand' (security), 'a role to play' (significance) and 'a world to which to belong' (solidarity).

The three 'S's are distinct enough for us to identify as the core components of a sense of community, but they are not discrete phenomena. Feelings do not have neat and tidy boundaries. Solidarity will enrich significance, security will enrich solidarity and so on. Where all three components are strong and mutually supportive of one another, what we call 'communal synergy' occurs. By this we mean that the sense of community as a whole becomes greater than the sum of its 'parts'. It is communal synergy that reveals the immense power of community.

Community as feeling is both a profound human need and also a dynamic driving force. It harnesses and expresses the power of feelings. If we fail to experience the three 'S's in a way that satisfies us (Boswell's 'gigantic omission'), we shall miss what makes being human worthwhile and ultimately sustains human civilization. We shall also find ourselves striving in one way or another to meet this unfulfilled need. Whether, as individuals, groups, institutions, cities or nations, we actually recognize what we are missing is another matter.

The communal dilemma

However, a serious impasse remains. We call this 'the communal dilemma'. If the strength of our three 'S's is the ultimate criterion for deciding the degree to which a collective can be called a community, then not only might the pre-school play group, the Rotary club and Amnesty International qualify as communities, but also the Mafia, the Red Brigade and al-Qaida. Even Hitler's SS, among the most active perpetrators of the Holocaust, could not be denied communal status on these grounds.

The dilemma faced here is the classic one of the part over against the whole. David Jenkins (1976, pp. 14–16) identifies the problem very clearly: 'That by which we identify ourselves and have our sense of identity, significance and belonging is also that by which we dehumanize others.' Thus *the communal dilemma is how social collectives can become ever more open to one another without undermining their own sense of community or that of others.*

Grey (1993, p. 75) puts the communal dilemma in this way: 'How can I connect with my authentic community group – nation, cultural group, religious tradition – in a way which both contributes to and draws strength from community memory, purpose and celebration, and yet remains receptive to and affirming of other communities?' And Colin Gunton (1993, p. 125) asks: 'Can there be found a vision of things which unifies without producing totalitarianism or homogeneity?' Any response certainly involves 'deconstructing a myth of "community" . . ., acknowledging that the dominant notion has typically been an ideal of homogeneous and exclusionary groups, and replacing it with a concept of communities . . . inclusionary and democratic' (Sandercock, 1998, p. 206).

But why bother to widen our communal horizons? It could well be a demanding and dangerous task, always likely to weaken the bonds that tie us to those we already know, and to threaten our identity, as the debate over the future of Europe demonstrates only too well. Yet we all recognize that our need for community cannot be satisfied in isolation. Our experience also tells us that whereas communal needs might once have been met within small local settlements, this is less and less possible. We must move on and move out. We have to recognize and meet the communal needs of others as well as our own if we are to avoid chaos and survive as human beings. Nevertheless, the hard questions remain. How far are we prepared to go to make the boundaries of our community more permeable? How far are we willing to acknowledge 'the stranger' and 'the foreigner' as fellow-travellers in the quest for community and thus 'one of us'?

The communal dilemma is also a critical issue for social collectives. Just as 'no man is an island', so no collective that wishes to develop fully as a community can do so in isolation. In a world that is becoming ever more a 'global village', the ability to live together as a community of communities becomes a matter of mutual survival. MacIver (1924, p. 260), writing soon after the traumatic experience of World War One, puts the issue as follows:

> The service of the large community is to fulfil and not to destroy the smaller. Our life is realized within not one but many communities, circling us round, grade beyond grade. The near community demands intimate loyalties and personal relationships, the concrete traditions and memories of everyday life. But where the near community is all community, its exclusiveness rests on ignorance and narrowness of thought, its emotional strength is accompanied by intellectual weakness. Its member becomes the slave of its traditions, the prisoner of his own affections. Without the widening of gates – nay, without the breaking down of walls – there is no progress. Herein is the service of the wider community, not only a completer 'civilization' but also the freedom of a broader culture.

It could be argued that the whole of history is about a human race caught on the horns of the communal dilemma. Our conditioned response has been to enhance our own sense of community by portraying the outsider or the foreigner as 'the enemy'. But the power of community turned inwards, creating defensive, self-seeking or aggressive societies, can become disastrously incestuous and hugely destructive. If the power of community is to save human civilization, there must be more to community than self-centred sentiment.

Community as value

Though sociological analysis may help us to understand that tackling the communal dilemma is a necessity for the survival of human civilization, the last century has taught us only too well that sociological analysis falls far short of giving us the vision and the will to do so. We need, with Plant (1974, pp. 8–36), to recognize that 'community' has to be about 'value' as well as 'fact'; that it must be an 'evaluative' as well as 'descriptive' word. The urgent task is to create what Bauman calls '*ethical* community' (2001, p. 72).

Our three 'S's, and the communal synergy that they are capable of producing, essential as these are, describe community only as fact. Until we also understand community as value, there is no way to free community as fact from its potential incestuousness and ultimate destructiveness. But what values are needed for this purpose and from where do they come?

It is our 'belief' (note the word), that the communal dilemma can only be resolved if we interpret community, following MacIver's eloquent plea, as an *inclusive* phenomenon. If we are to avoid chaos, we must be committed not only to fostering the three 'S's within the social collectives to which we ourselves belong, but across every social collective. The task before is *to build a global community of communities by creating an increasingly strong sense of security, significance and solidarity within and across social collectives.* In this definition the words 'and across' are vital. The well-being of human civilization depends on community being defined as an inclusive phenomenon.

'Inclusiveness' is a value. From where does it originate and on what grounds can it claim authenticity? The only way such questions can be answered is to move on to explore the realm of beliefs and the 'symbolic universes' on which they are founded.

'Symbolic universes'

Human civilization is on the move. Whether we are in the process of 'moving out' beyond tried and tested norms, or 'moving in' to try and protect these, we face a world in which the pluralization of values is going on apace. If we are to overcome 'the vertigo of relativity' (Berger, 1980, p. 9) which pluralization brings with it, we have to reclaim and reaffirm, with some urgency, those values that can bring community out of chaos.

Berger and Luckmann (1984) describe any nexus of all-embracing values, and the beliefs on which they are founded, as 'a symbolic universe'. Symbolic universes define our understanding of 'reality' and down the ages have guided generations to live and act as they have. Symbolic universes give purpose, meaning and power to our lives, individually and collectively. Whether or not we opt for community as an *inclusive* phenomenon will depend on the symbolic universe that we espouse.

A Christian perspective

There are numerous symbolic universes that have offered humankind a communal vision of some richness, but pre-eminent among these have been the great religions of the world. There is an important agenda ahead to discover what the major faiths have to say about the nature of community and how to tackle the communal dilemma. In this book, however, we concentrate on the Christian faith and the insights it continues to offer, despite the onslaught of the Enlightenment and of secularization, into the nature of community.

Two great Christian symbols or images are of particular relevance for our understanding of community: 'the Trinity' and 'the kingdom'.

The Trinity

The image of the Trinity lies at the very heart of the Christian understanding of the nature and purposes of God. It embodies the belief that 'human being in the image of God is to be understood relationally rather than in terms of the possession of fixed characteristics such as reason or will' (Gunton, 1993, p. 3). 'Relationally', there are four things about the image of the Trinity of especial note.

In the first place, the image of the Trinity as three 'persons' portrays *the cosmos as deeply and utterly personal*. The Trinity indicates that 'it is not . . . some*thing* which holds things together, but some*one*' (p. 179). This personal God is the ultimate 'universal' over against the false universals of, for example, 'the public, or "the people" – or history or the market' (p. 31). If God is 'personal', then the quest for community is a search for what it means to be 'persons', to be fully human, as part of a deeper and wider purpose for our universe. The image of the Trinity indicates that until this cosmic truth is recognized, there can be no ultimate human fulfilment, individual or corporate. It also means that *every human being*, because created 'in the image of God' (Sherlock, 1996, pp. 27–91), *is a person of divine worth* with both the right and responsibility to live out his or her unique human potential to the full. This divine valuing of each and every person challenges any circumscribed or exclusive understanding of community. It is a divine imperative that the communal dilemma is resolved not shelved.

Second, the three persons of the Trinity can be seen as possessing three divine attributes: *life*, *liberation* and *love* – what we might call the three 'L's'. These divine attributes are also offered to us as gifts. They are gifts intimately related to our three communal sentiments, a sense of security, of significance and of solidarity, but, when accepted, transform the latter into a completely new qualitative experience.

The first person of the Trinity, *God the Father*, is *the Creator* who transforms *a sense of security*, as the basic human need for food, clothing and shelter, into a profound experience of *life*. The doctrine of creation not only teaches 'about the origin of things in the unconstrained freedom of God but as an articulating of the way things are by virtue of the relation they have with their creator' (Gunton, 1993, p. 124). God the Creator offers us not only 'our daily bread', the necessities for survival, but the gift of life and the joy of living. Community is not just a sense of physical and material security, though these are essential for our communal health, but of experiencing the energy of life. As Irenaeus once put it: 'The glory of God is man fully alive.' For the Christian, therefore, community is about experiencing a sense of vitality, joy and well-being, and acknowledging these with thanks as the gifts of God the Creator.

The gift of life, however, carries with it the divine imperative that humankind cares for and nurtures the whole inhabited earth. Edward Echlin believes that the church has for too long accepted and collaborated with 'consumer societies which divorce man from nature, ravish the environment, and tolerate only a reductivist "redemption" that separates man from his world'. He argues for a 'fundamental convergence . . . of redeemed humanity with the redeemed earth' (1991, pp. 163, 164). God the Creator offers human beings the gift of life, but requires them to be stewards of his planet in return.

Christ, the second person of the Trinity, is *the Liberator* who transforms *a sense of significance* into a sense of *liberation*. We no longer have to prove our worth but are accepted as we are by 'the grace of our Lord Jesus Christ'. The only condition is that we 'repent and believe in the gospel' (Mark 1.15), that we are prepared to choose life and that we want to become what he all along meant us to be. Through his earthly ministry, death and ongoing life, Christ offers us forgiveness, liberation from self-seeking and a welcome into the divine community.

The Holy Spirit, the third person of the Trinity, is *the Unifier* who transforms *a sense of solidarity* into that of being at one with God and our fellow human beings. The Spirit enables us to move way beyond our earthbound experience of solidarity. Through the work of the Spirit, community becomes an experience of *being loved* and of being able to love, of belonging to God and to one another, in the deepest sense we can ever know.

The image of the Trinity as expressed through the Holy Spirit leads us one stage further. It reveals that the Trinity is not only an *inclusive* phenomenon, embracing each and all, it is *universal*, present throughout the whole of creation. Just as the Spirit 'blows where it wills' (John 3.8), so the Persons of the Trinity have a universal presence; they are omnipresent. Life, liberation and love are to be found in every situation, be that hell or heaven (Psalm 139.1–12).

A third thing to note concerning the image of the Trinity is that it reveals that the ultimate nature of *God is communal*. 'God is not simply shapeless, a negatively conceived monad, but eternal interpersonal life' (Gunton, 1993, p. 164). God as Father, Son and Holy Spirit represents both the personal identity of each part and the inclusiveness of the whole. 'Relationality that gives due weight to both one and many, to both particular and universal, to both otherness and relation, is to be derived from the one place where they can satisfactorily be based, a conception of God who is both one and three, whose being consists in a relationality that derives from the otherness-in-relation of Father, Son and Spirit' (pp. 6–7). The image of the Trinity describes community at its zenith, interpersonal relationships that bond without destroying identity. It offers a vision of a universal community undistorted by the communal dilemma.

Finally, the image of the Trinity symbolizes the nature of *divine power*. Haughton (1981) sees this power as that of a passionate God facilitating what she describes as a universal and ongoing 'exchange of life'. This is pre-eminently 'relational power', or, as Grey puts it, 'the power of connection' (1993, p. 99). It is a power offered to all those seeking to tap the resources of divine community in order to build human communities. It is a power that Christians believe gives us the means of transforming the incestuous nature of much that passes for 'community' into open, loving and redemptive relationships, through which alone the impasse of the communal dilemma can be overcome.

What the Trinity reveals to us about the meaning of community is reinforced, largely in the context of the early church, by the New Testament concept of *koinonia*.

> *Koinonia* (as life) is about Christians having the material and physical resources to live life to the full, a mutual responsibility as seen in a commitment to the sharing of goods (Acts 2.42; Romans 15.26).

> *Koinonia* (as liberation) emphasizes that within community each person is of special worth (Galatians 2.9) and that all matter as equal partners in the gospel (Philippians 1.5).

> *Koinonia* (as love) describes the solidarity of God with his people – as Father (1 John 1.3), Son (1 Corinthians 9) and Holy Spirit (2 Corinthians 13.14). This is witnessed pre-eminently in the mystery of the Eucharist where God and his people are drawn together in 'holy communion' (1 Corinthians 10.14 ff).

However, though the New Testament understanding of *koinonia* is helpful, it is the image of the Trinity that is pre-eminent in giving our sociological understanding of community a whole new dimension.

The kingdom community

The other great Christian image of particular relevance to our understanding of community is that of 'the kingdom'.

At first sight, it might seem that the image of 'kingdom' is hopelessly outdated because of issues of gender and authority now associated with the secular use of the term. Some have even suggested using the term 'kin-dom' (which carries some sense of community) to avoid this difficulty. However, we cannot downplay the fact that the image of the kingdom was absolutely central to the teaching of Jesus and that his commitment to it was a matter of life or death. The kingdom 'has therefore a primacy which cannot be denied' (Newbigin, 1980, p. 11). That Jesus used male language and referred to the kind of authority structure familiar to his audience was simply because, like us, he was a child of his own time and culture. This should in no way distract us from the dynamic vision of the kingdom as 'heaven on earth' that he put before his hearers, as powerful and challenging a vision for our age as it was for theirs.

'The mission of Jesus was to announce and embody the reign of God, a reign which claims jurisdiction over the whole created world and all that is in it' (Newbigin, 1983, p. 34). He also indicated that the kingdom embraced those who had discerned the purposes of God and committed themselves to fulfilling them. Thus the kingdom can be seen not only as referring to the sovereignty of God, but also to a divinely ordered *community*. We shall call the latter 'the kingdom community' (see also Clark, 1987). As such it embraces and gives public expression to the features of the Trinity as divine community described above. *In the image of the kingdom community, therefore, Trinity and kingdom come together as an integral whole.*

The image of the kingdom community offers us some profound insights into what it means to be a community. Like the Trinity, it also transforms our sociological understanding of community.

First and foremost, the kingdom community is not a place. It is about *a new order of relationships between God and his creation,* and thus between human beings themselves. It is an order of relationships not only embodying the three 'S's – a sense of security, significance and solidarity – but also the three 'L's, the Trinitarian gifts of life, liberation and love.

The kingdom community offers those who seek to enter it a *sense of security,* though this now becomes not just a sense of physical and material security, but a sense of the undergirding providence of God. That experience points us to the source of *life* that can transform our world into the kingdom community, as the tiny mustard seed grows into a great tree or the leaven transforms the dough into bread (Matthew 13.31–33). In John's Gospel, the image of the kingdom community is expressed 'in terms of "life" and "life eternal"' (Arias, 1984, p. 62), the gift of God the Creator.

The kingdom community offers its members a *sense of significance,* of being valued and loved as children of God, as Jesus demonstrated time and again in his ministry to the marginalized and the outcast. But the kingdom community offers much more than this. Christ promised *liberation* to all who recognized that they had fallen short of God's purposes for human-kind. Repentance and renewal are at the heart of this promise (Mark 1.15). Though, once a person 'puts his hand to the plough' there can be no look-ing back (Luke 9.62).

To enter the kingdom community is to be 'born anew' (John 3.3). In the Gospels, such rebirth is intimately related to more tangible forms of liberation. Thus, in what was probably his first sermon, Jesus spoke of his ministry as being 'to preach good news to the poor . . . to proclaim release to the captives and recovering of sight to the blind, to set at liberty those who are oppressed' (Luke 4.18). It was a message he continued to proclaim in word and deed throughout the whole of his ministry.

The kingdom community also offers *a sense of solidarity* to all those who enter it. As Arias writes:

> [The kingdom] was not reduced to a verbal proclamation: 'preaching and bringing the good news' was done by a small community that was itself a manifestation of the kingdom. There they were: the first fruits, the living signs of the coming kingdom, the transformed persons who made up the itinerant band of evangelists. (1984, p. 5)

Yet as the living signs of the kingdom community, this first small Christian group experienced more than a sense of solidarity. They received the gift of *love* and were transformed into a community bonded by love; love of God, love of others and love of self (Mark 12.30–31). It was a love so powerful that its recipients were prepared to sacrifice their lives for the well-being of their fellow human beings, be they friends or enemies (John 15.13; Luke 6.35). And so it has continued throughout history.

The kingdom community is 'a feast with unexpected companions', one that 'calls us to inclusive table fellowship and cross-cultural hospitality' (Murray, 2004a, p. 315). Thus the image of the kingdom community addresses the communal dilemma head on. Its gifts of life, liberation and love transform our feelings of security, significance and solidarity, which so easily become exclusive and even incestuous, into not only an *inclusive* but a *universal* experience. The kingdom community is always 'in the midst' of us (Luke 17.20–21); it is omnipresent. However, we will only find it if we are aware that it is at work making human boundaries permeable and breaking down social divides based on class, creed, culture, or religion itself.

To turn these reflections into a practical proposition, we offer the thesis that *the kingdom community is present wherever God's gifts of life, liberation and love are manifest within and across social collectives*. The sociological and theological dimensions of the kingdom community discussed so far are set out in Figure 1.

If we take the kingdom community's mission statement to be the Beatitudes (Matthew 5.3–12; Luke 6.20–23), its strategic plan to be the Magnificat (Luke 1.46–55) and its mantra to be the Lord's Prayer (Arias, 1984, p. 8), it not surprising that it is a community that presents us with a value system radically different from today's world. Humankind's value system

Figure 1: Sociological and theological dimensions of the kingdom community

Sociological		Theological		
FEELINGS (The three 'S's)	VALUES	BELIEFS	GIFTS (The three 'L's*)	
A sense of *Security*		God the Creator	*Life*	
A sense of *Significance*	*Inclusiveness*	Christ the Liberator	*Liberation*	*Universality*
A sense of *Solidarity*		The Holy Spirit the Unifier	*Love*	

(*In Chapter 3, we shall be adding a fourth 'L', that of *learning*, to these gifts.)

cannot solve the communal dilemma because, unlike the kingdom community, its priorities are not the needs of the marginalized (Luke 1.51–53), the outcast (Matthew 21.31), 'the poor' (Luke 12.34; Matthew 5.3) or the young (Luke 18.16–17). The kingdom community is a community concerned not only with peace and joy, but with justice (Romans 14.17). It is no wonder, therefore, that endeavouring to put the values of the kingdom community into practice, ending the advancement of 'my community' over against 'your community', will bring conflict and sometimes violent resistance (Matthew 11.12).

Yet the kingdom community remains 'good news' (Luke 8.1), as well as 'public news' (Newbigin, 1980, p. 15). It is a vision of immense hope that gives new meaning and purpose to the whole of human life. It is as valuable as the most priceless treasure (Matthew 13.44) or the finest pearl (Matthew 13.45). It is worth everything to discover it and to work for its coming (Mark 9.7; Luke 18.29). It is the epitome of every community. Its realization on earth means the fulfilment of all that humankind was meant to be.

Social collectives conducive to community

For the kingdom community to become incarnate in daily life, it must take the form of real human collectives. Have we any clues as to what such collectives might look like? The answer is that we have many clues, but that they lie scattered across a range of human experience. However, because sociology is one of the fields most concerned with this issue, we shall again make use of its insights here.

There is a wealth of sociological studies concerned with 'community' in general. However, there are only a few such studies that begin from the perspective that we have adopted in this chapter (Clark, 1996, pp. 73–6, 138–48; Wenger, 1998, 2002). Nevertheless, such studies suggest that there are four forms of social collective particularly conducive for creating and nurturing our three 'S's: the communal group, the network, the communal institution and the partnership. This being so, it is our conviction that the same four social collectives will be conducive to the nurturing of our three 'L's that greatly enrich but are intimately related to our three 'S's. On the basis of that assumption, we now explore the features of these four communal collectives.

The communal group

We define the communal group as one in which people who share a strong common interest are able to meet face to face, frequently and continuously. These features usually make the communal group rich in terms of our three 'S's. It is thus a uniquely important form of collective for communalizing larger collectives and, ultimately, society as a whole. As Vaclav Havel eloquently puts it (in words quoted towards the end of Chapter 1), our task is to 'set these fundamental dimensions of our humanity [love, friendship, solidarity, sympathy, tolerance] free from their "private exile" and accept them as the only genuine starting point of meaningful human community'. It is the communal group that, of all collectives, is best suited to nurturing these 'fundamental dimensions of our humanity'.

The communal group provides 'the starting point of meaningful human community'. It does so not simply because of the feelings (the three 'S's) that it fosters but because it is ubiquitous and multitudinous. Small is thus not only potentially powerful and 'beautiful' (Schumacher, 1974), it is everywhere. The communal group crops up on the margins of society and at the heart of institutions. Thus, communal groups can become vital change-agents in the life of society, able to operate in a host of different contexts and to give impetus and direction to the process of institutional transformation.

Just because human groups are human, they can be destructive as well as creative. They can become an arena of alienating tensions and for bitter conflicts, not least because close relationships are often difficult to handle. Such groups can also become introverted and self-seeking, using the power of human bonding to protect or exclude. Thus for groups to be communal, they must espouse a commitment to an inclusiveness that respects and validates as wide a range of other collectives as possible. Here Christian faith, which offers the image of the kingdom community as a vision and motivating force, becomes an immensely important dynamic for genuine community building.

The development of permeable boundaries and a commitment to inclusiveness are greatly strengthened where groups are motivated to link together to share experiences, skills or resources. In this context, networking, our second form of communal collective, becomes particularly important for the maintenance and development of communal groups and, ultimately, of a communal society.

The network

A network is a web of interconnecting lines of communication that enable participants to exchange ideas, insights and resources on an equal footing. A network is co-operative not hierarchical in nature. The modern example, par excellence, is the worldwide web, or 'Internet' (note the word). But there are a multitude of networks, actual as well as 'virtual', formal and informal, that enable people to communicate and, when appropriate and possible, facilitate their meeting together.

Networks tap into the synergy created by linking individuals or groups with one another. Humankind is only just beginning to articulate, appreciate and utilize for the common good the potential of networking. However, connectivity's potential for creative change is also manifest across a wide range of disciplines: from Capra (1983) with his reflections on the new physics, through philosophy and theology (Haughton, 1981; Grey, 1993), to its practical application in institutional empowerment (Wenger, 2002) and urban regeneration (Rockefeller Foundation, 1994).

29

Networks, like groups, can be communally destructive. They can be used to link those who have no desire to foster a sense of security, significance or solidarity in an inclusive way. They can be employed to exploit, manipulate and corrupt human relationships. Nevertheless, their potential to facilitate new and creative forms of community remains immense.

Networks have four major contributions to make to community building. First, they enable those with similar interests to communicate with one another in a way that can establish 'virtual communities'. Not infrequently, this leads to the emergence of actual communities. Second, networks have an inbuilt propensity to overcome the tendency of all collectives, even when intentions are otherwise, to fall prey to exclusiveness and the communal dilemma. Third, networks possess the unique ability to open up new communal possibilities by facilitating unexpected connections and surprise encounters. Fourth, networks can be a vital means of initiating and sustaining alliances and partnerships between all forms of social collective (Clark, 1996, pp. 130–48).

However, though communal groups and networks have a key role to play in the creation of inclusive communities, they cannot bring about significant and, above all, lasting change in the life of neighbourhood, city, nation and beyond, unless their endeavours lead to the creation of communal institutions. George Simpson's warning is apposite here (1937, p. 39): 'The challenge facing humankind . . . is the problem of carrying over the ideal of the primary or face-to-face group . . . to the larger group, and ultimately to nations and international action.'

The communal institution

The creation of communal institutions is of paramount importance if human civilization is to survive another millennium. By 'institution' we here mean well-established and formally structured collectives that maintain a society's cultural, social and economic norms and practices. Because of their propensity to become conservative and closed in nature, it is institutions that often imprison their members and prevent the development of a communal society, as we shall see only too clearly in Part 2.

Communal institutions have the crucial responsibility of maintaining continuity while facilitating change. The search is now on for ways in which institutions can fulfil this responsibility. Their role is increasingly being seen as that of helping to connect those communal groups and networks that give them substance, in a way that can offer all participants a corporate sense of identity. Institutions fulfil this role not by enforcing rigid boundaries but by enabling their members to cross boundaries so that 'innovative and unorthodox solutions are found . . . old ideas find new life and new ideas propagate' (Wenger, 1998, pp. 254–5). This kind of institution requires a new kind of legitimacy founded on corporate ownership and collective 'management'.

Institutions provide the locus of a further important aspect of community building, the maintenance of symbolic places (Clark, 1974), events or people. Places and buildings that represent shared memories or traditions, important social and cultural events, and notable public figures often become powerful symbols that strengthen a collective's sense of community (Cohen, 1985). (In subsequent chapters we shall keep an eye open for these symbolic representations of the common heritage and corporate life of the church as an institution.)

For institutions to become communal collectives, values and beliefs must be to the fore. But what values and beliefs? Where the symbolic universe of the market holds sway exclusiveness and the communal dilemma are reinforced. A market economy requires that institutions take 'a characteristically impersonal form' (Poole, 1991, p. 49) and operate on a competitive basis, the antithesis of the values that undergird the genuinely communal institution. The kingdom community offers a radical alternative to a market-driven society. Its gifts of life, liberation and love can nurture strong and inclusive communal institutions offering new hope to a world facing possible chaos. To help make that hope a reality, however, communal partnerships are essential.

The partnership

We define a partnership as an association or consortium of institutions, formal or informal, which commit themselves to one another in pursuit of some shared interest or concern to further the common good. Partnerships have an inherent communal quality about them resulting from exchanges, encounters and engagements of an inclusive and open kind. The inclusiveness of networks can be a matter of chance or convenience, and of access to the appropriate technology; the inclusiveness of partnerships is a more intentional matter, requiring ongoing commitment to a common goal. Partnerships are a powerful means of community building and of challenging the communal dilemma. They are thus of vital importance in enabling our world to become a global community of communities.

3

What is learning?

The creation of strong and inclusive communities, from the family to the nation, is humankind's hope of survival. But the creation of community is no easy option. It is an art that has to be *learnt*. If we are to foster a strong sense of community between groups, networks, institutions and partnerships as well as within them, we not only have to be open to learning about our own cultural norms and values but about those of others. Without such openness there is no way of overcoming the communal dilemma, the problem of how social collectives can become ever more open to one another without undermining their own sense of community or that of others. Community building and learning are inseparable.

But what do we mean by 'learning'? And what models of learning promote (or undermine) the creation and development of communities?

Models of learning

Figure 2 sets out five models of learning. These draw freely on the work of John Hull (1975, pp. 52–75) but are adapted to our particular concern with community building. Across the top are the titles of five models of learning. Down the left-hand side key aspects of the learning process are set out. These aspects refer to whether the learning process is closed or open, what its purpose is, where its focus lies, whether it embraces moral values, the extent to which it is rational, how it is undertaken, whether the learner has any choice in his or her learning, and what form of leadership it requires. We shall deal with these aspects in the following paragraphs. The question of leadership, which has critical implications for the well-being of learning communities, will be discussed in the following chapter.

We can deal with *indoctrination* briefly because it is clearly a learning process inimical to building community. Indoctrination is built on a closed understanding of learning. It aims to condition learners in order to recruit

Figure 2: *Models of learning*

Towards Education →

	Indoctrination	Nurture	Instruction	Training	Education
KEY CONCEPT	Closure				Openness →
PURPOSE	Conditioning	Socialization	Imparting knowledge	Imparting skills	*Learning to learn*
FOCUS	'The cause' or 'The system'	Culture	Subject	Technique	*The person and life*
MORALITY	Immoral (imposes values)	↓	Non-moral (accepts values) ↑	↑	*Moral (questions values)*
RATIONALITY	Irrational (ignores or distorts evidence)	↓	Non-rational (accepts evidence) ↑	↑	*Rational (questions evidence)*
MEANS OF LEARNING	Imprinting	Assimilation	Memorizing ↓ Understanding	Mastery →	*Discovery*
CHOICE	Determined by the teacher	Determined by the tradition	Determined by the syllabus		*Negotiated with the learner*
LEADERSHIP	Autocratic – imposes (avoids assent)	Paternal/maternal – guards and guides (fosters assent)	Directive – informs and explains (assumes assent) →	– demonstrates and practices →	*Democratic – fosters partnership (seeks assent) →*

them for a particular cause, or to bind them into a particular collective. It is immoral, in the sense that its values are imposed, and irrational, in the sense that bona fide evidence is ignored or distorted. Its methods are to imprint the information imparted on the mind of the learner in a way that brooks no questioning and allows no choice. Indoctrination is a learning model typical of those collectives that have become, on the one hand, totalitarian states, and, on the other, sects and ghettos. There is no way that such collectives can be regarded as learning communities.

Nurture, instruction and *training* share many features in common. All are important as learning processes. The purpose of nurture is to socialize new members of a collective into the culture of that collective. Instruction is about imparting knowledge. Training is about imparting skills. Nurture, instruction and training are non-moral in that they take the values of the society concerned as read. They are non-rational in that they take evidence as given. In contrast to indoctrination, nurture, instruction and training are 'open' models of learning, but only in the sense that their purpose is to prepare the learner for his or her role within their own society. Learning is not meant to question that role. The tradition and the syllabus dominate the learning process.

Learning as education

Nurture, instruction and training give the learner the experience, knowledge and skills to assimilate the norms and practices of his or her own culture. But in themselves they provide no means of engaging with and learning about other cultures. Thus they are inadequate models of learning for the task of overcoming the communal dilemma and enabling our world to become a community of communities. That task can only be tackled with any hope of success if we are prepared to engage in learning as *education*.

The problem that we face in the quest to create community is that we are operating with a totally inadequate understanding of 'education'. For example, New Labour has repeatedly proclaimed the importance of 'Education, education, education!' Yet its legislative programme has in practice espoused instruction and training rather than the educational model of learning depicted in Figure 2. The 'power of community' will never be realized if the learning required to liberate it remains circumscribed by nurture, instruction and training.

Nurture, instruction and training remain important when regarded as models of learning that lay the foundations for education. But unless they are seen as a means to that end, they lose their potential for openness and may become subtle forms of indoctrination. The competitive pressures of a market economy, the insecurity caused by loss of cultural identity in a pluralistic world, as well as a fear of terrorism carried out in the name of this or that fundamentalist ideology, are the kinds of pressure that can all to easily transform nurture, training and instruction into indoctrination.

Our contention is that the core quality of learning as education is *openness*. Defining the heart of education as openness takes us into the realm of values. In what follows, therefore, we shall first explore a number of key value-oriented aspects of education and then look at the how these aspects reflect the value system (symbolic universe) of the Christian faith.

In discussing learning as an educational process we shall move down the right-hand column of Figure 2, putting the main features of education in italics.

Education is not just about learning; it is about *learning to learn*. As Hull puts it (1975, p. 65), education 'has no purpose other than to make further learning possible'.

The focus of education is not a culture, subject or technique but *the person*, unique and of ultimate worth. Taking this as a premise, education works with the totality of human experience seeking to explore *life* as a whole, its nature, purpose and meaning. In education, the integration of what is learnt is seen to lie primarily with the learner, not with the subject matter or the teacher. 'The authority of education is . . . intrinsic to the person, the authority of other forms of communication [nurture, instruction and training] is extrinsic to the person' (Hull, 1975, p. 58).

Education is a *moral* enterprise in that it is about *questioning values*. This involves a process of what has been called 'double-loop learning'. Double-loop learning 'depends on being able to take a "double-look" at a situation by questioning the relevance of operational norms' (Morgan, 1986, p. 88). Double-loop learning is educational to its core because, as Morgan states, it encourages 'an openness and reflectivity that accepts error and uncertainty as an inevitable feature of life in complex and changing environments' (p. 91). It 'recognizes the importance of exploring different viewpoints' (p. 91) and does not attempt to 'impose goals, objectives and targets' (p. 92). It is about being what Schon (1983) calls 'a reflective practitioner'. Education as a moral undertaking questions values and beliefs rather than uncritically accept cultural norms or received wisdom. Thus the values and beliefs on which political, social and economic life is based are of central concern to education.

Because education is about questioning, it is also *rational*. It *questions the evidence* in search of the truth. Nurture, instruction and training simply accept 'evidence'; education is about analysing and challenging it. As a consequence, it fosters collective as well as personal ownership of the outcomes of such questioning and debate.

Education as learning is a journey of *discovery* with no predetermined end. Education does not impose goals, objectives and targets. It is open to all possible outcomes. Because education moves the learner into the unknown and carries an element of risk it also requires lifelong commitment. Education 'involves the ability to negotiate new meanings and become a new person' (Wenger, 1998, p. 219). That ability brings the capacity to forge a vision of how to advance and enrich the whole of human life. It is a process that is imperative if humankind is to create genuine learning communities.

In education, the learner's role is not determined by the teacher or instructor, the tradition or the curriculum, but *negotiated with the learner*. This entails learners taking personal responsibility for their own learning and making the best use they can of the skills and resources available. In education, the teacher also seeks to foster a *democratic* culture and to work in *partnership* with the learner so that 'all can learn from each' (Willie and Hodgson, 1991, p. 173).

Permeating all these aspects of education as learning is its core quality, *openness*. The functional tools for learning provided by nurture, instruction and training remain essential but circumscribed. Education breaks moulds and enables those involved to embark together on a journey of discovery that offers them a life-enhancing quality of learning. As Senge (1990, p. 284) puts it: 'Openness is more than a set of skills . . . (it is) a characteristic of relationships.' As such, education becomes an essential tool in our quest to transform the world into a community of learning communities. Morrell, an Assistant Under-Secretary of State at the Home Office in the early 1970s and architect of their pioneering 'community development projects', expresses this point in classic form (in Keeble, 1981, p. 44):

This is the purpose of education: to foster the growth of loving persons, who are aware both of their own individuality and of their membership one of another; who accept one another and who, understanding their own independent nature, choose to use their experience creatively in co-operation with one another.

36

In our search for forms of learning community that can enable us to avoid chaos and transform our world into a place of beauty, plenty, justice and peace, it is to learning as education that we must look. Therefore, when in future in this book we us the word 'learning' in relation to 'the learning community' it is always learning as *education* that we will have in mind. And when in future we use the word 'community', whether or not we add the word 'learning' to it, it is the *learning* community to which we will be referring.

A Christian perspective

The kingdom community as a learning community

The Trinity, as the pre-eminent Christian image of community, portrays three 'Persons', each with their own unique identity, yet intimately related. All relationships involve learning; and mature relationships involve that quality of learning we have described as education. If this is true of human relationships, and if we are created in the image of God, then it follows that the Trinity is itself a divine community that is engaged in learning. Or, as Hull puts it, God must be a 'divine learner' (1985, p. 224). Thus, this divine quality of learning becomes not only a fourth Trinitarian attribute but a fourth Trinitarian gift alongside the gifts of life, liberation and love. When accepted, it transforms human learning, even learning as education, into a completely new experience. Through our relationship with the Trinity as a learning community, our own learning is infinitely enriched.

When the gift of learning is accepted, our journey of discovery becomes a journey of spiritual discovery and growth. It is a journey that is different for every human being yet one in which all are guided by God's divine gift of learning. 'The fulfilment of an *educated* [our italics] spirituality lies on the far side of the Trinity, not in falling back from it' (Hull, 1985, p. 39).

The image of God as a divine learner has other implications for our understanding of God's relationships to human beings with their 'abyss of possibilities' (p. 225). If God has given human beings the freedom to learn, then even God cannot predict what will happen. Thus 'there appears to be no reason at all why [we] should not realize that God is learning from [us]' (p. 236). The journey of spiritual discovery and growth on which we are embarked thus becomes, as all true education requires, a shared journey of discovery in which all are open to learning from one another.

The image of *the kingdom community* also embraces the idea of God as

37

divine learner that is manifested by the Trinity. However, as Lesslie Newbigin puts it: 'The news is that "the kingdom of God" is no longer merely a theological phrase. There is now a name and a human face [to put to it]' (1980, p. 20), that of Jesus Christ. Hull sees the idea of God as a divine learner reflected in the life of Jesus as learner. He writes:

> When we ask whether God can learn we are not trying to reconstruct the divine life upon the model of our human experience any more than we are trying to reconstruct what our human experience should be like upon the model of what God is like. *We are, in fact, doing both* [our italics]. The movement of our thought is in both directions, from God to the human person and from the person back to God again, and in each case our thought passes through Jesus Christ, the Lord of Learning and the mediator between God and humanity. (Hull, 1985, p. 219)

The life of Jesus, as the personification of the kingdom community (Mark 1.15; Luke 4.21), shows us that learning lies at its very heart. It also shows us that the nature of that learning within the kingdom community is profoundly educational.

In what follows we will again be referring to Figure 2 and to the features of learning as education set out in the right-hand column.

In the kingdom community, the process of learning as education begins with the needs of the learner – body, mind and spirit – and the fulfilment of his or her possibilities as a *person* of infinite value and ultimate worth: young or old, rich or poor, upright or devious, in a position of power or socially marginalized. Learning in the kingdom community embraces the whole of *life*; whether the learner's needs be about food, health, money, family life, getting right with oneself and one's fellows, relations with other races or about being in communion with God. The purpose of our membership of the kingdom community is to enable us, individually and collectively, to learn how to become fully human.

Learning within the kingdom community is both a *moral (questioning values)* and a *rational (questioning evidence)* undertaking. Central to that process are questions about the meaning and purpose of life. Hawkins (1991, pp. 172–87) here adds an interesting extra dimension to what we described earlier as 'double-loop learning'. He believes that even double-loop learning is inadequate because it is bounded by an implicit 'philosophy of effectiveness' in a competitive world. He argues that the most important questions arise out of our potential for 'triple-loop learning', that which involves the learner in coming to terms with his or her mortality and related issues of meaning and purpose. He views such learning as a spiritual endeavour. Thus learning at its most profound engages us in triple-loop thinking, enabling us to see the cosmos as a whole, material and spiritual, and discover our place within it.

It was to help his hearers engage in such 'triple-loop learning' that Jesus posed so many searching questions. He deliberately jolted people into educational forms of faith development by compelling them to make value judgements and address moral issues of a personal and social nature. His teaching required people to question the origins and authority of the laws and traditions by which they lived their daily lives. In many cases the 'simple' stories he told raised penetrating questions about God's purposes and our response to them.

Learning of this kind cannot help but be an ongoing journey of spiritual *discovery*. For those prepared to 'seek first' the kingdom community, everything else that really matters is taken care of (Matthew 6.3). Yet though the kingdom community is all around us (Luke 17.21), it is hidden like the leaven in the lump (Luke 13.20–21) and its ways are not obvious (Mark 4.11). Discovering its true nature will bring many surprises (being *Surprised by Joy*, as C. S. Lewis (1959) put it) and, in the process, create energy and zest to pursue the journey. Learning that derives from asking real-life questions and being open to *The God of Surprises* (Hughes, 1985) is also about the importance of visions. The dream of what it means to be fully human within the purposes of God has to be continually revisited (Hull, 1985, p. 173). Such dreaming brings hope and life both to the learning process and to the learner.

A learning journey of this demanding nature requires commitment. Jesus was more than aware that it needed considerable determination to go on seeking the kingdom community when the way ahead was not at all clear and the track was very rough. Yet, unlike the scribes and Pharisees, he never sought to compel people to follow in his footsteps. As with the lawyer asking him about inheriting eternal life (Luke 10.25), Jesus was always ready to *negotiate with the learner* what the focus of the journey should be about.

Jesus' understanding of the kingdom community as a learning community was founded on an *openness* to God, to one another and to ourselves. It was about people becoming members of a community that enabled them to learn how to break clear of their cultural home (Luke 18.29b–30) without devaluing what it had offered them through nurture, instruction and training. It was about people gaining the inspiration and the courage to embark on a shared journey of spiritual discovery that could give them the hope of avoiding chaos and of building a new Jerusalem.

The image of the kingdom community, embracing the image of both kingdom and Trinity to form an integral whole, adds a rich faith-dimension to our understanding of learning as education. It is a dimension that enables us to see the kingdom community as the epitome and zenith of all learning communities.

Summing up, we can now take further our earlier thesis concerning the presence of the kingdom community in everyday life (Chapter 2). *The kingdom community is present wherever God's gifts of life, liberation, love and learning are manifest within and across social collectives.* We add a fourth 'L', that of learning, to the three other Trinitarian gifts and thus to the gifts of the kingdom community.

Social collectives conducive to education

Having explored learning as education from both educational and theological perspectives, our next task (as with our discussion of community in Chapter 2) is to explore which social collectives are most conducive to furthering the learning process in practice.

Like the strength of community, learning as education is not always easy to identify. In the last resort, it is the learner's own experience that indicates when it is taking place. If the observer has the time and opportunity to question the learner about that experience, all well and good. If this is not possible, other ways of determining which model of learning is being followed must be attempted. Here again certain forms of social collective prove themselves to be particularly conducive to an educational model of learning.

It should come as little surprise that those social collectives conducive to the development of community (the communal group, the network, the communal institution and the partnership) are also most conducive to learning as education (Clark, 1996, pp. 115–64, and see below in this chapter: 'No community without learning; no learning without community'). However, in the case of education, one other social collective needs to be added to our list: 'the hearing'. We shall look at this after we have discussed the communal group.

The communal group

A social collective especially conducive to learning as education is the communal group. Those features that distinguish it as a collective conducive to community also make it conducive to education. Particularly important here are its human-scale and its personal qualities. As a communal group, the family par excellence provides a vital foundation for learning as education. Outside the home, the peer group for young people and the interest group for adults can also have a profound educational impact. Indeed, such informal learning from practice, 'situated learning' as it is sometimes described, often has greater educational impact than formal learning.

Even in a formal context, however, learning has more chance of being educational in nature if it takes place within a small group. This is not just because of the interpersonal and inclusive nature of such a group, but because in a human-scale, face-to-face collective the learner has more chance to speak and be heard, as well as to listen and learn. The communal group also offers many more opportunities for the learner to be able to negotiate his or her learning aims and learning context.

The importance of the communal group as a fundamental form of educational collective has been continually neglected even by the so-called 'educational' world. For example, the teacher training college in which I taught for many years had no place in its curriculum for students to learn the skills of group work. In this respect it was typical of many other teacher training institutions across the country. The consequence is that many teachers have little knowledge of group work theory and their practice fails to benefit from its important insights.

The hearing

The primary purpose of the hearing, as we see it, is to help people 'to dream dreams and see visions' so that those ways of doing things that no longer build community can make way for new communal possibilities and alignments. Hearings tap into people's hopes and longings, using their concerns about the present as a springboard for visioning. Hearings open up creative ideas and new possibilities by encouraging double-loop and triple-loop learning. They encourage those involved to undertake a journey of discovery, one that can produce many surprises and new insights. Thus hearings are richly educational in character.

Hearings are founded on open-ended dialogue. They promote reflection on people's existing social constructs and the questioning of their existing norms and practices. Hearings foster what Chris Argyris (1990, pp. 106–7) calls 'social virtues'. These include increasing people's 'capacity to confront their own ideas, to create a window into their own mind, and to face their unsurfaced assumptions, biases and fears'. Hearings also foster Argyris' social virtues of encouraging people 'to say what they know yet fear to say', and enabling them to 'advocate [their] principles, values, and beliefs in a way that invites inquiry into them and encourages other people to do the same'.

Hearings can range from small focus groups to large forums (Clark, 1996, pp. 148–65), with many other forms in between. They can be formal or informal in nature. Dialogue often takes place across current social and cultural divides. They usually last for only a short time and a few sessions. Nevertheless, because they encourage intense and open debate, hearings often engender a strong, if short-lived, sense of community.

The network

The network has considerable educational potential because the learning involved is usually self-motivated and self-organized. It is the learner who here has the clear responsibility for determining the nature and pace of the learning process. Networking can offer especially rich educational rewards where it is used as a means of discovery and where the contacts established offer new or unexpected experiences.

This form of learning has come to the fore with the development of information technology and the Internet. These promise to extend learning opportunities to a vast number of those who have hitherto been denied them. The ongoing exchange of ideas and viewpoints between participants from different social, cultural and religious backgrounds, as in the case of many e-mail or discussion lists, can be highly educational.

However, it is difficult to predict just how educational, as opposed to simply informative or instructional, information technology networks as a whole will be. Because 'information' technology is frequently used to obtain or provide factual information, the user may not necessarily be involved in an educational process as such. For example, where Internet learning is circumscribed by a precisely designed programme or course, the learning process may be modelled more on instruction or training than education.

Nonetheless, the network, in its increasingly diverse manifestations, remains a form of social collective with huge potential to offer genuinely educational opportunities.

The communal institution and partnerships

Where the communal institution draws fully on the educational opportunities provided by communal groups and networks within its orbit, it can be a highly significant educational collective. Communal institutions take on even richer educational characteristics where they are involved in partnerships. Partnerships offer their participating institutions the chance of sharing ideas, experiences and resources, of breaking out of closed systems and of greatly enhancing learning as education in the process.

What is a learning community?

It is acknowledged that all the forms of social collective discussed above can become closed rather than open to learning. However, if this were to happen they would also cease to be *communal* collectives because, being closed to learning, they would inevitably become socially exclusive. Thus our contention that the social collectives we have been considering are conducive to learning as education assumes that they have retained their communal qualities. There can be no learning without community, and no community without learning.

'No community without learning; no learning without community'

In this and the previous chapter, we have been seeking a deeper understanding of the nature of the learning community by focusing, first, on the concept of community and, second, on learning as education. However, as just indicated, our key concepts of community and learning are not only complementary but also inseparable. We thus offer one further thesis: *A learning community is a social collective that is continuously involved in learning to be a community.*

43

'No community without learning'

Community needs learning because the importance of a sense of security, significance and solidarity, and of the inclusive values opening up the scope of these sentiments, are by no means self-evident. It is all too easy to allow the forces operating in today's world to drive us outwards into the wilderness or inwards into the fortress without realizing or questioning what is being lost in the process (Chapter 1). In the quest for community, nurture, instruction and training have their part to play. But no collective can hope to understand the true nature of community and how to create and sustain it, unless learning as education enables us to grasp that our three 'S's (and the first three 'L's that are intimately related to them) are key factors in creating a sense of community.

Community also needs learning because community is about inclusiveness. To practise inclusiveness requires openness to the importance of difference and diversity, an openness that education makes possible. An ability to understand and appreciate ways of life beyond the one in which we ourselves have been nurtured, instructed and trained is a constant challenge to our own communal identity. Unless learning can give us the tools to weigh evidence and to question values, we cannot hope to find a vision of a global community of communities that will give us the courage to join hands with those beyond our own collective while remaining true to our own.

The quest for community is an exhilarating yet demanding process of discovery. It is a journey motivated by a zest for life and a vision of how, individually and collectively, we can become fully human. In that undertaking, it is learning as education that reveals the nature, richness and power of community and offers us insights into the means of achieving it.

'No learning without community'

On the other hand, learning needs community. Without community, learning becomes a functional affair, often impersonal and arduous (Clark, 1986, pp. 56–61). The more that learning exposes the learner to experiences that appear strange and threatening, the stronger the sense of community (our three 'S's enriched by our first three 'L's) needed to make creative use of those experiences.

Having the security of a safe and healthy environment is vital if learning as education is to take place. It is very difficult to learn if food, clothing and shelter are lacking, though it is a tribute to the human spirit that this can happen, as we ourselves witnessed when visiting schools of impressive quality situated in the squalor of Soweto and the South African 'homelands' when apartheid was in force.

Learning is also a difficult task where the learner lacks a sense of significance. The alienation of students who have little sense of self-esteem has been documented time and again. Klein, in her seminal work on small groups, writes that 'peripheral or lower-status members [of any group] are less likely to learn' (Klein, 1963, p. 122). Because learning as education is founded on the ultimate worth of the person, anything that undermines that worth is educationally self-defeating.

Likewise, a sense of solidarity within the social collective concerned is vital if learning is to achieve its full potential. Solidarity not only enhances commitment and fosters enthusiasm, but releases essential resources for the learning task by facilitating the sharing of knowledge, skills and experience. 'Co-operative classrooms use the motto, "None of us is as smart as all of us",' write the Stainbacks (1992, p. 30) in their investigation of 'inclusive classrooms'. We fail to make use of a vast amount of untapped educational potential because sharing ideas and resources in the learning situation is either neglected or narrowly conceived. A whole world of experience thus goes to waste.

There can be no learning without community because learning as education can only take place when it draws on the communal synergy of our three 'S's (a sense of security, significance and solidarity complementing one another). But there can be no learning without community for one further reason. Learning as education, in its concern with the whole of life and the dignity of every person, can only achieve its full potential where restrictive practices and rigid boundaries are overcome and the communal dilemma resolved. Thus learning, as an open process, can only happen within collectives that are committed to the all-important communal value of inclusiveness.

Learning communities for a flourishing world

There can be no community without learning, and no learning without community. Therefore it is little wonder, as we have argued, that the social collectives that give the fullest expression to community and to learning are similar: the communal group, the network, the communal institution and the partnership.

The concept of the learning community embraces the inseparability of community and learning. Though community and learning have their own distinctive contribution to make to the learning community, the latter remains an integral whole. The learning community is a dynamic synthesis of community and learning. It represents the fundamental nature of the social collectives that we need to create if humankind is to survive and to thrive, be these families, neighbourhoods, cities or nations. Only by liberating the power of learning communities can chaos be overcome and our world be able to flourish.

A global community of learning communities

Social collectives are engaged in a vast variety of activities that, at least ostensibly, have little or nothing to do with building community. What is more, all such collectives have to achieve the task for which they were set up if they are to survive. Rice (1965, p. 17) has called this 'the primary task' of the collective. The primary task of few collectives is that of developing themselves, or other collectives, as learning communities. How then can learning communities come into being if it is the achievement of the collective's primary task, essential for the sustainability of the collective but apparently unrelated to community building, that dominates the scene?

No social collective can neglect its primary task. That would destroy its collective's purpose and ultimately threaten its survival. However, if we are to build community and avoid chaos, every social collective will now need to develop the art of integrating the task of learning to be a community into its primary task, and thereby into its ongoing life and culture. In whatever field a collective operates, be it health, welfare, trade, business, law and order, the arts, defence, government, or religion itself, it is imperative for the survival of our world that each seeks to integrate the task of becoming a learning community into the way it goes about its primary task. In this connection, it is crucially important that our so-called 'educational' institutions, currently so preoccupied with instruction and training, take far more seriously their function as role models for the whole of society of what learning communities should be like.

Only when social collectives of every kind and in every field commit themselves to becoming learning communities will we be able to transform neighbourhoods, cities and nations into learning communities. Only then will we be able to create that global community of learning communities on which the survival of human civilization depends.

46

4

What is leadership?

The community educator

To create a global community of learning communities requires a distinctive form of leadership at every level from the communal group to the communal institution. What is the nature of such leadership? In addressing this question we must first return to our discussion of learning models (Figure 2, page 33) in order to see why leadership styles related to models of learning other than education are unsuited to the learning community.

Autocratic and dictatorial styles of leadership, which are used to indoctrinate, are clearly anathema to the building of learning communities. Nurture, at its best, requires a supportive and caring style of leadership, be it maternal or paternal, which seeks to protect the learner while guiding him or her towards assimilating the indigenous culture, familial and societal. However, this style of leadership is concerned more with fostering assent than dissent, more with obedience than challenge. It is not involved in the questioning of norms and values that is such an important aspect of education and the life of the learning community.

Instruction and training are typically associated with a directive form of leadership, largely because the dominant purpose of instruction is to inform and explain, and of training to demonstrate and coach. Leadership in both these cases may encourage questions but these are expected to relate to the subject or skills being taught. An acceptance of the purpose and cultural context of the learning process is assumed by the instructor or trainer. In contrast to instruction and training, the leader's role in relation to education, and thus to the learning community, is different in kind.

We call the leadership role that we are seeking to identify that of *community educator* (see also Clark, 1996, pp. 99–114). It is a role that can apply not only to individuals but also to groups or organizations concerned with community building.

Leadership characteristics of the community educator

The community educator is a change-agent who ultimately serves the vision of a new global order. The nature and magnitude of the changes required to create such an order are daunting. We remind ourselves that Simpson (1937, p. 39) described the challenge as that of 'carrying over the ideal of the primary or face-to-face group which is most easily communalized, to the larger group, and ultimately to nations and international action'. And that Boswell spoke of our failure to tackle this communal undertaking as 'a gigantic omission' (1990, p. 3).

How then can the community educator most effectively exercise his or her leadership responsibilities as a visionary and change agent? A number of associated roles exemplify that of the community educator. Two are paramount: that of *catalyst* and that of *enabler*.

The community educator is a *catalyst* because the transformation of the values and attitudes needed to address the vision of the world as a global community of learning communities is formidable. Yet it cannot be a role exercised from a position of power whereby change is imposed on people. It has to be one that seeks to stimulate and foster a new vision of our communal future by the open questioning of established values, norms and traditions. The community educator may sometimes employ the surprise factor by encouraging new and seemingly risky encounters to break the mould of established ideas. He or she may employ double-loop (or triple-loop) thinking, a key educational tool in facilitating fundamental shifts in attitude and outlook. However, the nature of the community educator's role remains catalytic because the questioning of established mores is often a demanding and difficult process requiring the ability to challenge as well as to support the learner.

Complementing the role of catalyst is that of *enabler*. The community educator's skill to rouse people to think 'outside the box', to dream dreams and have visions, needs to be accompanied by the ability to help them make those dreams and visions a reality by acquiring the skills to become community builders. This enabling role is grounded in 'a culture of trust'. Unless the members of the collective feel that the community educator values them as persons, little will be achieved.

As an enabler, the community educator is both teacher and learner at the same time. Learning becomes a partnership. Wherever possible, the process of community building is openly negotiated and an agreement, or 'contract', to stick at the task entered into by all involved.

This enabling aspect of the community educator's task is sometimes described as working for 'empowerment'. However, there is often some confusion about the sort of 'power' to which the term 'empowerment' refers. 'Power' comes from a range of impersonal and external sources of influence that an individual possesses – status, wealth, information and so on. 'Authority', on the other hand, has a different source. It comes from a person's view of his or her own worth and from their affirmation by others.

Community building is a task that relies on, as well as enhances, the 'authority' of each and every member of the collective. Such authority may encompass 'power' but is never dependent on it. Thus the person who is an able organizer, competent secretary, teller of funny stories, good mother or caring friend may have little 'power' but considerable 'authority'. The task of the community educator is to help strengthen people's 'authority' in ways that encourage them to take increasing responsibility for their part in the community building process. This aspect of his or her task will involve the community educator in working to diminish the dependence of participants on himself or herself, and to create a situation where leadership is dispersed throughout the whole collective.

Two other roles are of special note in relation to the work of the community educator: those of *intermediary* and *resource person*.

The importance of the community educator's role as *intermediary* is founded on the premise that a wealth of human resources for community building is latent within every social collective. Therefore, a key aspect of the community educator's role is to foster creative connections within and between collectives so that visions, experience, ideas, skills and resources can be shared. It is the power of 'human fusion' that holds the key to the future communal well-being of our world. The task of the community educator as intermediary is to foster such 'human fusion' by enabling people to share their beliefs, insights, knowledge and skills across economic, social and cultural divides in new and imaginative ways.

The other important role that the community educator needs to play is that of *resource person*. Community educators should be well acquainted with the wide range of persons and collectives with whom they are dealing, and with their experiences, skills and abilities. They must also develop communally important contacts and connections with those who do not come under their immediate purview. Their competence in the field of information technology can be a great asset here. They also need to be skilled as group workers, 'community workers' and networkers. It is no surprise, therefore, that Leonie Sandercock (1998, p. 99), in the context of urban planning, describes the community educator's role as requiring 'nothing less than a new professional identity'.

Community educators will often be acting on their own. However, real benefits accrue where they are able to operate as part of a team that can offer a diversity of skills and resources. This kind of team is often to be found within communal institutions. Where this is the case, such institutions have a vital role to play as intermediary *agencies*.

'The learning organization'

A number of the leadership features of the community educator identified above appear in the abundant literature on 'the learning organization'. In fact, it is the business world, where the concept of the learning organization has been in vogue for some time, that has stimulated more reflection on the qualities of leadership needed to sustain and enhance contemporary organizations than either the public or voluntary sector (see, for example, Senge, 1990; Handy, 1990; Pedler et al, 1991; Garratt, 2001). Even so, the concept of the learning organization does not fully deliver the goods as far as we are concerned. It is relatively strong on education, but weak on community. It is our conviction that the concept of the learning *community* offers far deeper insights into the needs of today's world than that of the learning *organization*.

It is disappointing that the advocates of the learning organization fail to address the meaning and potential of community, and so fail to address at any depth the matter of the values that underpin (or undermine?) such organizations. As a result, they are on shaky ground when they advocate collaboration, champion 'inter-company learning' (Pedler et al, 1991, pp. 22–3) and talk of the creation of 'a good company' (p. 148), or even of a 'spiritual' ethos (pp. 12, 17), yet fail to address the issue of the dominance of market forces which mean that certain collectives must always 'win' and some always 'lose'. Our task, therefore, is to continue to explore what new light and fresh insights symbolic universes such as the Christian faith can throw on the kind of leadership needed for the creation of learning communities.

A Christian perspective

Christ as community educator

The kingdom community sets leadership in a very different context from the learning organization. If, as Adair argues (2001, p. 132), 'the "kingdom of God" [is] a *leadership* vision, [for] without a vision no real change can enter history; no significance progress can be made', then it has to be a leadership vision related to a kingdom that is communally inclusive and educationally open.

The good news preached by Jesus Christ was the vision of the kingdom community. Because 'Jesus was a man with a vision, [that of] "the kingdom of God on earth"' (p. 122), his leadership offers us a model of the kind of leadership needed to make the kingdom community a reality. As we see it, Jesus' leadership exemplifies that of the community educator. How then, by using Jesus as our model, might the role of the community educator be further informed and enhanced?

Jesus exemplified the community educator as *catalyst*. His first public appearance saw him calling people in no uncertain terms to 'repent and believe in the gospel' because the kingdom of God was 'at hand' (Mark 1.15). He provoked his hearers to ask questions about the way they lived their daily lives, to review their understanding of what it meant to be 'cured' of their ailments, to challenge received wisdom about how the laws of the land should be interpreted and, above all, to look at their relationship with God and one another in a new light. His aim was to stimulate them to fashion a new vision of what God was up to, not just for their benefit as 'the chosen people' but for the well-being of the whole of humankind.

Jesus refused to coerce people, yet taught with an 'authority' that was evident even to his enemies (Mark 1.22). When he took direct action, such as the occasion on which he threw the money-changers out of the temple (Mark 11.15–18), his purpose was not to engage in a unilateral act of defiance of the powers that be, but to get people to rethink their understanding of the nature of God and what he required of them.

Jesus exemplified the role of community educator as *enabler*. It was a role rooted in his affirmation of all whom he met and in the trust that people placed in him as a result. He revealed a relationship to God and an understanding of his purposes for the world that seemed utterly authentic. At the same time, Jesus sought to help people to stand on their own feet (sometimes literally) and claim the kingdom community for themselves. This entailed encouraging them to take responsibility for their own lives and to exercise the 'authority' they already possessed. So, for example, Jesus deliberately sent people away after he had cured or assisted them, with instructions that they too become enablers. He did not seek to hold on to leadership but to disperse it.

Other leadership roles figure prominently in the ministry of Jesus. One of these was that of *intermediary*. Jesus sought to impart his vision of the kingdom community by making redemptive connections between God and his people, and between human beings themselves. It was an undertaking that involved him in being a go-between, mediator and bridge-builder. Rosemary Haughton describes the role of intermediary as one that enables people to break through the divides that separate them from God and each other, and to bring about 'an exchange of life, whose name is love' (1981, p. 22). This exchange, and the flow of divine–human energy which derives from it, gives access to the gifts of the kingdom community and promises the transformation of human society. Jesus as an intermediary was pre-eminent in facilitating such 'an exchange of life' between all those he met.

Jesus also exemplified the community educator as a *resource person*. He possessed a deep understanding of people and their concerns, born of 30 years of living among them as his family, neighbours and friends, listening to them and learning from them as a true leader must. He had a profound understanding of God's purposes that came from reflecting on everyday life, doing so in the light of his knowledge of the Jewish scriptures. As a result, he was able to relate to an amazing diversity of people and to offer them deep but accessible insights into the nature of the kingdom community. He also offered them the gifts of the kingdom community (life, liberation, love and learning) so that they might be able to live according to its values. As a resource person, Jesus served people in ways that often drained him (Mark 5.30): he asked a lot of others, but gave more.

As a community educator, Jesus demonstrated one further aspect of leadership that the analysis of the role of the community educator earlier in this chapter did not bring to the fore. Jesus not only proclaimed the coming of the kingdom community and called people to commit themselves to it, but saw himself as its *servant*. Thus Hull argues that our understanding of the nature of leadership within the kingdom community 'must be accompanied by a restored and more faithful image of Jesus Christ as the servant-saviour and the learner-leader' (Hull, 1985, p. 209). For Jesus, servanthood did not mean slavish obedience or abject servitude, but total commitment to the service of God and his kingdom community.

Jesus always saw this servant ministry as one in which he walked alongside others as a partner. He was God incarnate: God *with* us. Hull writes (1985, p. 208): '[Normally] the teacher is the minister to the learner. In the Christian kingdom things are reversed. Just as the one who will be first and most powerful must become the servant and slave of all, so the one who would be teacher must become the learner from all (Mark 10.42–45).' The store that Jesus set on partnership is demonstrated in his relationship with those whom he called to share in the building of the kingdom community. 'True leaders do not seek to create followers, but partners,' writes Adair (2001, p. 117). Jesus went further and called his 'followers' his 'friends' (John 15.14–15). Unlike secular partnerships, their relationship with him was not a contract but a 'new covenant' founded on mutual affirmation and trust.

Leadership in the kingdom community is not only an individual matter. 'Jesus expected his disciples to live the vision of "the kingdom of God" and thereby fulfil their calling,' writes Adair (2001, p. 133). Thus from the outset Jesus sought to delegate the task of bringing in the kingdom to a group of people. As the years passed such groups proliferated, leading to the emergence of the church as an organization called to make the good news of the kingdom community a reality in everyday life. In that capacity, the church as a body assumes two particularly important leadership roles. First, it is called to be an *intermediary agency*, seeking to connect human beings with God and with one another and, in that process, break down the divides that destroy redemptive relationships. Second, it is commissioned to fulfil this calling as a *servant*. In what follows, we explore what it means for the church to be a servant church.

Part 2

The diaconal church – a model

Introduction

In the face of the choice between community and chaos, the purpose and nature of every institution is called into question. We have argued that until institutions become learning communities on a global scale, the communal dilemma will prove impossible to resolve, social collectives will turn in on themselves and chaos will win out. What is true for other institutions is also true for the church. But the church has a unique responsibility. It is called by God to witness to the epitome of all learning communities, the kingdom community, and to build communities that manifest the kingdom community's gifts of life, liberation, love and learning. What, then, would a church seeking to fulfil this calling look like?

The church as model

In order to address this question we need to introduce the concept of the 'model'. We define a 'model', with Avery Dulles (quoted in Bevans, 1992, p. 24), as 'a relatively simple, artificially constructed case, which is found to be useful and illuminating for dealing with realities that are more complex and differentiated'. As Titmuss puts it (quoted in Martin, 1987, p. 23): 'Model building is not to admire the architecture of the building but to help us to see some order in all the disorder and confusion of facts, systems and choices.' What we describe in this part of the book is not a blueprint. It is a model of a church whose nature, form and leadership enable it to reflect and communicate the essence of the kingdom community.

The church is not the kingdom community. The church is the 'servant' (*diakonos*) of the kingdom community. The church that God is calling into being to serve the kingdom community and to meet the needs of our age is a 'diaconal church'. Part 2 of this book focuses on the theological and ecclesiological features of our model of the diaconal church. In Parts 3 and 4 we explore what the diaconal church might look like in practice.

Unfortunately, the diaconal model of church is not the one that currently informs and shapes the life of the church in the West, and in many places beyond. It is the model of the Christendom church that dominates the scene. Its legacy remains so all-pervasive that unless the mould of Christendom can be broken, the diaconal church will never come into being. In Part 2 we shall be looking at the differences between the Christendom and diaconal models of church. First, however, we need to outline the Christendom model of church in order to give us a template against which we can set our model of the diaconal church.

Christendom

The model of church that we in the West have inherited is that of Christendom. We define 'Christendom', in the words of Aidan Nichols (1999, p. 1) as 'a society where the historic Christian faith provides the cultural framework for social living, as well as the official religious form of the State'.

In the past, Christendom was both a religious and a geo-political entity. Most historians are agreed that the Christendom era began in 313 when the Emperor Constantine declared that Christianity should have official recognition throughout the Roman Empire, though others look to Theodosius's reign (379–95) as the time when Christianity first became the empire's majority religion.

Christendom was of profound importance. 'The experiment of a Christian political order had to be made,' states Newbigin (1983, p. 34). For many centuries, Christendom shaped and sustained the life of an entire civilization, from princes and pontiffs to peasants and priests. Reflecting our earlier definition of community, it offered people a strong sense of security, significance and solidarity: a sense of security founded on shared territory and a common heritage, and a sense of significance and solidarity founded on family and parish life. Christendom was also a civilization in which the 'seven ages of man' were clearly marked out, the rules well defined, sanctions formidable and boundaries firm. To this world the church offered the resources of the Christian faith to sustain and enrich communal life. The Christendom church had many assets, so much so that some people, like Aidan Nichols in his *Christendom Awake*, long for its renewal.

Yet Christendom was also founded on 'coercion, control and domination' (McLeod and Ustorf, 2003, p. 218). As the world became increasingly mobile geographically, cognitively, socially and culturally, Christendom sought to retain its coherence by rejecting new expressions of community and resisting changes that threatened its identity and power. Far from addressing the communal dilemma – how to become open to other cultures without weakening itself as a community – it sought to impose its own culture on an ever wider scale. Hence, as a geo-political entity, it became the model for competing land-based empires that lasted into the middle of the twentieth century. However, as Howe notes (2002, p. 6), although such great historic imperial systems have collapsed during the past half-century, their legacies still shape every aspect of global life.

Throughout Christendom, the church was closely identified with secular power. Not only did it exercise spiritual domination over the lives of men and women, it frequently sought to order affairs of state as well. Even in the post-Reformation era, the church continued to carry forward its mission in Christendom mode. Indeed, Dulles argues that the Counter-Reformation led to a more imperialistic form of centralization and institutionalization within the Roman Catholic Church than ever before (1976, p. 189). As Christendom merged into empire, 'the most powerful and widespread early-modern argument vindicating empire was a religious one' (Howe, 2002, p. 84) even if, as Porter (2004) argues, Christian missionaries were not uncritical propagandists of empire. As empire-building continued apace, the attitude of all churches was that 'not only should new worlds be won for Christendom but specifically for one's own particular version of it, denying opportunities of conquest and conversion to the heretics' (Howe, 2002, p. 84).

What is still disputed is when Christendom's decline commenced. Hugh McLeod (McLeod and Ustorf, 2003, p. 16–19) identifies three different periods that scholars claim are the decisive ones in precipitating that decline. Some see the seventeenth and eighteenth centuries, in particular the Enlightenment, as the main period of Christendom's demise. Another school of thought sees Christendom's decline as running from the French Revolution in 1789 to the end of World War Two. However, more recently, it has been argued that it was 'the "long 1960s" from 1956 to 1973 [that] appear as a cataclysm for the place of religion in British [and European] society' (Callum Brown in McLeod and Ustorf, 2003, p. 35).

Whenever Christendom's decline began, there is 'no way back to the Constantinean alliance between church and state' (Newbigin, 1983, p. 34). Nevertheless, McLeod and his fellow writers believe that 'we are still living in its [Christendom's] shadow' (McLeod and Ustorf, 2003, p. 2). Indeed the hypothesis upon which their book is based is 'that the coercion, control and domination that were part of the Christendom model of church and mission carry within themselves the seeds of the modern repudiation of Christianity in Europe' (p. 218). We accept that hypothesis.

McManners (1990, p. 665) spells out the implications of this legacy:

> Even if the dream of a culturally integrated 'common Europe home' were to be achieved, a united Europe that imagined itself to be Christendom once again could do only harm to the world-wide Christian movement ... The choice between the open, diversified church and the church behind institutional and mental barricades emerges yet more clearly as the supreme issue for the next century.

Yet the fact remains that the church in the West is still moulded by the Christendom model of church. Loren Mead (1991, p. 18) puts it as follows:

> We are surrounded by the relics of the Christendom Paradigm, a paradigm that has largely ceased to work. But the relics hold us hostage to the past, and make it difficult to create a new paradigm that can be as compelling for the next age as the Christendom Paradigm has been for the past age.

We believe that it is this continuing captivity to the legacy of Christendom that prevents the church from making its communal contribution to a world that can only survive if it becomes a global community of learning communities. The task before us is to liberate the church from a Christendom model of church that is exclusive and closed by discerning how the gospel can be expressed through a model of church that is inclusive and open. Newbigin describes this task as follows (1980, p. 35):

> What we have now to seek are forms of church and ministry which neither draw men and women out of the world into a private society, nor seek to dominate the world through controlling centres of power, but enable men and women to function within the secular life of the world in ways which reflect the reality of Christ's passion and thereby make the reality of Christ's resurrection credible to victims of the world's wrongs.

At the beginning of the twenty-first century, therefore, the church is called upon to undertake yet another journey of discovery. This time, however, it is a journey that will necessitate the biggest revolution that it has faced since the emergence of Christendom. Furthermore, as that body called by God to discern and make known the gifts of the kingdom community, the church's ability to reshape its own life and mission will have critical implications for human civilization as a whole. Grace Davie (2002) asks whether *Europe is the exceptional case* in still being held fast by the mould of Christendom. We believe that the need for the church to break that mould is as crucial for the future of every other continent as it is for Europe.

This journey is 'a divine risk' (Holloway, 1990), yet it is also a divine imperative without which the resources of the kingdom community will remain untapped. It is our conviction that the church that God is calling into being to undertake this journey is the diaconal church.

Sources of the diaconal model of church

To construct our model of the diaconal church we draw on three sources. The first source is the academic insights of sociology, education and theology: a source that has provided us (as we have seen in Part 1) with the concepts of the learning community and the kingdom community, the latter transforming our understanding of the former. In describing our model of the diaconal church, we will be drawing extensively on these sociological, educational and theological insights into the nature and gifts of the kingdom community.

The second source that we draw on is empirical. Here we face something of a chicken-and-egg problem because our investigation of the diaconal church in action does not appear until Part 3. We have decided to outline our model of the diaconal church before presenting these case studies because we need that model to assist us in our analysis of the diaconal church in action. However, those features of the case studies that have important implications for our model of the diaconal church (for example, the role of the laity in the life and mission of the church) will be integrated into our model at the appropriate points in Part 2.

A third source for our model is historical. We begin here. Our question is how our model of the diaconal church can be informed by the nature of 'diaconal ministry' from the early church onwards, and especially by what happened to that form of ministry from the middle of the nineteenth century to the present day.

The history of diaconal ministry

In reviewing the history of diaconal ministry, and the lessons to be learnt from it, we draw freely on the findings of a number of working parties that over the past few years have been investigating what a so-called 'renewed diaconate' might have to offer to the life of their churches. The documents on which we draw most frequently are Roman Catholic (*From the Diakonia of Christ to the Diakonia of the Apostles*, 2003), Anglican (*For such a time as this. A renewed diaconate in the Church of England*, 2001, and *The Distinctive Diaconate*, Diocese of Salisbury, 2003), and Methodist (*What is a Deacon?*, Methodist Conference, 2004).

The early church and after

A wide diversity of diaconal forms of ministry permeated the life of the early church (Collins, 2002). These led to the emergence of the title of deacon well before the end of New Testament times, though the nature of the office during that period remains controversial. In the second and third centuries, deacons appear to have gained in status and power, in part because they developed a role as assistants to bishops and in part because they accumulated important administrative and financial responsibilities (pp. 109–10).

After Constantine offered the Christian church official recognition in 313, bishops gradually assumed the oversight of larger and larger areas. At the same time, priests took increasing responsibility for the local church, which together with a greater focus on eucharistic worship considerably enhanced their status. As a result, from the fourth century onwards the influence of deacons steadily declined. 'They became subordinate to the priests, their direct link with the bishop faded away, and they ended up having no specific function' (*From the Diakonia of Christ*, p. 30). 'The functions [of deacons] which had in the past been autonomous and practical, [gradually] became stages in the career path towards priesthood.' By the tenth century, a hierarchical order of ministry, with the deacon at its base, became the norm (p. 31). This has remained the case, notably within the Roman Catholic Church, Orthodox Church and the Church of England, up to the present day.

The nineteenth century to the present day

In the early nineteenth century, there was an unexpected upsurge of interest in diaconal ministry. In 1836 Pastor Theodor Fliedner of the German Lutheran Church founded the first deaconess institute at Kaiserswerth, training women for welfare work, nursing and teaching. The Church of England admitted its first deaconesses in 1862 (*The Distinctive Diaconate*, p. 19). In 1878 the Methodist Church began training Sisters of the Children, and in 1890 the first training institute for the Wesley Deaconess Order was set up in London (Staton, 2001, p. 103). Similar developments, mainly confined to women, were seen in other churches across Europe, especially in Scandinavia.

The reasons for this renewed interest in diaconal ministry were largely threefold. First, churches were possessed by a growing concern to re-engage with a 'working-class' culture. They were fast losing touch with working people as the industrial revolution gathered momentum and hundreds of thousands of people moved from the countryside to the city. Second, churches became increasingly aware of the needs of those for whom migration brought massive deprivation. Many people not only lost touch with their communal roots but were forced to live and work in appalling conditions in the new industrial heartlands. Trying to meet their material as well as spiritual needs demanded more trained and dedicated personnel than the church then possessed.

Third, women were beginning to look for ways of gaining an independent identity in a still dominantly male culture. Offering to work as deaconesses was one way of enhancing their status and self-esteem, as well as fulfilling their own sense of vocation. 'The deaconess movement in the nineteenth century,' writes Staton (2001, p. 94), 'was a pragmatic response to the needs and demands of contemporary society, not least the demands by women for recognition and fulfilment.'

The deaconess movement gathered momentum up to the middle of the twentieth century. As a result, in 1947 DIAKONIA, now a worldwide federation of diaconal associations, was founded (see also Chapter 14). DIAKONIA began to hold international assemblies every few years and to promote contacts, debate and reflection on the role of the diaconate across many denominations.

After World War Two, however, the picture becomes more confusing. The deaconess orders in England declined in strength. There were a number of reasons for this. The coming of the welfare state to some extent blunted the cutting edge of the church's involvement with those in poverty, were socially deprived or unemployed. This meant that the social ministries of the urban settlements and inner-city churches and missions, on whose staff many deaconesses served, were less in demand than in decades past.

At the same time competing forms of ministry, particularly presbyteral ministry, were gradually opening up to women. The Salvation Army had begun to commission women officers as early as the mid-nineteenth century. In 1904 the Unitarians, and in 1914 the Congregational Union accepted women ministers. In 1972 the Methodist Church opened presbyteral ministry to women, and in 1992 the Church of England followed suit. Within the last two churches, many deaconesses and deacons who had been 'priests in waiting', often for some time, opted to be ordained as presbyters.

These post-war developments, combined with the church's continuing ambivalence about the status of the diaconate, led the Church of England's Advisory Committee for the Church's Ministry in 1974 to recommend the abolition of the diaconate (*For such a time as this*, p. 8). The recommendation was rejected. However, in Methodism the Wesley Deaconess Order was closed to new candidates in 1978. At that time, therefore, it looked as if the diaconate, at least as it had developed over the preceding century, was reaching the end of the road.

However, other factors were at work paving the way for a renewal of interest in the diaconate. Vatican II had restored the 'permanent diaconate' (the term used by Roman Catholics to describe an ordained order of deacons who remain as such, and do not see their role as a stage en route to the priesthood). It was a decision that stemmed from a renewed theology of the church that accepted 'the diaconate as a stable order of the hierarchy' (*From the Diakonia of Christ*, p. 54). It was also given impetus by the hope that a permanent diaconate might help to relieve the workload of a declining number of Catholic priests. Although the Catholic Church initially saw the restoration of a permanent diaconate as of particular importance to the African and Asian churches, it was in fact in Europe and the United States where the restoration had most impact. By 1998 there were over 25,000 permanent (male) deacons in the Roman Catholic Church world-wide, the majority being located in the West (p. 63).

In 1986 the British Methodist Church reopened its Diaconal Order to men as well as women and by 2004 there were over 100 active deacons. In 1988 the Church of England produced a report entitled *Deacons in the*

Ministry of the Church, which encouraged the church to make provision for a permanent diaconate. A second Anglican report, *For such a time as this*, was produced in 2001. This urged that the permanent diaconate be considerably expanded, though at the discretion of each diocesan bishop. By the turn of the millennium the Church of England had some 75 permanent deacons. In 2003 the Diocese of Salisbury produced a lengthy report entitled *The Distinctive Diaconate*, urging that the church should encourage many more people to become permanent deacons.

The current debate

In using the history of diaconal ministry as a source for our model of the diaconal church, we need to recognize that 'there is no single normative model of the diaconate to which we can hark back' (*For such a time as this*, pp. 4–5). Or, as *The Distinctive Diaconate* states (p. 27), 'There is no suggestion that there is a first century model of diaconal ministry to which we can ascribe "authority" for diaconal ministry today.' Thus, although the New Testament and the early church offer us important insights into the nature of a diaconal church, it is to the history of the diaconate since its renewal in the nineteenth century, and especially to the quest for a renewed diaconate over more recent years, that we must give particular attention in our task of discernment. This is not just because 'today's theology works from today's need' (*The Distinctive Diaconate*, p. 119). It is because 'it seems that the diaconate has been particularly important in the church's mission at times of acute political and social change and upheaval' (*For such a time as this*, p. 1).

It is perhaps not surprising, therefore, that in recent years the literature on 'a renewed diaconate' has proliferated worldwide. The so-called 'Lima' document of the Faith and Order Commission of the World Council of Churches (*Baptism, Eucharist and Ministry*, 1982) was widely regarded as setting the pace for a renewed interest in the ministry of the whole people of God, with deacons seen as exemplifying the people of God's calling to a servant ministry (*For such a time as this*, p. 16). This document also witnessed an important shift from a hierarchical concept of ordained ministry to a more integrated approach that grounded ministry in the nature and mission of the church (see also Chapter 14). However, it was not until the early 1990s that interest in the diaconate began to move to centre stage, with John Collins' first book, *Diakonia: Re-interpreting the Ancient*

Sources, exploring the meaning of the *diakon-* words in the New Testament, a task he continued to pursue assiduously over the next decade and more (1992, 2002).

In 1992 Christine Hall edited a symposium entitled *The Deacon's Ministry*, a book described as filling 'an important gap' in the literature about the church's ministry, both ordained and lay. In 1996 the Anglican–Lutheran Commission published the Hanover Report, *The Diaconate as Ecumenical Opportunity*, and 'for the first time in the history of bilateral ecumenical dialogue, the diaconate was the sole focus of a report' (*For such a time as this*, p. 17). In 1997 an ecumenical and diaconal consultation was held at St George's, Windsor. It produced *The Windsor Statement*, a radical interpretation of the ministry of deacons that, among other roles, described it as 'pioneering' and 'prophetic' (see also Chapter 14).

At the end of the 1990s, the Anglo-Nordic Diaconal Research Project published two volumes of papers entitled *The Ministry of the Deacon* (Borgegard et al, 1999, 2000). These papers underlined the diverse interpretations of the ministry of the deacon in different countries and churches, and raised important ecclesiological issues concerning the future of the office. Methodism contributed to the ongoing debate with the publication in 2002 of *What is a Minister?* (Shreeve and Luscombe) which included a chapter by Sue Jackson on 'What is a Deacon?' In 2003 the Roman Catholic International Theological Commission produced a comprehensive report entitled *From the Diakonia of Christ to the Diakonia of the Apostles* in which it traced the development of the role of the deacon from biblical times to the present day and explored the office's future potential. In 2004 the British Methodist Conference approved a document entitled *What is a Deacon?* that confirmed Methodism's understanding that the diaconate was both an order of ministry and a religious order.

Why has there been this upsurge in interest in the ministry of the deacon over the past decade or so? Why, as *For such a time as this* puts it, 'across the Christian traditions and around the world [are] the churches ... rediscovering the diaconate'?

More cynical observers point to a shortage of priests. However, in the West at least, what appears to be driving the interest in a renewed diaconate is the church's consciousness of the growing gap between itself and a secular society. There is an increasing awareness that the church has to re-engage with contemporary cultures and that, as it has been shaped by Christendom, it can no longer fulfil that task. There is also a slow but growing realization of the need to enhance the role of the laity in the mission of the church, an undertaking that will require new forms of leadership for which the ordained ministry as we have it seems ill-equipped.

There are signs, however, that the upsurge of interest in the possibilities for renewal opened up by the recent interest in the role of the diaconate could wane. The response of the Church of England to its report *For such a time as this* has so far been lukewarm, other than in one or two dioceses such as Salisbury (*The Distinctive Diaconate*, p. 85). Within British Methodism, there are still many differences of view about the nature and potential of the diaconate. And the reinstatement of a permanent diaconate within the Roman Catholic Church has so far failed to herald any major changes in its understanding of hierarchical ministry or the role of the laity within the life of the church. All this is evidence of the church's habit of only half exploring avenues of renewal that could lead to a breakthrough in its approach to mission and ministry. Yet it is only as we are prepared to question some of the foundational assumptions of Christendom that we will be able to look at the nature of diaconal ministry with fresh eyes and to discover its radical, redemptive and recreative message for the life of church and world alike.

Nevertheless, we believe that the forces leading to the current debate over the role of a renewed diaconate are here to stay, and that it is a debate that has profound implications for the future. We take this position because we believe that the concept of *diakonia* (which we interpret as 'servanthood', as we will see later) relates not just to a particular order of ministry, but to every aspect of the church's life and work. As *For such a time as this* puts it, 'the diaconate remains the fundamental stratum' of all ministries, ordained and lay (p. 9). Because Christ's ministry was utterly diaconal, 'so by analogy the church is a diaconal body' (*The Distinctive Diaconate*, p. 40). *From the Diakonia of Christ* makes a similar point (p. 3): 'The Kyrios, Lord, becomes the diakonos, servant, of all,' thus 'Christian existence is a sharing in the *diakonia* or service which God himself fulfilled in favour of mankind: it likewise leads to an understanding of the fulfillment of mankind.' It is this all-embracing understanding of the meaning of *diakonia* that informs the model of the diaconal church which we set out below.

Overview of the model of the diaconal church

Figure 3 lays out an overview of our model of the diaconal church. In the first column are set out the main themes to be explored later. In the second column are those features of the Christendom model of church that continue to mould the life and work of the contemporary church. Though these features apply particularly to the church in the West, their influence extends across every continent and shapes not only the mainstream denominations but also many new expressions of church (Chapter 13). The third column summarizes the transition that needs to be made if the mould of Christendom is to be broken and a diaconal church is to come into being.

The themes of mission, culture, stance and the laity are explored in this chapter. The types of social collective conducive to the ministry of the diaconal church are examined in Chapter 6. The themes of church leadership and governance are discussed in Chapter 7.

The features of the Christendom model of church and their diaconal counterparts are also used to analyse and evaluate the case studies set out in Part 3, the movements of Christian renewal discussed in Chapter 13 and the role of a renewed diaconate in Chapter 14.

Figure 3: *From the Christendom church to the diaconal church*

Theme	The Christendom Church	The Diaconal Church
MISSION	Proselytism	From church-centred to *kingdom community-centred*
	Exclusivism	From exclusive to *inclusive communities*
	Dogmatism	From indoctrination to *education*
CULTURE	Sacralism	From a sacred to *a secular society*
	Conservatism	From preservation to *transformation*
STANCE	Imperialism	From domination to *servanthood*
THE LAITY	Clericalism	From priest to *people*
	Conformism	From dependency to *autonomy*
SOCIAL COLLECTIVES:		
Hearing	Legalism	From venerating the status quo to *visioning*
	Didacticism	From instruction to *dialogue*
Group	Parochialism	From community of place to *communities of interest*
Network	Isolationism	From insularity to *interconnectedness*
Institution	Institutionalism	From controlling the whole to *serving the parts*
		From guarding the boundaries to *facilitating connections*
Partnership	Separatism	From competition to *co-operation*
CHURCH LEADERSHIP	Élitism	From hierarchy to *servant leaders*
	Authoritarianism	From director to *community educator*
	Paternalism	From men to *women and men*
GOVERNANCE	Centralism	From centralization to *subsidiarity*
	Unilateralism	From autocracy to *democracy*
	Statism	From establishment to *self-government*

5

Mission, culture, stance and the laity

Mission

From church-centred to kingdom community-centred

The mission of the diaconal church is to be the servant of the kingdom community, the epitome of all learning communities (Part 1). In pragmatic terms, its mission is to help create a global community of learning communities transformed by the gifts of the kingdom community. As Giles Fraser puts it, the mission of the diaconal church is to be a 'vanguard of a new world order known as the kingdom. Our job is to rattle the cages of those who believe the kingdom is make-believe, and that, deep down, things can never really change' (*Church Times*, 15 April 2005).

As the servant of the kingdom community, the diaconal church is a *kingdom community-centred* church. As such, it is called by God to make manifest the kingdom community's gifts of life, liberation, love and learning within its own life. 'Neither truth nor love can be communicated except as they are embodied in a community which reasons and loves' (Newbigin, 1989, p. 85). It is called to build communities that, in their turn, manifest the gifts of the kingdom community. And it is called to enable others to discern, comprehend and receive those gifts.

The diaconal church serves a kingdom community whose membership is known to and determined by God alone and which requires no church-defined or church-defended boundaries. The diaconal church bears witness to a God who is both beyond us yet with us, showing us the meaning of servanthood in the life of Christ. The diaconal church is the servant of a kingdom community already omnipresent within the church and beyond, through which the grace of God is freely offered to humankind.

The mission of the diaconal church is the transformation of our world so that the kingdom community might come 'on earth as in heaven' (Clark, 1993). It is a mission concerned with the 'integrity of creation', of the preservation and sustainability of 'one inhabited earth', the stewardship of which has been entrusted to all of us. It is a mission that challenges poverty, injustice and oppression and all that destroys the image of God in men and women. It is a mission that embraces the whole of humankind, those who hold power as well as those on the margins of society. Thus it is called 'to speak of God not [only] on the boundaries but at the centre, not [only] in weakness but in strength; and therefore not [only] in death and guilt but in man's life and goodness' (Bonhoeffer in Bethge, 1979, p. 155). The mission of the diaconal church is one that calls all to account, but it is one that also offers 'an explosion of joy' (Newbigin, 1989, p. 116).

Within Christendom, by contrast, the church regarded itself as synonymous with the kingdom, or as near as human beings could get to the kingdom in this life. It was the kingdom in ecclesiastical garb. The church's rituals, symbolism and buildings offered the most visible and tangible demonstration of God's rule here on earth. The church was humankind's means of salvation, a saved and saving community. God's grace was bestowed on men and women primarily through the church and through its sacraments. The Word, when read or preached, was God-given, to be heard and then obeyed.

The Christendom church sought to ensure that its members remained safe and secure within its fold, their reward being membership of a divinely ordered society and the blessings of eternal life. Such a protectionist perspective meant that the Christendom church needed to guard its boundaries – geographical, political and doctrinal – with great care. It engaged with 'alien' communities, sacred or secular, only when it felt impelled to convert them, as heathens or heretics, to the one true faith (not infrequently at the point of the sword or through threat of divine punishment). *Proselytism* (see Figure 3), the attempt to bring everyone into the fold of mother church, permeated its church-centred approach to mission.

The mission of the diaconal church is far removed from proselytism. As we have seen, its task is to be the servant of the kingdom community. In that undertaking, the diaconal church is called to enter wholeheartedly into partnership with all those furthering the purposes of the kingdom community, whether or not they are aware of that which motivates and inspires them.

From exclusive to inclusive communities and from indoctrination to education

The kingdom community-centred nature of the diaconal church impels it to challenge the church-centred *exclusivism* and *dogmatism* that are so prominent within the Christendom model of church (see Figure 3). The diaconal church sees as a divine imperative its task of enabling the world to move from exclusive to *inclusive communities*, and from indoctrination to *education*, so that it can build communities that manifest the kingdom community's gifts of life, liberation, love and learning (see the discussion in Part 1).

Desmond Tutu sums up the nature of such communities:

> You and I are made for goodness, for love, for transcendence, for togetherness. God has a dream that we, God's children will come to realize that we are indeed sisters and brothers, members of one family, the human family – that all belong, all white, black and yellow, rich and poor, beautiful and not so beautiful, young and old, male and female. There are no outsiders, all are insiders – gay and straight, Christians, Muslims, Jews, Arabs, Americans, Protestants, Roman Catholics, Afghans – all belong. And God says: 'I have no one to help me realize my dream except you – will you help me?' (Addressing Georgetown University, Washington DC, quoted in *Look to Christ*, 2004, p. 35)

Culture

From a sacred to a secular society

The diaconal church fully acknowledges the realities of life in today's world. It accepts that, in the West, we now live in *a secular society*; 'in the brave new world of secular secularization – that is, the permanent decline of religion' as we have known it (Callum Brown in McLeod and Ustorf, 2003, p. 29).

By 'secular' and 'secularization' we here mean an open-ended process characterized by four main developments. First, 'differentiation': functions that the church once fulfilled are being taken over by many other institutions. Second, 'disengagement' (see Glasner, 1977): responsibility for such functions is being transferred from church to state or to the latter's many associated agencies. Third, 'pluralism': there is great diversity among and competition between all those institutions, of which the church is only one, now seeking to 'market' themselves to a global constituency. Fourth, 'technical rationality': the increasing influence of a process whereby 'supernatural influences and moral considerations [are gradually displaced] from ever-widening areas of public life, [and are replaced] by considerations of objective performance and practical expedience' (Steve Bruce in McLeod and Ustorf, 2003, p. 14).

The diaconal church recognizes and accepts the increasingly secular nature of society. However, it sets its face against the hegemony of secularism, an ideology that denies the reality of any sacred order or, in its less extreme form, an agnosticism that treats the sacred as irrelevant to public life. At the same time, the diaconal church resists the hegemony of sacralism (see Figure 3). Sacralism is an ideology that reifies the sacred. In a sacralistic world, it is religious systems that reign supreme and deny the legitimate authority of the secular. Sacralism permeated the culture of Christendom from top to bottom. It buttressed the Christendom church's claim that it had the right to control every aspect of human life because God had placed everything under its jurisdiction.

The diaconal church's response to both secularism and sacralism is to espouse what we have termed elsewhere 'secular faith' (Clark, 1984, pp. 26–7). Secular faith rejects the closed ideologies of secularism and sacralism, but it remains open to learning from the secular milieu within which we all now live and work. Secular faith is a Yes to God, of which Alan Ecclestone has written with such profound insight (1975). But it is also a Yes to Life (Clark, 1987), the whole of life. It is a faith founded on 'reality'. As Bonhoeffer once put it, 'There can be no reality without Christ and no Christ without reality' (in Bethge, 1979, p. 156). Secular faith liberates the diaconal church to build a world transformed by the gifts of the kingdom community because it knows that our 'Yes to God' and our 'Yes to life' are always met by God's 'Yes' to us.

From preservation to transformation

The diaconal church is committed to radical change. Unlike the Christendom model of church, it is not founded on conservatism (see Figure 3) or primarily concerned with preservation. The diaconal church acknowledges and affirms its Christian heritage of which Christendom has been a major part. But it knows that it can no longer be bound by 'Tradition' spelt, as by Aidan Nichols (1999), with a capital 'T'. Its concern is with the *transformation* of a world that has lost touch with the kingdom community, a transformation brought about by its making manifest and sharing of God's gifts of life, liberation, love and learning.

Stance

From domination to servanthood

'The church of the next [millennium] will be a servanthood church' (*Diaconal Reflections*, 1998). The concept of *servanthood* (*diakonia*) is of fundamental importance for the diaconal church because the relational qualities of servanthood are those at the very heart of the kingdom community.

Servanthood characterizes the entire life of the diaconal church. The Anglican report on a renewed diaconate, *For such a time as this* (p. 37), states that 'all Christian ministry, ordained and lay, is grounded in *diakonia* because it is all dependent on the fundamental divine commission of the church in the service of the kingdom'. *The Distinctive Diaconate* (p. 40) comments that '*Diakonia* belongs to the whole life of the church'. *From the Diakonia of Christ*, a Roman Catholic perspective (p. 3), adds that 'Baptism confers this *diakonein*, power of service, on every Christian.' The Methodist document *What is a Deacon?* (para. 3.1.1) maintains that 'being and acting as a deacon is a particular expression of a calling to discipleship that is shared by all Methodists'.

Biblical and historical background

There are numerous biblical words that fill out the meaning of servant and servanthood. In the Old Testament, the Hebrew word *ebed* is used, while in the New Testament it is the Greek word *diakonia* that is most relevant to our concerns.

For the diaconal church, the meaning of what it is to be a servant derives first and foremost from the life and ministry of Christ. In turn, Christ's understanding of his own ministry drew freely on the meaning of servanthood in the Old Testament. '[The] tradition of the servant of God runs from Moses through Elijah to Jeremiah and into the portrayal of the nation of Israel as the suffering servant in the beautiful Servant Songs of Isaiah 40–55' (Croft, 1999, p. 57). These servant songs must have had a profound influence on Christ's understanding of his own ministry, and of the nature and cost of being God's mediator in the creation of redemptive relationships. Christ's public declaration of his own calling when he preached in the synagogue in Nazareth (Luke 4.18–19) also resonates with Isaiah 61.1–2.

A number of passages in the Gospels exemplify the servanthood of Christ. In Mark 10.45 ('For the Son of Man came not to be served but to serve, and to give his life as a ransom for many'), Christ indicates the fundamental stance of his life's work. John Collins (2002, p. 28 ff) insists that 'service' in this passage is intimately linked with suffering and salvation. In Luke 22.24–30, when dealing with his disciples' dispute about greatness, Christ says, 'I am among you as one who serves', dramatically reversing the expectations of those who looked to him as 'master'. In John 13.1–16, at the Last Supper Christ takes the towel and basin and washes the feet of his disciples. Here, though the word *doulos* (a meaning more akin to that of 'slave') not *diakonos* is used, Christ's actions exemplify the caring and self-effacing nature of servanthood. It is interesting to note that, by the early second century, when the office of deacon had emerged more clearly, the role was directly associated with the person of Christ (Collins, 2002, p. 13) who was at that time given the title of 'the great Deacon' (*For such a time as this*, p. 35).

The early church recognized the essence of Christ's ministry as fundamentally that of servanthood, a quality that should be seen to permeate the lives of his disciples and followers. As *From the Diakonia of Christ* (p. 8) puts it:

> The first fundamental fact of relevance from the New Testament is that the verb *diokenein* designates Christ's actual mission as servant (Mk 10.45 and parallels; cf. Mt 12.18; Acts 4.30; Phil 2.6–11). This word or its derivatives also designates the exercise of service or ministry by his disciples (Mk 10.43ff; Mt 20.26ff; 23.11; Lk 8.3; Rom 15.25) [as well as] ministries of different kinds in the church.

Thus the apostles are entrusted with a servant ministry (Acts 1.17; 6.4; 20.24), and Paul often refers to himself as *diakonos* (1 Corinthians 3.5; 2 Corinthians 3.6; 6.4; 11.23). Christopher Moody writes (in *The New Dictionary of Pastoral Studies*, 2002, p. 85):

> In the developing order of the churches of the New Testament, *diakonia* ... was shared by the whole community. It described a way of living with each other and in the world brought about by the revelation of God in the ministry of Christ as 'the one who serves' ... and in the outpouring of the Spirit to equip God's people for the proclamation, service of the kingdom, and the ministry of reconciliation. The term can be applied to

any individual ministry in relation to the whole church and to the whole church in relation to its service to the world (2 Cor. 3–5).

Collins (2002) argues that during the early years of the Christian church, the word *diakonos* came increasingly to be used to identify the role of deacon. In the process, its more all-embracing meaning as 'servant' became overlaid by other meanings, such as those of attendant, agent and messenger. Nevertheless, Collins also acknowledges that when the diaconate re-emerged in the nineteenth century, 'the leading edge of the new ministerial model was service . . . the kind of selfless, caring and loving service that characterized Jesus in his dealings with the lame and rejected men and women who people the gospel narratives' (pp. 7–8). It is quite clear that the diaconal communities and associations that came into existence at that time saw their ministry as one primarily of service, in particular nursing, welfare work and teaching, often among the most marginalized and destitute members of society.

In recent years, the theme of the servant church has come increasingly to the fore. Dulles sees it as the fifth (and most recent) model of church (1976). The Roman Catholic International Commission report (*From the Diakonia of Christ*, p. 3) states that 'Christian existence is a sharing in the *diakonia* or service which God himself fulfilled in favour of mankind; it likewise leads to an understanding of the fulfillment of mankind.' The current interest in a renewed diaconate can be seen as 'a sign of the church's vocation to be the servant of Christ and of God . . . which could renew the church in the evangelical spirit of humility and service' (p. 57)'. 'Deacons represent to the church its calling as servant in the world', states the Lima document from the World Council of Churches (quoted in *For such a time as this*, p. 16).

'Servanthood' and 'service'

In the light of the life and ministry of Christ, the witness of the early church and, not least, the needs of the world today, we believe that it is the model of the church as servant, the model of the diaconal church, that must take precedence over all others.

Nevertheless, it is extremely important that we distinguish between two interrelated but different interpretations of the nature of 'servanthood' as found in the discussions about a renewed diaconate: servanthood as 'service', and servanthood as what it means to be a 'servant'. The legacy of diaconal communities and associations founded over the last century and a half has generally been one where servanthood is equated with service, as personified in the often sacrificial endeavours of the deaconess movement. It is also this understanding of servanthood as service that permeates many of the more recent reports on the restoration of a renewed diaconate. See *For such a time as this*, pp. 53–5 and *The Distinctive Diaconate*, pp. 65–6, where pastoral care figures prominently; *From the Diakonia of Christ*, p. 68, which stresses 'the service of charity'; *What is a Deacon?*, para. 5, 'Core emphasis of Methodist diaconal ministry: a ministry of witness through service' – though here the concept of 'service' is given a more radical interpretation than in the other reports.

'Service' is, of course, an essential aspect of servanthood. Compassion and care for others are an integral part of a servant ministry and the life of the servant church. Service embodies love for God and love for neighbour in a way that can be seen and responded to by a world that challenges the credibility of a church that does not practise what it preaches. But service does not in itself get to the heart of the biblical meaning of servanthood, and thus of the nature of the diaconal church as a servant church.

'Service' is action-focused. Being a 'servant' is person-centred. The meaning of being a servant is derived from who or what is served. The diaconal church is the servant of the kingdom community and of the Trinitarian God who rules that kingdom. Thus the diaconal church is a servant of God, a servant of Christ (2 Corinthians 11.23) and a servant of the Spirit: in short, of One God in three Persons. It is also a servant of humanity, of the world God created and which he loves. As a servant of the kingdom community, the diaconal church is called to offer the gifts of life, liberation, love and learning to all in the name of Father, Son and Holy Spirit.

Features of servanthood

The diaconal church is 'a good and faithful servant' (Matthew 25.21). It obeys the Triune God's call to follow him, trusts that his purposes are for the well-being of his creation, orders its life in accordance with his divine priorities and seeks to be worthy of its calling. That calling it lives out in and for the world, and throughout the whole of life.

As a servant of the kingdom community, the diaconal church is deeply concerned about the planet earth. However, as Archbishop Rembert puts it, our stewardship of God's creation 'is more than just a question of not polluting the earth; it becomes a whole question of what lifestyle we must live as followers of Christ, in order that the earth can be constantly regenerating itself and, as it were, renewing itself from our waste and pollution. A kind of Christian cosmology has to accompany a Christian anthropology' (quoted in Echlin, 1991, p. 165).

Being the servant of the kingdom community commits the diaconal church to the kingdom's work of redemption, of bringing 'human integrity and wholeness' to all of creation (Grey, 1989, p. 4). It is a ministry of reconciliation and renewal offered to the whole of society (*What is a Deacon?*, paras 5.5, 5.7). It is a calling to address whatever causes chaos in public affairs, as well as in private life. But it is a costly calling; it involves the way of the cross (para. 5.6). The diaconal church follows the example of Christ who became 'a suffering servant' so that through his suffering a broken world might be forgiven and healed, and God's kingdom come.

The power of the servant church is not coercive power. It is the power of redemptive love. As Collins (2002, p. 39) puts it, all the sayings of Jesus on the matter of the first and the last, the great and the lowly, are teaching his followers that 'the kingdom of God establishes itself in a community of relationships' undistorted by the misuse of power. Such servanthood 'is neither menial nor servile' for 'service in Christ is true greatness and to be great is to be a servant' (*For such a time as this*, p. 35). The servant church also bears witness to what Stanley Hauerwas (1986) calls a 'peaceable kingdom', a community that transforms the world through quiet authenticity and authority, not by frenetic endeavour.

Servanthood involves being open to learn, to embark on a journey of spiritual discovery. The diaconal church knows that it can only begin to manifest the gifts of the kingdom community when it has the humility to become a genuine learning community. Such learning is about openness to the movement of the Spirit which 'blows where it wills' (John 3.8), and about listening to 'the still small voice' however faint. The diaconal church also recognizes that it has an immense amount to learn from a secular world, a world wherein the kingdom community is omnipresent even if unrecognized.

Servanthood brings great rewards. The servant church is invited 'to enter into the joy of [its] master' (Matthew 25.21) whose 'service is perfect freedom'. Servanthood brings to members of the servant church the most profound experience of life, liberation, love and learning that human beings can experience. These are gifts that the servant church cannot help but want to share with others.

As a servant church, the diaconal church presents a very different picture from that of a Christendom church that has been shaped over many centuries by belief in a kingdom founded on power and control. If the church is once again to be able to respond to its commission to proclaim the gospel and to witness to the centrality of the kingdom community in all that Christ taught and did, then such *imperialism* (see Figure 3) must end. There has to be a fundamental shift of stance from domination to servant-hood. The preoccupation of the Christendom church with controlling and moulding, still prevalent today, has to give way to a spirit of affirmation, listening, learning and of 'self-giving sacrificial love'.

Comparing what he calls 'empire' and 'discipleship' (2002, pp. 36–7), Collins writes:

> [Christ's] words 'servant' and 'slave' are introduced into [his] sayings for the purpose of identifying the extreme contrast between two social groups. The two words stand opposed to 'great' and 'first'. The imperial group pursues values which are immediately recognizable and which have been part of our historical understanding and of folklore from time immemorial. But the sayings of Jesus are insisting that discipleship does not operate by the principles that make one 'great' or 'first'. Instead discipleship operates by principles that no social organization has ever known . . .

If this last sentence is true, then the servant church offers a radically new vision of the future. It is a vision that will mean the most profound change in the life of the church since Christendom began. But without a vision we perish. The church, of all bodies, does not exist to dismiss the words of Christ as naive, but to use them as pointers to the nature of the kingdom community and to seek, as far as is humanly possible, to make manifest that community for the benefit of the whole of humankind.

Joe Holland (Holland and Henriot, 1983, p. 85) puts this commission in a contemporary context:

> The symbolic interpretation has shifted from the Davidic image of 'Christ the King', dominant since Constantinean Christianity, to a mosaic image of a 'Prophetic Servant Jesus' . . . We are entering not simply a new response to industrialization, but a whole new form of church – one that is altering elements that have dominated the church since the time of Constantine and perhaps since the apostle Paul and the rise of the Greek Church. The radical strategy, therefore, is not merely a short-term traditional strategy. Rather, it is a profound shift that termi-nates Constantinean Christianity, retrieving neglected elements of the pre-Constantinean and perhaps pre-Pauline forms.

But how can the diaconal church pursue this radical and demanding agenda? It can only do so if the church is acknowledged, in principle and practice, to be the *laos*, the whole people of God whose calling it is to be servants of the kingdom community across the world.

The laity

From priest to people

The diaconal church is first and foremost a body of people, the *laos*. The *laos* is comprised of the whole people of God and is theologically prior to any distinction between laity and clergy. In the Gospels, the servant passages were 'directed to the church as a whole' (Collins, 2002, p. 122). Throughout the New Testament church, 'the [diaconal] emphasis was on the ministry of the whole Christian community through the use of God-given gifts which included prophecy, evangelism, teaching and pastoral care (Ephesians 4.11)' (Staton, 2000, p. 18). Thus diaconal ministry becomes a way of life that reflects the servant ministry of Christ through the life and work of the whole people of God (Staton, 2000, p. 298; see also *What is a Deacon?*, para. 3.2). 'Ordination does not take anyone out of the *laos*' (*For such a time as this*, p. 26).

The all-embracing nature of servanthood has two important implications for the diaconal church. First, both clergy and laity are called to servanthood as the hallmark of their Christian discipleship. Whatever role they might be fulfilling, from the leadership of worship within the church to witnessing to the nature of the kingdom community beyond it, it is as servants that both clergy and laity undertake their responsibilities. Second, because all are servants of Christ the Servant and his kingdom, there can be no question of those ordained claiming or being given higher status than the laity.

(Note: For the sake of clarity, in the rest of this book we use the term 'laity', as generally employed, to identify those members of the church who are not members of its ordained ministry.)

Christendom failed to grasp or, where it did, to acknowledge the importance of the laity in the ministry and mission of the church. Instead, *clericalism* gradually gained strength, setting the position and standing of priest above that of *the people* (see Figure 3). For a variety of reasons, from a distorted sacramental theology – which took the breaking of bread to be of deeper significance than the washing of feet – to a concern to guard 'the truth', and the status and power which thereby accrued to its guardians, clericalism came to dominate the ethos of the Christendom church.

'Clericalism is the domination of the "ordinary" people by those ordained, trained and invested with privilege and power' (Stevens, 1999, p. 52). It is a 'division between clergy and laity [that] undervalues the lay lifestyle, lay talent, lay leadership, lay experience and lay spirituality' (Lakeland, 2003, p. 195).

In the diaconal church, Christendom's understanding of the relationship of clergy and laity is radically changed. We shall see later that this has important lessons to teach us about the nature of ordained leadership within the diaconal church (Chapter 7). Here, we simply note that in the diaconal church it is the laity who move centre stage, though the clergy remain their fellow travellers. Thus the diaconal church is one in which the focus moves from priest to people, to the whole people of God, as *Lumen Gentium*, one of the most important documents of Vatican II, made abundantly clear (Ker, 2001, pp. 9–10).

From dependency to autonomy

A laity that breaks clear of clericalism also breaks the mould of *conformism* (see Figure 3). Alan Gilbert (1976, p. 13) describes this as ending 'the dependency system' that dominated the social and political scene in pre-industrial England. Throughout Christendom, it was the church, in alliance with the state, at all levels of society but especially at parish level, that controlled and directed the lives of lay people. Other factors colluded to maintain this situation, such as a relatively immobile society, strong kinship ties and bonding based on a shared locality and a common heritage. The outcome was a laity so dependent on a Christendom church that their experiences, insights and skills, both religious and secular, were constantly undervalued.

The diaconal church is a church in which there has been a transition from dependency to *autonomy*. This is not a self-centred autonomy that focuses on the desires and interests of the self-sufficient individual, but what moral educators term 'altruistic autonomy', that form of autonomy that embraces both the fulfilment of self and the welfare of others.

Within the life of secular institutions the transition from lay dependency to autonomy has been ongoing for some centuries, even if it has only gained real momentum during the second half of the twentieth century, not least as a result of the coming of universal educational opportunities.

Within the church, however, clericalism and conformism have retained a powerful hold. Even within much of 'Evangelical Nonconformity', the nineteenth century saw the ordained ministry gradually reasserting its authority over an initially pro-active laity (Gilbert, 1976, p. 58), even though the ongoing contribution of lay people remained significant in the development of some denominations, such as certain branches of Methodism. Yet, writes Gilbert (1976, p. 158), 'the impetus within the professional ministry of Nonconformist organizations towards role differentiation between ministers and laymen, and the consequent marked reduction in the scope for lay initiative in pastoral and evangelistic work, was successful, in the final resort, only because the laity acquiesced with the process'.

Nor has the recent rise of Pentecostalism (and its near relative, the charismatic movement) very much altered this situation (Chapter 13). In many cases, the professional leaders of these movements have promoted their own role and image in such a way that their followers have remained dependent on them as symbolic figures and conformist to the religious culture that they have fostered. Thus clericalism and conformism have made their mark even in churches with an ecclesiology that, at first sight, appears very different from that of the Christendom church.

Within the diaconal church, lay and ordained exercise their ministry as equal partners. The laity's experience, knowledge and skills are acknowledged and affirmed. The responsibility of all those ordained is to encourage and equip lay people to use their talents and skills to fulfil their calling as servants of the kingdom community wherever they live or work (Chapter 7). At the same time, lay people have a responsibility to encourage and support the ministry of the ordained. In the diaconal church the relationship of lay to ordained is one of interdependence not dependence.

The laity as community builders

The ministry to which the laity are called is that of fulfilling the mission of the diaconal church. Their vocation is to be the servants of the kingdom community throughout the world. As such, they are called to be community builders by making manifest the kingdom community's gifts of life, liberation, love and learning within the church. But they are also called to be community builders within the world, empowered by and offering to others the gifts of the kingdom community.

As community builders, the laity will often have a more hands-on and proactive role than that of community educators, the role we associate with the ordained leadership of the diaconal church and will explore further in Chapter 7. Nevertheless, the role of the community builder has much in common with the role of community educator. Thus, it is likely that lay people will be called to act as catalysts, enablers, intermediaries and resource persons (see Chapter 4).

As *catalysts*, lay people will not only seek to share their vision of the kingdom community with others, but confront those things that deny its values, and challenge people to acknowledge where they have ignored or rejected its gifts.

As *enablers*, lay people will affirm all as human beings created in the image of God, each having his or her distinctive part to play in building the kingdom community. They will invite people to claim membership of the kingdom community and to commit themselves to its fulfilment. They will work alongside all those, Christian or not, who share their vision of a world transformed by God's gifts to be a community of communities, supporting their endeavours and learning from their example.

Lay people will be involved in breaking down barriers and divides which bring hatred, injustice and oppression in order that that there can be a divine–human 'exchange of life' (Haughton, 1981). As such they will be called to act as *intermediaries*, mediators or bridge-builders.

As *resource persons* lay people will offer all fellow travellers the spiritual resources of the diaconal church on which they themselves draw: its scriptures, its worship and sacraments, its experience and wisdom, its teaching and its pastoral care.

The laity, liberated from clericalism and conformism to play their full part in the mission of the diaconal church, offer to church and world a wealth of expertise and skills. The sheer diversity of lay experience makes available to the church a vast resource of human imagination, knowledge, talents and energy hitherto latent, but for years undervalued and underused by the Christendom model of church. The liberation of the laity means that the diaconal church can be present wherever lay people live, work or play, on the margins as well as at the heart of society, to discern, to make known and to participate in making manifest the kingdom community.

For lay people to rediscover their calling to be servants of the kingdom community, it will be necessary for the concept of Christian vocation to become as important to them as it is to those ordained (see Adair, 2000). Unless this happens, the laity will continue to see the clergy as those with the 'real' responsibility for the life and mission of the church, and themselves as the supporting cast. It is thus a top priority for the diaconal church to find ways of reinstating Christian vocation as the high calling of all lay people. It is a calling both to be about God's work of building communities that manifest the gifts of the kingdom community and also to keep moving forward on the journey of spiritual discovery by means of which those gifts can be better appreciated, understood and used.

Coming to realize that God is calling them to be servants of the kingdom community will offer many lay people new inspiration, purpose and fulfilment, over against the debilitating passivity so often forced on them by the Christendom model of church. However, this does not mean that we are assuming that lay people are waiting eagerly to be liberated from Christendom's legacy of clericalism and conformism. It will be no easy transition for *God's Frozen People* to become *God's Lively People* (Gibbs and Morton, 1964, 1971). The changes required for this transformation to happen are just as radical and demanding as those required for the diaconal church itself to come into being. How these changes might be brought about is a question that will concern us throughout the rest of this book.

6

Social collectives

In Chapters 2 and 3 we identified a number of types of social collective conducive to developing learning communities that manifest the gifts of the kingdom community, the epitome of all learning communities. Because the diaconal church is also called to manifest the gifts of the kingdom community, we believe that the same sort of collectives will be integral to its own life and work. In this chapter we explore the nature of these collectives when associated with the diaconal church.

The hearing

From venerating the status quo to visioning and from instruction to dialogue

In this chapter we look at the hearing before we consider the communal group. This is because although the communal group is the building block of all larger social collectives, it is the visioning process typifying the hearing that often prepares the way for the emergence of new kinds of community, including new kinds of communal group.

The hearing has two key features. Its primary purpose is to help people 'dream dreams and see visions' so that ways of doing things that can no longer sustain the life of their communities can make way for new communal possibilities and alignments. Visioning is a process that depends on dialogue. Thus the hearing's second key feature is facilitating open-ended dialogue across social, cultural and religious divides.

Because it is a forum that enables people to share their visions, the hearing is a social collective of the utmost importance to the diaconal church. The process of *visioning* (see Figure 3, page 69) that the diaconal church seeks to facilitate is one in which people feel safe to question their basic assumptions, to share their values and beliefs and to challenge the status quo. Hearings offer Christians an opportunity to communicate with passion their vision of the kingdom community. Hearings also offer those who are not Christians the opportunity to present their own visions of the future. The hearing offers a forum in which there need be no dumbing-down of convictions.

Hearings are founded on *dialogue*. The diaconal church is committed to bringing people together across the divides that would normally keep them apart so that they can advocate their principles, values, and beliefs in a way that invites inquiry and lively discussion.

Hearings are a far cry from the Christendom church's culture of *legalism* and *didacticism* (see Figure 3, page 69). The mindset of the Christendom church was a 'legalistic' one in which the divine order was seen as 'the same yesterday, today and for ever'. Legalism venerates the status quo. It permits no questioning of the past and no visioning for the future. Of course, Christendom had its 'visions'. They were evident in the massive output of world-renowned architecture and art that it has bequeathed to posterity. But they were reified 'visions', like that of the heavenly city towards which the Christian's pilgrimage was leading humankind. Thus though these 'visions' were expressed in a multitude of different forms and through the work of a host of different craftsmen and artists, they drew on essentially traditional images.

Closely related to this static view of the divine order, the Christendom church saw instruction not dialogue as the way in which Christian faith should be handed down from generation to generation. What passed for 'education' was based on a model of church resembling 'a unique type of school – one in which the teachers have the power to impose their doctrine with juridical and spiritual sanctions' (Dulles, 1976, p. 35). The Christian's journey was not one of discovery but of pilgrimage, where the destination and the route were already mapped out, the main uncertainties being the temptations along the way. The idea that the journey might actually be the 'destination', or that there might be a diversity of journeys, was never contemplated. Indeed, the worst crimes of the Christendom church were perpetrated by some of its so-called 'guardians' who sought to force recalcitrants to walk a predetermined path.

The legalism and didacticism of the Christendom church still retain their hold. As a result, many Christians remain at what James Fowler (1984, pp. 57–62) calls the (fourth) 'synthetic-conventional' stage of faith development. This stage brings 'a supportive and orienting unity' (p. 60) but, unquestioned and unchallenged, can result in the continuation of a religious 'dependency system' which inhibits spiritual growth and development. The Christendom church has no reason to encourage its members to move beyond this stage of dependency because, as Hull puts it (1985, p. 189), 'the authority of institutions is challenged by people [who progress to later stages]' and especially to the final stage of 'universalizing faith' (Fowler, 1984, pp. 67–71). The diaconal church cannot accept such constraints on spiritual growth and development because they prevent Christians realizing their God-given potential as human beings.

Legalism and didacticism also inhibit the mission of the church. In a highly mobile world, and one in which plurality is now the norm, those new forms of communal identity imperative for the survival of the planet can only be discovered through dialogue and visioning. For this reason, the hearing must remain an essential component of the diaconal church's life and mission.

Hearings reflect the nature of the kingdom community as a learning community. They reflect the teaching ministry of Jesus, one in which his ability to listen to others was of paramount importance. 'Listening begins with the acknowledgement that we are servants and have so much to learn,' writes Croft (1999, p. 75) in his reflections on the ordained ministry as *diakonia*. Listening is a much neglected activity. Yet those who talk about it most often listen least. Genuine listening involves affirming the one listened to as a person of unique value. It requires being present in the 'now' (Tolle, 2001). It demands attentiveness and ongoing reflection. Listening also means being open to learning from the diversity and richness of others' experience. Because this kind of openness can threaten our existing values and beliefs, hearings can feel risky and uncomfortable. Yet without a preparedness to listen to others, and engage in an open exchange of views, there can be no dialogue, no visioning and no hope for the future.

Hearings, in their diverse forms, contribute to the worship of the diaconal church. Worship is about enabling us to dream dreams and see visions, not of utopia, but of the kingdom community and how that community might come more fully. Worship within the diaconal church seeks to bring together God and people, world and church, person and person in a dialogical process that can open minds and hearts to a new understanding of who they are, and of what it means to be servants of the kingdom community. Worship at its richest is a dialogue with God and thus a boundary-breaking experience. However, all too often worship remains part of Christendom's dependency system, perpetuating 'the unpopularity of monologue' and leading to people 'leaving churches, weary of dogmatism and rhetorical performances, of being spoon-fed and patronized' (Murray,

2004a, p. 265). As such, worship neither facilitates people's growth in the faith nor enables them to envision new communal possibilities for a new kind of world.

Wherever hearings, large or small, bring people together to share their visions of the world as a community of learning communities, they become a tool of mission. They offer especially rich rewards when undertaken in 'the middle ground' between collectives, religious and secular, that would otherwise be exclusive or closed. For it is in the space between such collectives that we are most likely to meet fellow travellers trying to work at what it means to acknowledge our common humanity.

Nobody illustrates the importance of dialogue in the middle ground better than John Hull (1993). He writes:

> There is a Christianity that says, 'I am holy and you are holy but the ground between us is not holy. If we meet on that ground, if we touch, we shall be contaminated.' There is another Christianity that says, 'I am not holy; I am on the way; my spirituality and that of the tradition I represent is incomplete. But I have an affinity with you, my Muslim brother, my Jewish friend, my Hindu colleague, if you are prepared to say, "I am not holy; I am on the way; the tradition I represent is not complete." ' Then we will both say, 'But the ground where we meet is holy ground because this is the place where we claim our complete humanity.'

Charles Davis (1994, pp. 144–5) describes the hoped-for outcome of this kind of dialogue:

> A post-conventional [we would say 'post-Christendom'] or universalistic religious identity is . . . realized when people, belonging to a religious tradition but not tied to its fixed contents of norms, engage as free, autonomous persons in a process of unrestricted and unconstrained communication with others of the same tradition, of other traditions, or of no tradition on matters concerning religion with the aim of achieving agreement, not conformity.

Hearings facilitate such dialogue and the visioning that results from it. In this way they help to break through the legalism and didacticism of the Christendom church. However, as Davis stresses, dialogue of this kind is never iconoclastic. It is always looking for a new and creative vision of the kingdom community. As Jeffrey Cox argues (in McLeod and Ustorf, 2003, p. 206), visioning is the quest for 'a new narrative'. Not the narrative that the historian offers us. Not even a 'master narrative', such as that currently dominated by the theme of 'secularization'. Genuine visioning seeks to tap into a 'grand narrative, the whole story, the story God would tell if God could tell a story'. What emerges from this process, writes Newbigin (1989, p. 120),

> is not a movement which will take control of history and shape the future according to its own vision, not a new imperialism, not a victorious crusade. Its visible embodiment will be a [Christian] community that lives by this story, a community whose existence is visibly defined in the regular rehearsing and reenactment of the story which has given it birth, the story of the self-emptying of God in the ministry, life, death and resurrection of Jesus.

Secular institutions need a new communal vision as urgently as the church. Thus an essential missionary enterprise for the diaconal church is to mount hearings that bring together those from secular institutions to enable them to share their concerns, experiences and, above all, visions, across the divides that separate them from each other or from the church (Chapter 11). As Kevin Walcot puts it, the task of a diaconal church is to reconstruct 'mission as dialogue' (in Clark, 1997, pp. 81–5), or, as Staton writes (2001, p. 347), 'the key word in the new model of mission is dialogue'.

If the church is to engage in genuine dialogue beyond its own walls, it will need to engage in and learn from genuine dialogue within them. 'The crux of the matter is that dialogue between the church and the world cannot have credibility unless there is dialogue within the church itself,' writes Walcot (Clark, 1997). To foster this dialogical process within the life of the church will not be easy as it will require a radical review of the way in which its liturgy, its preaching and its teaching is undertaken.

The diaconal church recognizes that only as we affirm the right of others to hold and articulate their views will we earn the right to speak about our experience and understanding of the kingdom community. Walcot is right to call the church to take up a servanthood stance in its missionary endeavours. He longs to hear the voice of a 'church hesitant [which] may yet become as sweet a sound as the church militant and triumphant used to be to our ears'.

However, the church 'hesitant' does not mean 'the church somnolent' or 'the church unprincipled'. Mission as dialogue does not mean a church apologetic for, or passionless about, its message to a world that at times appears hell-bent on self-destruction. Nor does it mean a church that sits lightly to the horrendous inhumanities that our 'enlightened' civilization is still capable of perpetrating. What mission as dialogue does mean is a diaconal church wholeheartedly committed to sharing its vision of the kingdom community with those of other faiths and convictions, using all the passion it possesses, yet a church that remains open to learn from the vision and advocacy of others.

Hearings reflect the nature of the kingdom community. They offer us an all-important glimpse of the kind of inclusive and open communal alignments and identities now needed by church and world. However, because they are usually short-lived, hearings cannot become sustainable communities. The encounters they facilitate, though often intensely communal, are too brief to provide those more enduring communal collectives that are needed to address such deep-rooted issues as poverty, injustice, oppression and the destruction of the planet. For this reason, the diaconal church needs to embrace other types of social collective that are able to sustain and enhance its ongoing life as a learning community. One such collective is the communal group.

The communal group

From community of place to communities of interest

Because we now live in a highly mobile world, 'membership of a permanent religious body that confronts us as a fixed objective entity cannot give us our basic social identity as religious persons', writes Davis (1994, p. 148). Hearings are essential because they provide the all-important visioning process out of which can emerge new communal collectives crucial for the emergence of the diaconal church. Key requirements of such collectives are that they are diverse and available to all. At the same time, they must be inclusive and open if the church is to address the communal dilemma, end exclusiveness and make its essential contribution to the creation of a global community.

Not only are the structures of Christendom unable to meet this need, but their legacy locks the church into an anachronistic past. In particular, *parochialism* (see Figure 3, p. 69), the idea of 'church' being equated with a parish or local neighbourhood, has to be superseded if new social collectives conducive to the growth of the diaconal church are to emerge. 'The parochial system of the Church of England [has] been one of the most durable of the nation's institutions,' writes Gilbert (1976, p. 127). The problem is, however, that the parish remains 'a fixed objective entity' too closely associated with a specific and limited geographical area. It cannot provide communities of faith adequate to support and equip a highly mobile laity who, unlike previous generations, live, work and play in many different locations.

For new communities of faith to emerge, the church must acknowledge the importance of *communities of interest*. It needs to embrace such communities, encouraging its laity to come together around common interests related not only to the parish or the local neighbourhood, but to occupation, social and political concerns and leisure interests. At the same time, faith communities based on common interests must provide their members with a sense of security, significance and solidarity strong enough to match the demands of a mobile and volatile society. It is here that the communal group, a mini community versatile enough to embrace a wide variety of common interests and concerns, comes to the fore.

The small group as such has played a key role throughout Christian history. The Christian church originated from a group of twelve people. 'The church in the house' was the normative form of the early church's gatherings, in many cases the homeowners, male or female, being identified by name (Acts 12.12; Romans 16.5; 1 Corinthians 19; Colossians 4.15; Philemon 2). The term *ekklesia* (church) was used to refer to the small home-based gathering and to the wider Christian community. For many years the church was composed of small communities of faith, meeting where secrecy and safety permitted, linked by preachers and pastors mobile enough to keep them closely in touch with one another.

Subsequent centuries witnessed the small group at the heart of the church's missionary endeavours, often providing the springboard for movements of Christian renewal. From the Desert Fathers to Benedict of Nursia and the monastic cells that gathered round him, from the Celtic missionaries keeping the faith alive on the fringes of a fragmenting Roman empire to the Franciscans and the Dominicans, from the explosion of small Christian groups after the Reformation to the Counter-Reformation spearheaded by the Society of Jesus, from the rise of 'nonconformity' typified by the small independent church, the Quaker meeting and the Methodist 'class meeting', small groups shaped and sustained the life and mission of the church (Clark, 1984, pp. 74–5).

The nineteenth century also saw the small group at the forefront of renewal and mission. New Roman Catholic orders appeared on the continent and new Anglican orders were founded in England. From the middle of the century, first the Salvation Army and then the Pentecostal movement strove to create small Spirit-filled bands of Christians. As we have noted (Chapter 5), it was during this period, too, that a new form of diaconal movement emerged, first within the German and Scandinavian churches and later within the Anglican and Methodist Churches in Britain.

In the latter half of the twentieth century, renewal movements throughout the church continued to be pioneered by small groups of Christians. Such was the case with the Christian Community Movement in the UK (Chapter 9), the basic ecclesial communities in Latin America (Chapter 13), the so-called 'house churches' (Clark, 1984, pp. 87–91) and the more recent 'emerging churches' worldwide (Chapter 13).

However, we must recognize that not every small group is a communal group. If we had time to examine the history of the small group in the life of the church, we would find many instances of groups that were exclusive and closed, that had distorted the church's understanding of its call to be the servant of the kingdom community and distorted attempts at Christian renewal.

The communal group forms the collective foundation of the diaconal church. It offers its members a sense of security, significance and solidarity (see Figure 1, page 27). It is inclusive in its relationships with other groups. As an integral part of a diaconal church seeking to reflect the nature of the kingdom community, the communal group is also a community of faith through which the kingdom community's gifts of life, liberation, love and learning are offered to its members. It is a mini learning community pursuing a journey of spiritual discovery and, in that undertaking, always open to learning from others. Within the life of the diaconal church, every communal group becomes 'a kingdom community group'.

The communal group, as a kingdom community group, is a key resource for nurturing the life of the diaconal church within and beyond the parish or local neighbourhood. One of its great assets is that it can be located anywhere. It is neither restricted to a particular place, such as the parish, nor to a particular organization, such as the institutional church. Work and voluntary interests, as well as concerns about issues such as justice and peace, can bring small communities of faith into being. The human potential of the communal group lies in the fact that it is ubiquitous, able to draw Christians together wherever they live, wherever they work or whatever their interests.

However, the diaconal church recognizes that the kingdom community is omnipresent. It knows that the kingdom community is not encountered and its gifts received only within communities of *faith*. Thus it does not attempt to corral its lay people within church-centred groups that, at best, can encompass only a narrow range of their interests, skills and needs. It welcomes their membership of any group, religious or secular, that can provide the opportunity for them to fulfil their calling to create communities that manifest the gifts of the kingdom community. Because of this, the diaconal church is able to re-engage with many areas of the life of society with which the Christendom church has lost touch.

Nonetheless, in a global village, the word 'globe' is as important as the word 'village'. The whole is as essential as the part. Larger social collectives are as important as the small group for building a global community of learning communities. Without devaluing the importance of the communal group, the responsibility of the diaconal church is to share in creating forms of social collective that can create a trans-world community. In this task networks and networking have a key part to play.

The network

From insularity to interconnectedness

The parochialism that typified much of the Christendom era led to community of place, especially rural place, shaping the day-to-day life of the Christian church. It was the boundaries of the parish that defined the interests and concerns of most people. But it was also a situation that led to *isolationism* (see Figure 3, p. 69). The spatial immobility of the population, with only the most laborious means of communication available to them, led to what we have described as cognitive and cultural as well as social and economic immobility (Chapter 1). The sense of being part of a universal church was still there, though largely mediated through common rituals and symbolic figures.

The diaconal church faces a quite different world. Since the middle of the twentieth century mobility in every sense has gathered momentum. Vastly increased spatial mobility, notably through air travel, and cognitive mobility, given impetus by a dramatic revolution in information technology, has presented humankind with unimagined opportunities for greater cultural and social mobility. If the church is to re-engage with this world of so-called 'flows', then the small groups that still provide its communal life-blood will need to become integral parts of a much greater whole. Insularity must be replaced by *interconnectedness*. For this purpose networks assume great importance.

The word 'network' is a relatively recent term. It refers to a web of inter-connecting lines of communication that enable participants to exchange experiences, ideas, insights and resources quickly, easily and on an equal footing (Chapter 2). 'Networks' of small Christian groups have characterized the church from its inception, even if communication between such groups was extremely slow right up to the Victorian era. Such networks represent a model of the church as 'movement' rather than as 'institution'. The early church was for many decades (if not centuries) a movement, consisting of networks of Christian groups linked by itinerant missionaries like Paul and his associates. Indeed, Collins (2002, p. 113) states that 'the first written record of a church building is said to be [not until] the year 200 in the writings of Clement of Alexandria'.

With the coming of Christendom, mission gradually gave way to 'main-tenance' and the church as institution gradually took precedence over the church as movement. Only when the call for the renewal of the church as institution, or the conversion of those outside it, came to the fore, did the need for the church as movement re-emerge. Thus the religious orders over many centuries, the post-Reformation 'churches' and the Methodist revival (note that Methodism still calls itself a 'Connexion'), as well as the Pentecostal and charismatic movements of more recent years, have all made use of networks to link the diversity of the small groups that initially gave them life and momentum into corporate and sustainable renewal movements.

The diaconal church welcomes the emergence of networks that can give identity and sustainability to the diverse and dispersed communities of faith that make it up. It recognizes, as has always been the case, that the church as movement is complementary to the church as institution. Thus the diaconal church seeks to create networks that can enrich its life, work and mission. To that end, it has a special concern to create networks that facilitate communication that is open, immediate, direct, informative and interactive (Clark, 1996, p. 76).

For the diaconal church networking is also about linking the local and the global. Holland and Henriot describe such a strategy as follows (1983, p. 85):

While [this] radical strategy is centred on the activities of small grass-roots groups that constitute the basic Christian community, there is also a significant *transnational character* to the strategy. The (diaconal) church is a genuine transnational actor, one that is present and active across national boundaries. Thus, there is a paradoxical two-way thrust to the strategy, the first towards the grassroots and the second towards the transnational arena. Thus, within the new strategy, there is a combination of decentralization and broad networking.

Though the diaconal church employs the network as pre-eminently a means of linking communities of faith, it also recognizes the network as a means of connecting Christians as individuals. This is particularly important where the mission of the laity as the church widely dispersed throughout society is concerned. The network here offers a way of enabling lay people to share their experiences, insights and skills. It makes resources available that would not otherwise be accessible. The network, too, can sometimes offer lay people a 'virtual' faith community when they might otherwise find themselves in isolated and lonely situations.

It is one of the great assets of a new millennium that the information technology needed to create networks of diverse kinds is rapidly becoming available to everyone, not least to the church. Yet, as with all types of social collective, networks can be used for good or ill. The power of information technology can promote interests (such as pornography) and activities (such as terrorism) that are deeply destructive of those values for which the kingdom community stands.

Nevertheless, the sustainability of the diverse and dispersed groups and individuals that make up the diaconal church and enable it to engage with the global challenges of a new era will in large part depend on the creative development and maintenance of communal networks. To further that development, the diaconal church will need to assume the character and functions of a communal institution.

The communal institution

From controlling the whole to serving the parts and from guarding the boundaries to facilitating connections

Institutions are well-established and formally structured organizations that link past and present through the maintenance of cultural, social and economic norms and practices. They enable their members to tap into a common heritage and, through socializing them into an established culture, enable them to experience a sense of community. However, the communal strength of any institution will gradually decline if it fails to adapt to cultural, social and economic change. We have called such inflexibility and solidity *institutionalism* (see Figure 3, p. 69). As Dulles notes (1986, p. 39), the Christendom model of church has increasingly taken on this character.

The early Christian church retained fluid and open structures for a long period. But as the need for continuity and the preservation of both the message and its medium increased, notably from the Constantinean era onwards, a more all-embracing and formalized model of church emerged. Within Christendom, that model was one of 'a total institution' (Goffman, 1961), a church that sought to become all things to all people. The primary concern of the Christendom church was to order and control the social, economic and religious milieu in which the populace lived the whole of their lives.

The Christendom church fulfilled this role in a number of very effective ways. It offered rituals, acts of worship geared to both sacred and secular seasons of the year, together with rites of passage, that gave a familiar framework to every stage of human life, as well as offering the assurance of a life hereafter. It provided catechetical instruction that ensured the Christian tradition was passed on unchanged from generation to generation. It provided pastoral care to the entire parish and alongside this built and maintained hospitals and welfare agencies, schools and colleges.

Symbolic events, places and people were also of particular importance in maintaining the Christendom church as an institution. Its festivals were major symbolic events shared by everyone. The towers and spires of parish churches dominated the countryside, and its cathedrals were gigantic symbols of the glory of God, as well as of the glory of man. Its parish clergy were symbolic figures on the local stage and its 'higher' clergy symbolic figures on the wider scene of church or state.

Particularly important aspects of the Christendom church's institutionalism were the enduring structures by means of which it carried on its life and work. These structures reflected the hierarchical nature of a society in which social stratification was normative and unchallenged. Within the Christendom church, 'the rich man in his castle and the poor man at his gate' was a way of life accepted without question as part of the divine order.

The Christendom church not only defined its boundaries, religious and geopolitical, with dogmatic exactitude but guarded them at all cost. Beyond those boundaries was presumed to be a hostile and godless world holding to heretical 'faiths' or none. Thus 'mission', where it was an issue, was a matter of either enforcing conformity among the faithful or persuading the infidel to surrender to the embrace of mother church, more often than not at the point of a sword.

The world in which the Christendom model of church held sway is passing. If the church is to address the needs of a radically different era, then it has with some urgency to develop a radically different model of the church as an institution. The diaconal church is such a model. It is a communal institution that seeks to *serve the parts*. It gives its members, individually and collectively, a sense of security, significance and solidarity (see Figure 1, p. 27). However, the diaconal church is more than a communal institution in sociological terms. It is 'a kingdom-community institution' that serves its members because it is itself a servant of the kingdom community. It offers to all, individuals and groups alike, God's gifts of life, liberation, love and learning.

As an institution, one of the most distinctive and important functions of the diaconal church is to nurture the life of the communal groups and networks that are at the heart of its life and mission. Thus a core task is *facilitating connections*.

Unlike the Christendom church, the diaconal church makes no attempt to control every aspect of life. Nor does it define its boundaries with exactitude, and then guard them at all cost. On the contrary, its main concern is to serve the needs of the diverse and dispersed groups that make it up, and to link and connect them in creative and sustainable ways. In the process, it deliberately allows the church's institutional boundaries, though still identifiable, to become flexible and permeable. We remind ourselves how Wenger (1998, p. 247) defines this all-important intermediary role of institutions but in this case relate his words to the diaconal church:

> [The diaconal church] connects communities of practice [communal groups] into an organization by crossing boundaries. It does not sit on top; it moves in between. It does not reign; it travels, to be shaped and appropriated in the context of specific practices ... The fundamental principle is to connect and combine the diverse knowledgeabilities that exist in a constellation of practices.

How does the diaconal church as an institution 'connect and combine' its groups and networks into a holistic learning community?

Like the Christendom church, the diaconal institution recognizes the importance of 'the symbolic construction of community' (Cohen, 1985) and of the power and efficacy of Christian symbols. Thus one way in which it enables its members to (re)gain a collective identity as 'church' is to provide a range of symbolic events, places and people that enhance their sense of security, significance and solidarity. However, unlike the Christendom church, the concern of the diaconal church is to ensure that these symbols help its members to experience the church as an inclusive and open communal institution whose mission is to work with those of other faiths and none to transform our world into a global community of communities.

The key symbolic event in the life of the diaconal institution is the gathering for worship. Where gatherings for worship take place, when and how often they are held and how the ministry of word and sacrament is offered on these occasions are matters that will be determined by all the factors that have been discussed in this and the previous chapter. But, as a symbolic event, worship within the diaconal church is of supreme importance in giving its laity, dispersed throughout a secular society, a strong communal identity (see also Chapter 14).

The diaconal institution tries to enhance its members' sense of community through symbolic places (Clark, 1974). In a mobile and cosmopolitan world, buildings can still offer a sense of the dependability of God and the holistic nature of church. However, they need to be communal in architecture and character, places that symbolize life, liberation, love and learning, and not a remote, exclusive and closed religious world. Thus churches that were made too large and grandiose for the population they were meant to serve (as in the case of many buildings constructed when the church sought to transplant itself into the industrial city), or churches that display features that largely glorify their benefactors (typical of numerous Nonconformist chapels), cannot serve the purposes of the diaconal church. Nor can churches that for the most part remain shut, that are enclosed by high walls or imposing railings separating them from the wider world, or that are in a state of disrepair, hope to be symbols of the kingdom community.

The diaconal church maintains buildings that symbolize inclusiveness and openness and offer a sense of community to those who use them. Local (parish) churches that fulfil this requirement have an important part to play within the diaconal church. At the same time the cathedral, or its equivalent, not least because it links past and present, seems to be gaining in communal importance and could remain a focal point of symbolic note. The cathedral is also in a position to 'combine and connect' diverse and dispersed Christian constituencies, a function we have identified as a core concern of the diaconal church.

The diaconal institution also contains symbolic people who could help in 'combining and connecting' its constituency. Though these people would not be the grandiose figures of Christendom, they could play an important part in giving a corporate identity to the diverse groups and networks making up the diaconal church.

The diaconal institution is the servant of its laity. Its task is to affirm, equip and support lay people in their calling as community builders. This is a task where resource centres, which collate, document and disseminate 'good practice' and encourage the telling of stories and the exchange of insights, knowledge and expertise, would be of great value. Such centres would also provide the diaconal institution with a base for workshops and meetings, including hearings, and research.

The diaconal church is a missionary institution engaged in ongoing encounters and exchanges with secular institutions. Its vocation is to create transformed institutions. The gifts the kingdom community offers to its own members, it offers to a secular society. The hearings, groups and networks that shape its own life as an institution are engaged in reaching out into and fostering community within the wider world. Its symbolic events, places and people are inclusive of and open to those who do not express any allegiance to the Christian faith. Its resource centres are concerned not only with the life of the church, but with the public arena.

Nevertheless, the diaconal church can lose its way if it becomes cut off from other institutions, sacred or secular, with similar passions or concerns. Just as communal groups need to network in order to remain inclusive and open, so the diaconal church needs to forge partnerships with institutions in education, health, welfare, business, law and order, and government, among others, if it is to remain faithful to its task of global community building.

The partnership

From competition to co-operation

Partnerships are associations or consortia of institutions (Chapter 2). They are major players in humankind's attempts to build a global community of learning communities. By connecting institutions and encouraging the exchange of ideas, skills and resources, partnerships address the communal dilemma head-on and help to raise hopes for the creation of a communal world. Partnerships open up the possibility of overcoming social and economic divisions based on occupation, class, nationality, race or creed.

Christendom represented an all-embracing 'partnership' between church and state, pope and emperor, priest and feudal lord. However, this was often a marriage of convenience, disguising deep vested interests that frequently disintegrated into bitter rivalry. It was a 'partnership' concerned to preserve the balance of power, with the seeds of competition and conflict lying just below the surface, rather than to further the well-being of church and world.

The Christendom church was a self-contained and self-sufficient Rome-centred church. As time passed, other churches such as the Eastern Orthodox appeared on the scene. Yet the Catholic Church still identified itself as 'the one true church'. What we have called Christian *separatism* (see Figure 3, p. 69) began its long and destructive life. In later centuries, such separatism continued to determine the relationship between Rome and other churches, an attitude that, as Dulles notes (1976, p. 33), hardened considerably from the time of the Reformation and Counter-Reformation onwards.

If the church of the future is to be able to communicate a radically new understanding of partnership, separatism and the conflicts that result from it must give way to *co-operation*. The mould of Christendom has to be broken. For the diaconal church, the foundation on which Christian partnership is built is a commitment by all involved to build transformed communities. Christian 'unity' lies in sharing our visions of the kingdom community and in working together to make these visions a reality. Partnership also has many practical outcomes, not least reducing the enormous waste of energy and resources created by denominational duplication. Yet what matters most is that, as the tenacious grip of Christendom is loosened, partnership leads all parties to rethink and reshape what it means to be church in a new age.

An essential aspect of the mission of the diaconal church is to overcome secular as well as religious separatism and so to end humankind's fear of inclusiveness and openness. This requires it to enter into partnership not only with religious institutions, but with any institution that shares its concerns. In this kind of co-operative enterprise the church has many lessons to learn, as Alison Webster reminds us (CIPL, C43, 2000):

In terms of ecclesiology, inter-agency working and participation in partnerships is as about as theologically exciting and challenging as it gets. Will it be an arena through which the churches discover the uniqueness of our identity, or the one in which we run for cover in shame because we are not like everyone else? Who do we think we are? What are the areas where the 'big wide world' rightly challenges us to get our act together, and what are we proud of? . . . We need a lot more clarity, a lot more courage and a lot more corporate sharing of expertise and experience if we are to grasp the ecclesiological opportunities that inter-agency working affords.

The diaconal church is committed to facing up to these questions and to furthering any kind of partnership, sacred or secular, that is concerned with the building of a more communal world.

7

Leadership and governance

Church leadership

To understand and describe the nature of church leadership within the diaconal church, it is necessary to use the insights of all the academic disciplines at our disposal. We recognize that there are a significant number of people, especially among those who remain committed to the Christendom model of church (Nichols, 1999), who reject what they see as a 'functional' rather than a sacramental approach to church leadership. Others are put off by what they regard as 'management-speak' (Pattison, 1997). In what follows, we are not claiming that the nature of the church and its leadership can be fully understood in terms of the human sciences. The church, as a servant of the kingdom community, will always retain its mystical and sacramental character (Dulles, 1976, pp. 43–70). However, we are convinced that if the church is to have any hope of addressing the communal needs of a new millennium, it will require a form of leadership radically different from that which characterized the age of Christendom. Thus in discerning the nature of the kind of leadership needed by the diaconal church we need to draw on useful insights wherever available.

For the purposes of our analysis and of clarity, we here use the terms 'church leader' and 'church leadership' to refer to those appointed and employed (usually) on a paid basis by the church, and (usually) ordained, to oversee its life and work. This chapter focuses on the roles of church leaders within the diaconal church, and in particular on how these roles relate to the ministry of the laity.

To understand what will be required of church leaders within the diaconal church, we first need to look at the forms of leadership that we have inherited from the Christendom church. We start with a brief resumé of how the leadership of the church developed from New Testament times onwards.

The historical context

As the early church grew and spread, a wide diversity of leadership roles emerged that were inevitably shaped by the missionary nature of the church's life and work. Even so, as John Collins reminds us, the Christian world is now familiar with 'the profound obscurity surrounding the rise of forms of church order' (2002, p. 97). Nevertheless, before any clear and definitive leadership roles emerged within the early church it was commonly believed that all forms of ministry should be 'diaconal' in nature.

Collins presents a wide-ranging discussion of the diverse use of diaconal words in the New Testament. He acknowledges their highly contextual meaning, but comes to three main conclusions. First, he argues, in the face of current assumptions about the word, that 'it is no longer possible to continue claiming that social work expresses what the early church meant by the term *diakonia*' (2002, p. 121).

Second, Collins believes that the word *diakonia* describes a broad range of ministries. These appear to be focused on three functions (*For such a time as this*, p. 32, and Jackson, in Shreeve and Luscombe, 2002, p. 119): that of messenger – one who is entrusted with carrying good tidings; that of agent – one who is commissioned to carry out a task on behalf of someone in authority; and that of attendant – one who waits on a person on whose behalf he performs various duties. In practice, it is not easy to distinguish between these three aspects of diaconal ministry. Nevertheless, what they appear to have in common is that they embrace the concept of servant-hood (Chapter 5), that they stress the role of intermediary and that they include the task of spreading the good news of the kingdom.

Third, with respect to the last of these tasks, Collins states that *diakonia* includes a responsibility for proclaiming 'the Word' (*For such a time as this*, p. 50) and is thus a role carrying a clear missionary connotation.

Over the first few centuries of the Christian church, three specific leadership roles identified by the titles of *diakonos*, *episcopos* and *presbyteros*, probably in that chronological order, gradually began to appear. At the local level the role of priest or presbyter came to dominate the scene, and at the level of the region that of bishop. As the church became more an institution and less a movement (especially after Constantine extended official recognition to Christianity in 313), the role of deacon, which had early in the life of the church gained some prominence, declined in importance. At the same time, the laity came increasingly to be seen more as the recipients than the instruments of ministry, and the church more as 'a community of followers' than 'a community of leaders' (Adair and Nelson, 2004, p. 190).

As the Christendom church became part of the warp and woof of society, bishops and presbyters, as its overseers and guardians, gained in power and status. The consequences were the emergence of forms of church leadership that reflected power and status, and in particular the attributes of Christendom that we have called *élitism, authoritarianism* and *paternalism* (see Figure 3, p. 69).

There were, of course, even within Christendom, exceptions to this pattern of church leadership. When the renewal or mission of the church came to the fore, the roles of priest and bishop could not suffice. Such times required new movements and new forms of leadership able to nurture faith and communicate the gospel with fresh vision, zeal and energy. The monastic movement was one such movement. Other movements were associated with the Reformation and the Counter-Reformation. Likewise, Nonconformity was a movement before it developed into different denominations. So were the Methodist revival and subsequent 'evangelical' revivals, as well as the international missionary movements associated with the age of empire.

Movements of this kind have continued up to the present day (Chapter 13). Those leading them have pursued ministries that have far more in common with the New Testament understanding of *diakonos*, in particular the role of the messenger who proclaims 'the Word', than with that of *presbyteros* or *episkopos*. Despite this fact, such movements have done little to break the mould of Christendom, of the élitism, authoritarianism and paternalism of its leadership and of the lowly position occupied by the laity.

Church leadership within the diaconal church

From hierarchy to servant leaders

Leadership within the Christendom church was élitist in the sense that there was a clear and unassailable order of 'merit', with lay people at the bottom, the priest in the middle and the bishop at the top of that order. The church was a hierarchical institution where those who were 'above' ruled, and those who were 'below' obeyed.

The failure of the Christendom church to acknowledge that the church is 'a community of leaders', and that different 'orders' of ordained ministry are of equal value and status, is one of the most tenacious of all problems facing the emergence of the diaconal church (Barnett, 1981, pp. 161–2). The assumption, within society as well as the church, that there is a hierarchy of ministries that reads 'bishop, priest, deacon and laity', in that order of precedence, remains deeply entrenched. The diaconal church radically questions this legacy of Christendom. It believes that all (ordained and lay) are servants of the kingdom community, and that all ministries (ordained and lay) have equal standing even though they entail different responsibilities. The only 'privileged' position enjoyed by the ordained leadership of the diaconal church is that of being 'servant leaders' of the laity (Philip Mawer, in Adair and Nelson, 2004, p. 92).

Reports from recent working parties on the nature of a renewed diaconate argue that the deacon has a special responsibility to model a servanthood ministry (see Chapter 5). A 'diaconal, servanthood ministry means being a healing, accepting, encouraging presence to others, enabling them to experience God's unending, unconditional love and forgiveness' (*Diaconal Reflections*, 1998). However, though servanthood is 'the key to understanding the call to diaconal ministry' (*Diaconal Reflections*, 1998), it is not an attribute of the ministry of the deacon alone. Servanthood is also a hallmark of the ministries of presbyter and bishop. Thus for the diaconal church to single out the deacon as having a particular calling to exemplify the meaning of servanthood would not only be invidious but also deny the fact that presbyter and bishop, as well as deacon, are servant leaders.

One would have hoped that the recent literature on a renewed diaconate would have produced a radically new vision of church leadership. One would also have hoped that these reports would have recognized the laity as the leaders in mission and those ordained as supporting them, with lay and ordained alike being seen as having equal value and status. However, the conclusions, in particular of the Anglican and Roman Catholic working parties on a renewed diaconate, are ambivalent if not contradictory on these issues. Their reports assert with some conviction that all ordained ministries are diaconal (servant ministries) in nature, but then go on to argue for the retention of a hierarchical order of church leadership.

On the one hand, the Church of England working party set up by the House of Bishops states that the diaconate is 'the *sine qua non* of all ordained ministry, the base line, the template on which it is fashioned' (*For such a time as this*, p. 37), a sentiment echoed by the Diocese of Salisbury report *The*

Distinctive Diaconate (p. 5). The Roman Catholic Church's International Theological Commission believes that the 'representation of Christ as Servant . . . should be considered a characteristic common to every ordained minister' (*From the Diakonia of Christ*, p. 80).

On the other hand, the hierarchical threefold order of bishop, priest and deacon remains firmly entrenched. The Anglican Church, in *For such a time as this*, states that (permanent) deacons operate 'under the oversight of the parish priest and both deacon and priest are subject to the oversight of the bishop' (p. 56). The Diocese of Salisbury report at least acknowledges that 'there may appear to be a tension between our desire for an integrated approach to ministry and the seemingly hierarchical context of the Anglican church (as well as the Roman Catholic and Orthodox churches) whereby from the *laos* some are called as deacons, of whom some are called as priests, of whom some are called as bishops' (p. 39). But the report's attempt to resolve this dilemma by talking of 'cumulative responsibility for the edification of the church', still leaves the diaconate at the bottom of the ladder, a fact brought home by its recommendation that the deacon's stipend is to be 'as other *assistant* clergy' (p. 83, our italics). In the Church of England all deacons remain 'junior clery' (Borgegard and Hall, 1999, p. 211).

The Roman Catholic Commission similarly notes that Vatican II, despite reinstating the permanent diaconate, still upheld 'different "degrees" of Holy Orders' wherein 'deacons represent the "lowest" degree in the hierarchical scale, in relation to bishops and priests' (*From the Diakonia of Christ*, p. 83). In short, the relegation of the deacon to a transitory grade of ministry 'placed after the bishop and the priests' (p. 20), remains the norm.

From director to community educator

Authoritarianism (see Figure 3, p. 69), in the literal sense of taking authority to oneself, typified the leadership of the Christendom church. Its leaders were certainly not into the business of equipping the church to be a learning community. Their task was to instruct and train, not to educate. As guardians of the church, they were there to direct its affairs and protect the souls of the faithful.

In contrast, church leaders of the diaconal church are *community educators* (Chapter 4) not directors. As such, presbyter, deacon and bishop have two major responsibilities. The first is that of enabling the church to become a *community* that makes manifest the gifts of the kingdom community. All its church leaders are working to nurture and sustain a body of people who are open to receiving God's gifts of life, liberation, love and learning and who are passionate that others should have the opportunity to receive these gifts. Presbyter, deacon and bishop are also there to enable the church to become a *learning* community. Their task is to help the laity to interpret the Christian faith not as a closed book, but as an ongoing journey of spiritual discovery in search of the meaning of the kingdom community.

The second major responsibility of presbyter, deacon and bishop is that of equipping the laity to be community builders. This means helping them to discern and make known the gifts of the kingdom community already omnipresent in the world. It also means helping lay people to be community builders empowered by the gifts of the kingdom community in whatever situations they find themselves.

Presbyter, deacon and bishop fulfil their role as community educators in four main ways. They are *catalysts*, rousing a Christendom church from its slumbers and challenging the laity to break clear of their dependence on the clergy. They encourage lay people to engage in visioning what a world manifesting the gifts of the kingdom community would be like. They work to raise the awareness of the laity to their vocation to be the servants of the kingdom community in the world.

As community educators, church leaders within the diaconal church are *enablers*. They build up the confidence of lay people by affirming the knowledge, experience and skills that they already possess. They encourage them to reflect on how these attributes can enrich their life as a faith community and enhance their ministry in the world. They help lay people to learn how faith can inform work, and how work can inform faith, and to discover how both processes can inform their calling as community builders. They work with lay people to enable them to become 'reflective practitioners' (Schon, 1991).

As community educators, presbyter, deacon and bishop are also *intermediaries*. Their responsibility is to link lay person with lay person so that beliefs, experiences and ideas can be shared, learning advanced and the sense of being a team be strengthened. They work to create local team ministries that bring together presbyter, deacon and laity. They seek to foster links with other churches committed to an ecumenical vision of mission. They are also on the lookout for creative connections that can be made between the church and a secular society, especially connections that can create networks and partnerships to further community building.

Through all these facets of their role as community educators, presbyter, deacon and bishop operate as *resource persons*. They offer the resources of the church, through worship, education and pastoral care, to enable lay people to gain a deeper understanding of Christian faith, to learn what it means to be a learning community and to prepare for their calling to represent the church in the world.

At the present time, when we still await the freeing of the diaconal church from the legacy of Christendom, it is our belief that the deacon has a particular responsibility to fulfil the role of catalyst and enabler (see Chapter 14). Complementary to this diaconal role, the presbyter might be seen as having a special responsibility to undertake the role of resource person, and the bishop to fulfil that of intermediary. Nevertheless, in suggesting such a 'division of labour', we would not in any way want to undermine the all-important fact that deacon, presbyter and bishop all remain community educators and, at one time or another, will be called upon to play out every facet of that role.

From men to women and men

All positions of leadership within the diaconal church are open to *women and men*. This is a far cry from the Christendom model of church in which patriarchy and *paternalism* (see Figure 3, p. 69) were the norm.

In the early church, women appear to have worked as equals alongside men in exercising informal leadership, despite the gender discrimination evident in certain of the Pauline letters and the reservations about the role of women as leaders in the pastoral epistles. Even though the status of Phoebe, designated a *diakonos* (Romans 16.1), and that of the women 'deacons' mentioned in 1 Timothy 3.11, is disputed (see Collins, 2002, p. 99, as against *From the Diakonia of Christ*, p. 21), there is little doubt that women leaders figured prominently during this period. However, as the leadership of the church became more formalized, women were increasingly excluded from positions of authority. Even when designated 'deaconesses', women were only in evidence in the Eastern Church and then exercised a ministry largely confined to the needs of other women. Indeed 'in the West there is no trace of any deaconesses for the first five centuries' (*From the Diakonia of Christ*, p. 26). From then on deaconesses continued to fulfil a lowly 'ecclesiastical function' in both East and West (p. 27), though their ministry developed unevenly in different regions.

With the emergence of female monastic communities, a number of women came to exercise a notable ministry as their leaders. However, in relation to the order and governance of the institutional church they continued to be treated as subordinate to men.

It was not until the nineteenth century, as we have seen (Chapter 5), that deaconesses, as members of a reinvigorated diaconate undertaking a ministry of social welfare, nursing and teaching, again came to the fore. However, they were usually seen as exercising a 'lay' ministry of service, and few were given any voice in matters of church governance. In fact, the deaconess associations of this era did not press for such a voice, did not take a great interest in church politics and were not much involved in 'feminist causes' as a whole (Staton, 2001, p. 68).

During the twentieth century, deaconess associations began to lobby for their role as church leaders to be recognized by their being accepted into the presbyteral ministry of the church. Women were ordained as presbyters within the Congregational Union in 1914. In Methodism, the Wesley Deaconess Order began debating the ordination of women as early as 1920 (Staton, 2001, p. 159). In 1947, the Methodist Diaconal Convocation again pressed for deaconesses to be given the opportunity to be ordained as presbyters, a request declined by the Methodist Conference (p. 210) even though many deaconesses were then working in presbyteral appointments because of a shortage of male ministers following the war. Not until 1972 was the Methodist ministry opened to women. Staton goes so far as to describe the treatment of the Wesley Deaconesses in the Methodist Church during the period from 1932 (the union of Methodism in the United Kingdom) to 1972 as 'a paradigm of subordination and the exploitation of feminine good nature!' (p. 250).

In the second half of the twentieth century there were similar moves to ordain women as priests within the Church of England. Increasing numbers of women opted for the diaconate but mainly in the hope of eventually being able to become priests (700 women were ordained deacon in 1987). In 1992, the General Synod at last voted to open the priesthood (though not the episcopate) to women. The first ordinations of women to the priesthood of the Church of England were held in 1994 (*For such a time as this*, p. 8).

It is worth noting here that the coming of greater gender equality also raised the issue of equal opportunities for men. Thus many diaconal associations and communities, once entirely female, are now open to men, though women continue to be a large majority.

However, within the Roman Catholic and Orthodox Churches the reinstatement and revival of the permanent diaconate relates only to men.

Nor in those churches has there been any official movement towards the ordination of women to either the diaconate or the priesthood. At the same time, a similar male-dominated form of church leadership characterizes many Pentecostal and charismatic churches (Chapter 13).

The ordination of women to presbyteral ministry has certainly challenged Christendom's legacy of paternalism. Thus it could be a major step towards the emergence of the diaconal church in which positions of church leadership are open equally to women and men. However, there is some danger that the opening of presbyteral ministry to women could inadvertently continue to perpetuate the Christendom model of élitism and clericalism. For if the opportunity for women to be ordained only leads to an increase in the number of priests and presbyters, it could perpetuate rather than challenge hierarchical orders of ministry. Of major consequence too, the diaconate could continue to be seen as a subordinate office, and the ministry of both deacon and lay people continue to be devalued as a result.

Church leadership roles: presbyter, deacon and bishop

(Note: At this point we put on hold our discussion of how the diaconal model of church differs from that of Christendom in order to look in more detail at the roles of presbyter, deacon and bishop within the diaconal church.)

The gathered church and the dispersed church

Before we examine the roles of presbyter, deacon and bishop, we need to identify two forms of the diaconal model of church that are vital to its life and work: the *gathered* church and the *dispersed* church. By the gathered church, we mean the people of God as servants of the kingdom community gathered to worship, learn, care for one another and enjoy each other's company. By the dispersed church, we mean the people of God dispersed throughout society to serve the kingdom community by building communities that manifest its gifts, wherever they live, work or play.

One of the most crippling weaknesses of the Christendom model of church is that no form of church leadership is specifically designated to serve the laity as the people of God in the world. This is a huge omission. It is one that we believe lies at the heart of the church's marginalization in our day and age. Thus it is our contention that the diaconal church needs to create a form of church leadership explicitly concerned to equip and support the laity as the church dispersed in the world. We argue below that this responsibility should be that of the deacon. This would mean the deacon's role being interpreted in a way that differs radically from how it is seen today, even in the recent literature on a renewed diaconate.

In the discussion of church leadership roles that follows, we distinguish three main spheres of church leadership within the diaconal church. That of 'presbyter' we see as related to the gathered church; that of 'deacon' to the dispersed church; and that of 'bishop' as concerned with integrating the life and work of both the gathered and the dispersed church. (Note: In what follows, the title of 'presbyter' is taken to be synonymous with the titles of 'priest' or 'minister'.)

We here keep the titles of presbyter, deacon and bishop because they are the ones in common usage today, as well as linking us with the early church and our Christian heritage. However, we need to make clear that we see the titles as such as relatively unimportant. It is the leadership *roles* that relate to these titles that are of real concern. Indeed, in future years these titles may well be superseded by new ones that have greater affinity with the everyday language of a secular society, as well as with the ethos of the diaconal church.

(Note: Throughout this discussion the male gender is used but should be regarded as interchangeable with the female gender.)

Figure 4 outlines what we see as the main features of the role of presbyter and deacon within the diaconal church. Each role is described as what, in sociological terms, is called an 'ideal type'. Each ideal type brings together the key features of a particular leadership role, though all the features will rarely be evident in the ministry of any one individual. We do not include the role of bishop because, as we explain later, we see his role as supporting and integrating the roles of presbyter and deacon.

Figure 4: *The roles of presbyter and deacon in the diaconal church*

	Presbyter	Deacon
COMMON FEATURES	*Servant leaders of the laity* *Community educators* *Women and men*	
FORM OF CHURCH	Gathered	Dispersed
PEOPLE SERVED	The laity in the church	The laity in the world
PRIMARY TASK	Church as medium of the kingdom community The church as 'the Body of Christ'	Church as messenger of the kingdom community The church as 'the people of God'
FOCUS OF MINISTRY	Community of place The church as workplace	Communities of interest The church as home base
BOUNDARIES OF MINISTRY	Working within the boundaries of the church	Moving across the boundaries of church and world
WORSHIP	'The Word' for the church Baptism as a sign of belonging Holy communion as 'the breaking of bread' Christian rites of passage	'The Word' for the world Baptism as a sign of discipleship Holy communion as 'the washing of feet' Secular 'rites of passage'
LEARNING	Learning about the faith Doctrine Spirituality of growth in the Christian life Learning about the church Reflection on faith Discussion	Learning about Christian vocation Ethics Spirituality of work Learning about the church in the world Reflection on practice Dialogue

PASTORAL CARE	The laity in the church Those in need associated with the church	The laity in the world Those in need beyond the church
MANAGEMENT RESPONSIBILITIES	The gathered church Team ministry co-ordinator	The dispersed church
AS SYMBOLIC FIGURE	Represents the church as an institution	Represents the church as a movement
'ECUMENICAL' MINISTRY	Working with other churches	Linking Christian and non-Christian collectives
PIONEERING MINISTRY	'Planting', supporting and developing 'emerging churches'	Exemplifying, advocating and working for the acceptance of the gifts of the kingdom community in the world

The presbyter

Within the diaconal church, the presbyter is both a servant of the kingdom community and a servant leader of the laity. He is also a community educator and his style of leadership will reflect this.

The *form of church* with which the presbyter is mainly concerned is the gathered church, and the *people served* who are his particular responsibility are those lay people who are members of that gathered congregation. His *primary task* is that of building the laity into a learning community that makes manifest the gifts of the kingdom community: life, liberation, love and learning. The corporate image most clearly associated with this expression of church is 'the Body of Christ'.

The *focus of ministry* for the presbyter is the church as a community of place, usually meaning a particular building within a particular locality (such as a parish), even though the members of his congregation may come from further afield. The local church building also serves as the presbyter's main place of work, in the sense that his office may be there, that he meets people on church premises during the week and that worship takes place there. The *boundaries of ministry* for the presbyter are defined largely by the church as a community focused on the local neighbourhood, and as an institution.

In the context of *worship*, the presbyter is seen as a minister of 'Word and Sacrament'. He celebrates the sacrament of baptism as a sign of belonging, and holy communion as 'the breaking of bread', as well as other Christian rites of passage. For the presbyter, *learning* has faith and doctrine as its main focus, as well as the history and traditions of the particular denomination he represents. As with any community educator, the presbyter encourages reflection and discussion. He also seeks to nurture the laity in a spirituality that helps them grow in the Christian life. For the presbyter, *pastoral care* is focused on the members of the gathered church, especially on their personal and family concerns, and on the needs of others closely associated with the church or living in the immediate neighbourhood.

The presbyter's *management responsibilities* encompass organizational, administrative and financial matters related to the life of the gathered church. The presbyter has the important task of co-ordinating any team ministry associated with the work of the local church. Such teams will be made up of ordained (including deacons) and lay members. Their style of operating will be collaborative and consensual.

As a *symbolic figure*, it is with the church as a public institution that the presbyter is most clearly identified.

The presbyter's wider ministry has two main foci. *Ecumenically*, his main concern is working in partnership with (local) churches of other denominations. Where he undertakes a more *pioneering* role, his work will often be focused on church growth or how 'emerging' forms of gathered church, usually linked to his own, can be created and nurtured.

The deacon

Within the diaconal church, the deacon, like the presbyter, is a servant of the kingdom community and a servant leader of the laity. He, too, is a community educator.

However, it is of importance to recognize that the *form of church* for which the deacon takes the main responsibility is the dispersed church, the people of God called to be the servants of the kingdom community in the world. Thus the *people served* by the deacon are the laity as that church dispersed in the world.

The *primary task* of the deacon is to challenge and equip lay people to fulfil their calling as messengers of the kingdom community. This means that he will be equipping them to be community builders empowered by and offering to others the gifts of life, liberation, love and learning.

The deacon's task is 'to enable [lay people] to see that mission is not an optional extra, but central to what it means to be the church ... called not merely to maintain itself but to proclaim God's kingdom' (Atkinson, 2005). He helps 'the church to have confidence in God by recognizing his constant presence' (Atkinson) throughout the whole of society. The deacon's responsibility is to maintain 'a permanent focus on the servant ministry of Christ by attempting to embody that role and encouraging and enabling the church to do so too' (Atkinson). The corporate image most clearly associated with this expression of church is 'the people of God'.

The role of the deacon as one facilitating the ministry of the laity receives attention from a number of commentaries on a renewed diaconate. For example, *For such a time as this* (quoting the Anglican–Lutheran Hanover Report of 1996) describes the deacon's role as 'enabling and resourcing the ministry of the laity' (p. 18). *For such a time as this* argues that a renewed diaconate should 'model, encourage and coordinate the diaconal ministry of the people of God' (p. 36). It adds that 'a renewed, distinctive diaconate, operating as a catalyst for Christian discipleship, in the mission space between worship and world, can help the church to become more incarnational' (p. 30). *The Distinctive Diaconate* report for the Diocese of Salisbury states that 'the deacon does not do the work of others but encourages and enables the ministry of others' (p. 106). For the Methodist Church, *What is a Deacon?* contends that 'the primary purpose' of diaconal ministry 'is to help all Christians discover, develop and express their own servant ministry' (para. 5.4), adding that the deacon 'encourages and enables others to undertake their ministry with greater effectiveness in their daily lives' (para. 3.3 (b)).

Although, like the presbyter, 'the central community of the diaconal minister's life and ministry is the congregation' (Lambert, 1999, p. 16), the *focus of ministry* for the deacon is the communities of interest, occupation or concern in which lay people are involved on a daily basis. The deacon is thus involved not only with community education within the local church as such but, following up the ministry of the laity, with community education well beyond. The local church is not so much the deacon's place of work as a home base and launching pad for his ministry within wider society.

The *boundaries of* the deacon's *ministry* do not limit him to working within the institutional church. He criss-crosses the boundaries of church and society in order to discover ways in which he can better equip the laity to fulfil their vocation as the dispersed church. He also moves across these boundaries to enhance his own knowledge, experience and resources.

In this connection, some reports on a renewed diaconate misinterpret what it means for a deacon to be 'a boundary worker'. These speak as if it is the deacon himself who is the 'go-between', the 'bridge' or the 'envoy' (*For such a time as this*, p. 22), or the 'ambassador' or 'agent', on behalf of the church (*The Distinctive Diaconate*, p. 42). Within the diaconal church, however, it is the laity, not the deacon, who are the 'go-betweens', 'the envoys' and 'agents' linking church and world. The responsibility of the deacon is to inspire, enable and resource the laity to fulfil that ministry. If the deacon's boundary role were interpreted in this way, then fears that a renewed diaconate could devalue the ministry of the laity, and a new form of clericalism thereby reassert itself, would be allayed (see *For such a time as this*, p. 46; *The Distinctive Diaconate*, pp. 46 and 73; *From the Diakonia of Christ*, p. 65–6).

The deacon's boundary role gives depth and breadth to his understanding of the communal needs of society. It is a role that 'may also involve social and cultural analysis' (Lambert, 1999, p. 11). It offers him a unique vantage point from which to discern the presence of the kingdom community in church and world. It is a position that enables him to keep the servant ministry of the dispersed church constantly under review, and from which he can identify the most appropriate resources for educating and equipping the laity for that ministry.

The laity, as the dispersed church, also need to gather in order to renew themselves for mission. When this happens, it is the deacon's primary responsibility, through worship, education and pastoral care, to help the laity reflect on and renew their calling as the church in the world and to equip them for that ministry. (Practical examples of these aspects of the deacon's role are discussed in greater detail in Chapter 14.)

In the context of *worship*, 'liturgical involvement holds great potential for expressing a diaconal minister's identity as a *public* [our italics] minister of the Word' (Lambert, 1999, p. 12). The deacon ensures that 'the Word', through preaching or prayers of intercession, is applied not just to the life of the church but also to the needs of the world. His presence shows baptism to be a sign of discipleship, and holy communion to be a sacrament of servanthood symbolized by 'the washing of feet'. The deacon's act of sending the congregation out with a prayer of dismissal emphasizes their calling as the people of God in the world. The deacon can also help the church to acknowledge and celebrate secular 'rites of passage'; those important transitional experiences that mark significant stages in everyday life: from home to school, from school to work, from job to job, from work to retirement, and from place to place.

Recent reports on the renewed diaconate affirm a number of the features of the liturgical role of the deacon mentioned above. For example, in the Anglican reports, the deacon's responsibility is seen as reading the Gospel, offering prayers of intercession and dismissing the people with an appropriate blessing (*For such a time as this*, p. 55 and *The Distinctive Diaconate*, p. 63). In the Diocese of Salisbury's report, it is argued that the deacon should also preach (p. 72). At the Roman Catholic mass, the deacon reads the Bible and occasionally preaches (*From the Diakonia of Christ*, pp. 61–2). However, these Anglican and Catholic commentaries fail to make a clear connection between the deacon's liturgical role within the gathered congregation and his ministry to the laity as the dispersed church. Their approach is dominated by the deacon's liturgical responsibilities as an assistant to the presbyter (priest), especially in relation to the celebration of the Eucharist or Mass.

The deacon has a key role in relation to *learning*. An important focus of the deacon's ministry in this context is to strengthen the laity's sense of vocation as the people of God in the world. In this his task is to challenge, inspire and equip them to become community builders. Facilitating theological reflection on daily life and work, and developing the idea of dialogue as mission are other tasks central to the deacon's role as community educator. Christian ethics will figure prominently in the deacon's repertoire. All these responsibilities will involve the deacon exercising his educational skills through the use of hearings and groups. He will also enable lay people to develop a spirituality of work related to their working situation and their personal needs.

These aspects of the deacon's role as applied to learning are far removed from the catechetical role of the deacon portrayed in recent reports on the renewed diaconate. In those reports, the 'educational' role of the deacon is generally interpreted in the narrow sense of instructing the faithful in the faith and preparing people for Christian rites of passage. In few commentaries is the deacon's role explicitly associated with strengthening and developing the vocation of lay people as the church dispersed in the world.

The deacon, along with the presbyter, exercises *pastoral care*. However, the deacon's caring ministry is primarily concerned with nurturing, encouraging and supporting the laity as they seek to live out their calling in daily life. His job is to understand and address the inevitable strains and stresses experienced by those seeking to serve the kingdom community in a secular and sometimes hostile society. At the same time, the deacon is always ready to care for those outside the church, as the situation demands and his time and energy allow.

Recent reports on the renewed diaconate again miss the point. They see the deacon's pastoral role as relating primarily to the needs of the gathered church and the local neighbourhood and not to those of the dispersed church as such. For example, in the Anglican reports, the deacon is regarded as the person who 'spearheads pastoral care in the parish' (*The Distinctive Diaconate*, p. 64). This is seen as his 'pivotal' responsibility (p. 65). The Roman Catholic International Commission goes a good way to reinforcing this approach with its emphasis on the deacon's ministry as being 'the service of charity' within the parish (*From the Diakonia of Christ*, p. 68).

The deacon's *management responsibilities* require him to oversee the work of all those facilitating the ministry and mission of the dispersed church. Ideally, he will build up groups of people with relevant skills, especially educational skills, to assist him on a paid or voluntary basis. At the same time, 'diaconal ministry is not a "lone ranger" activity' (Lambert, 1999, p. 17). Thus he will be an active member of any team ministry that seeks to integrate the work of the gathered and dispersed expressions of the diaconal church.

As *a symbolic figure*, the deacon is most closely identified with the church as a movement. He represents a diaconal church that is mobile, dispersed and able to respond to the call to serve the kingdom community anywhere and anytime. The fact that, for the public at large, it is still the presbyter who symbolizes the church, and a church that is modelled on Christendom, simply reveals the difficulties that lie ahead for a diaconal church attempting to offer a new interpretation of the church as the servant of the kingdom community in the world.

The deacon fulfils an *'ecumenical' ministry*. His role here is primarily that of an intermediary. He seeks to link Christian collectives, of whatever denomination, wherever this can enrich the quality of their life and work as learning communities. The presbyter focuses his attention on connecting gathered church with gathered church. The deacon looks to build and promote creative connections between the church and a diversity of Christian collectives active in society (groups, voluntary organizations, church schools, religious orders and so on), as well as between the church and non-Christian collectives that share its concerns for the communal renewal of our world.

On occasions, the deacon's intermediary role will take him into other fields of work. He may operate as a person seeking to connect secular collective with secular collective in an attempt to build a more communal society (Chapter 11). On an even broader front, he may sometimes interpret his 'ecumenical' role as relating to 'the whole inhabited earth' (the literal meaning of the word) and become involved in ecological issues of preservation and conservation. Here, however, we are touching on the role of the deacon as pioneer.

Like the presbyter, the deacon may sometimes be called upon to undertake a *'pioneering* and prophetic' *ministry* (*Windsor Statement*, 1997).

Though most of the commentaries on the renewed diaconate major on the deacon's liturgical, catechetical and pastoral responsibilities in relation to the gathered church, some do touch on his role as pioneer. *For such a time as this*, for example, claims to be offering 'a vision of the renewed diaconate at the cutting edge of the church's mission' (p. viii). *The Distinctive Diaconate* believes that 'the deacon is the church's representative person in a liminal ministry among those who would never cross the threshold of the church on their own' (p. 106). *From the Diakonia of Christ*, for the Roman Catholic Church, notes that 'in various places particular efforts have been made to make the diaconate a "threshold" ministry, which aims to look after "the frontier church"' (p. 69). The Methodist Church is particularly strong on this aspect of the deacon's role, stressing the deacon's pioneering role as 'crossing boundaries, making connections between alienated and fragmented groups, including those beyond the margins, overturning unjust structures, standing in solidarity with the vulnerable and helping them discover their own voice' (*What is a Deacon?*, para. 5.7).

The role of deacon as pioneer is expressed in three main ways. He identifies with the marginalized (see *Voices from the Margins*, 2005). As *Diaconal Reflections* puts it (1998, p. 2): 'In identifying with Christ, [the deacon is] identifying with the suffering of the world, with the oppressed, the poor, the disenfranchised, the abused.' Second, the deacon as pioneer is an agent of change: 'The prophetic role of diaconal ministry is to see God's intention for the creation, to critique what is going on in church and world, to protest against evil and injustice, and to call the church and world – all people – to respond in ways that will transform the world' (p. 2). Third, the deacon as pioneer is pro-active in striving for a more just world, in working for peace and in serving those in need, especially where those needs are acute. It is a role that entails 'prophetic, political, social and environmental action directed towards peace, justice and reconciliation . . . ' (*What is a Deacon?*, para. 5.4).

Nevertheless, in interpreting the role of deacon as a pioneer it is important to remind ourselves of the nature of the diaconal church and of the deacon's role within it. Within the diaconal church, the deacon only assumes the role of pioneer where this role cannot be fulfilled by lay people. Within the diaconal church, his primary responsibility is to educate and equip the laity to be the pioneers. His task is not, as is suggested in *From the Diakonia of Christ* (p. 56), 'to penetrate secular society in the same way as lay people' unless lay people are just not available to meet the need concerned.

If the deacon is called to take up a pioneering role, he will seek to move aside as soon as possible so that the skills, energy and resources of the laity can come to the fore. Such 'stepping aside' is of the essence of the deacon's ministry as a servant leader. This does not mean that he is unconcerned about the needs of a world facing a stark choice between community and chaos. Rather, he is attempting, as his role requires, to encourage and to support lay people to fulfil their pioneering ministries. Any deacon, indeed any church leader, however dynamic, courageous, or sacrificial his ministry, who takes over what should be the ministry of the laity, devalues the church's greatest resource and perpetuates clericalism.

One final but important point needs to made. When the mission (though not the maintenance) of the diaconal church requires it, there may sometimes be circumstances in which a presbyter is required to play the role of deacon, or a deacon to play the role of presbyter. In these circumstances the presbyter must be given the authority to undertake diaconal responsibilities. For the same reason, the deacon must be given the authority to undertake presbyteral responsibilities, including if necessary the administration of the sacraments. Nonetheless, it remains essential to maintain a clear distinction between the role of the presbyter, which is primarily focused on the gathered church, and the role of the deacon, which is primarily focused on the dispersed church, if we are to understanding the dynamics of leadership within the diaconal church.

The bishop

As with the role of presbyter and deacon, there is only 'fragmentary New Testament evidence about the office of *episcopos*' (bishop) (Croft, 1999, p. 146). In the early church, the broad picture is that of an *episcopoi* initially exercising oversight of local churches alongside presbyters, but gradually assuming a wider remit as the church expanded numerically and geographically. In time, the bishop came to oversee both presbyters, who were beginning to take greater responsibility for the life of the gathered church, and deacons, who were assuming a more itinerant and administrative brief, the latter often acting as the eyes and ears of the bishop who authorized their ministry. As we have noted, with the emergence of Christendom this threefold order of ministry became normative, with power and influence accruing to the bishop at regional level and to the presbyter at local level, while the office of deacon lost its itinerant brief and was eventually relegated to a first brief stage en route to the priesthood.

We here use the title 'bishop' as that which encompasses not only the office of bishop as witnessed in the Anglican and Roman Catholic Churches, but any office (such as that of chair of district or moderator) with which it is equated in other denominations. The Christendom church has left us with the problem that the title remains equated, in the eyes of both church and society, with those at the 'top' of the ecclesiastical pyramid. However, our interpretation of the role of bishop within the diaconal church will differ markedly from that with which it is currently associated.

Within the diaconal church, the bishop, like the presbyter and deacon, is a servant of the kingdom community and a servant leader of the laity. Like the presbyter and deacon, he is also a community educator.

A key aspect of the bishop's role as community educator is that of *intermediary* (as against the common interpretation of *episcope* as an 'overseer' or director). To use Wenger's words on the leadership of organizations again, the role of the bishop is not to 'sit on top but to move in between, not to unify by transcending but to connect and disconnect, not to reign but to travel and to be shaped and appropriated in the context of specific practices' (1998, p. 247). The bishop is 'a go-between leader' serving a 'go-between God' (Taylor, 1979). From his 'go-between' position he is able to learn, to monitor (Rudge, 1968, pp. 55–7), to connect and, if necessary, to initiate.

The bishop serves the whole *laos*. His task is to integrate the gathered and dispersed forms of church, across a wide area, into a dynamic whole. It is a task he fulfils largely by affirming and supporting the ministries of presbyter and deacon. His responsibility is to enable them to share their visions, experiences, knowledge and skills so that the church can manifest the gifts of the kingdom community and, through the laity, offer those gifts to all.

The bishop helps deacon and presbyter to recognize their ministries as complementary. He enables them to hold together baptism as a sign of belonging and baptism as a sign of discipleship; worship as 'the Word' for the church and worship as 'the Word' for the world; holy communion as 'the breaking of bread' and holy communion as 'the washing of feet'; learning about the faith and learning about Christian vocation; pastoral care to nurture the laity 'at home' and pastoral care to support the laity 'at work'. The bishop also has the task of maintaining strong links between the church as an institution and the church as a movement.

The bishop is servant leader, always seeking to discern and understand more clearly the workings of the kingdom community in church and world. The exercise of *episcope*, of being an intermediary, is crucial in enabling the whole church to see and acknowledge the ministries of presbyter and deacon as complementary and collaborative. But it is also crucial in enabling the laity to recognize that their ministry as the dispersed church is as important as their work within the gathered church, and that, unless these two expressions of Christian ministry are given equal validation, the church's mission will remain unfulfilled.

The bishop, like the presbyter and deacon, is a symbolic figure. However, his authority as such derives not from any kind of historically ascribed status, but from the fact that he represents the holistic nature of the church, gathered and dispersed, as a servant community.

Though the bishop's primary role within the diaconal church is to support and connect the ministries of presbyter and deacon and, through them, to affirm the ministries of the laity, he also has ecumenical responsibilities. Here, the bishop's task is to link the servant ministry of the groups of churches in his care with that of groups of churches within other denominations. Likewise, he helps to link the groups of churches for which he has responsibility with secular organizations also engaged in seeking to create learning communities.

On occasions the bishop may exercise a pioneering role. As a pioneer, the bishop may be engaged with urgent issues or critical needs that the dispersed church, for whatever reason, is not able to address, or that need the involvement of a person representative of a large Christian constituency.

However, the bishop's role should not become that of a focal person on which the ultimate success of such interventions comes to depend. Thus he will assume a pioneering role only where the ministries of presbyter or deacon, and above all the ministry of the laity, are not operative or adequate.

Equipping the leadership of the diaconal church

The diaconal church is a learning community called into being to manifest the gifts of the kingdom community. Its mission is to enable all social collectives to become learning communities that likewise manifest those gifts. This being the case, the diaconal church needs church leaders with the knowledge, skills and experience of community educators, attributes very different from those associated with the leaders of Christendom.

We highlight below a number of key elements of a curriculum that might be of value to all church leaders fulfilling the role of community educators within the diaconal church. (Note: In Chapter 14, we focus on those features of a curriculum of especial importance in the training of a renewed diaconate.)

The elements of the curriculum we outline below are intended to reorient the knowledge and skills normally associated with the training of presbyters, and the management, administrative and financial expertise required by all church leaders today.

Even so, the new elements of a diaconal curriculum that we suggest constitute a substantial list. It is recognized that no student in preparation for church leadership would be able to study the whole curriculum. Indeed the range of talents needed for the leadership of the diaconal church are such that only through team ministries operating on the basis of a division of labour could the diaconal church find the skills and expertise it requires. Thus the purpose of the curriculum outlined below is neither to lay down a blueprint, nor to suggest that any one person is capable of mastering the whole. It is to pinpoint a range of important themes and skills that appear only infrequently in the still pervasive Christendom model of ordination training.

An outline curriculum

- Those preparing for professional leadership roles in the diaconal church would major on the theology of community, in particular on Trinitarian theology and the theology of the kingdom, the importance of which we stressed in Part 1. In the process, they would also draw on other disciplines such as sociology and education.
- In ecclesiological studies, they would explore the diaconal model of church, especially in relation to the role of the laity and its forms of church leadership.
- In missiology, students would focus on models of mission and how these can enable a diaconal church to re-engage in communally creative ways with a secular society. An interfaith component of the curriculum, to help students to compare and contrast the contribution of Christianity and other faiths to civilization's quest for community, would be important here.
- Students would explore the biblical understanding of servanthood and how this applies to the life and ministry of the diaconal church.
- A knowledge of Christian ethics would be important, especially in helping church leaders to equip lay people to bring their faith to bear on their working lives in an informed and creative way.
- To help church leaders develop the diaconal church as a learning community, adult education would be an important skill, together with the skills of group work and networking. Competence in pastoral work and counselling would be useful.

Informing all these aspects of the curriculum would be the skills of 'the reflective practitioner' (Schon, 1991), the ability to analyse, review and, when necessary, adapt one's own practice as circumstances required.

Governance

In our exploration of the main features of the diaconal church, we have made only passing reference to issues of governance. How is the diaconal church to govern itself, make decisions, look after its finances, maintain its buildings, and, especially, handle organizational conflict over matters both spiritual and temporal?

We recognize that these are critical concerns, and that the diaconal church could all too easily be undermined by the day-to-day challenges of running an institution within which convictions will inevitably diverge and passions run high. We recognize, too, that breaking the mould of Christendom would be little more than iconoclastic if no appropriate form of church governance were put in its place.

Our conviction is, however, that it is more important to set out a number of principles on which the governance of our model of the diaconal church is based rather than to make any attempt to present a detailed blueprint for governance. Thus we offer three principles of diaconal governance: *subsidiarity*, *democracy* and *self-government*. We believe that they have the potential to break the mould of Christendom because they are the antithesis of the principles on which the governance of that model of church is based: *centralism*, *unilateralism* and *statism*.

From centralization to subsidiarity

Over against *centralism* (see Figure 3, p. 69), the diaconal church is committed to the principle of *subsidiarity*. It encourages the dispersal of leadership and the devolution of power. Interestingly enough, for a church that is perhaps still the one most influenced by the legacy of Christendom, it was the Roman Catholic Church, in a papal encyclical of the late nineteenth century, that first enunciated the principle of subsidiarity. Stamp quotes Hans Küng (CIPL, G3, 1992): the principle of subsidiarity states that 'the behaviour of the community in regard to the individual, and that of the superior community in regard to the subordinate community, is subsidiary'. Küng continues, the principle of subsidiarity

allows as much liberty as possible and as much association as necessary. But this implies, too, that the community has no right to shut itself off like a sect. Its autonomy is not absolute, but in many ways relative, inasmuch as subsidiarity carries with it an obligation to solidarity . . . with other communities, with the regional church and universal church.

From autocracy to democracy

Unlike governance within the Christendom church, decision-making within the diaconal church is never *unilateral* (see Figure 3). It is *democratic* not autocratic. We define democracy here, with the Oxford Dictionary, as 'government by all the people, direct or representative', as well as 'a form of society . . . tolerating minority views'. This form of church governance is derived on the one hand from the principle of subsidiarity, and on the other from the assumption that the leaders of the diaconal church are servant leaders of the laity.

Some people reject the idea of the church being a democracy, not only on theological grounds, but because of the dangers of 'heresy', conflict and fragmentation to which such a form of governance could lead. Some evidence for this is offered by Werner Ustorf who informs us that 'Christianity today is split into approximately 34,000 separate denominations' and is 'a massive Babel of diversity' (McLeod and Ustorf, 2003, p. 220). However, the fundamental issue here is, how much longer can the church continue to reject democratic forms of governance in an era in which the autocracy that characterized Christendom is no longer tenable?

We remind ourselves that human civilization is facing a high-risk future and that we must learn how to create a global community of learning communities, or chaos will ensue. All of us need to be involved in that enterprise and all of us are responsible for its outcome. The governance of the global community we seek cannot be based on anything other than democratic principles, whatever form such democracy may take. If the church is to be true to its calling to be the servant of the kingdom community, the latter offering a vision of community desperately needed by a world in crisis, then the church too must find ways of taking democracy into its system. The risks it faces in so doing are no greater than those faced by the world of which it is an integral part (Holloway, 1990). Unless the church is prepared to take such risks, not only will it deny its divine calling, it will have nothing to offer to a world in crisis.

From establishment to self-government

The diaconal church is a *self-governing* church. The principles of subsidiarity and democracy reinforce this requirement. Thus *statism* (see Figure 3), the Christendom model where the church is supported by the state and civil law in respect of its doctrines, worship and discipline (often described as 'establishment'), is no longer an option.

All established churches, and especially those in a relationship with the state exemplified by the position of the Church of England, benefit in one way or another from the privilege, patronage and power bestowed on them by the legacy of Christendom (Hobson, 2003). In England, for example, the Church of England's senior bishops sit in the House of Lords, its cathedrals are nationally symbolic places and its leading clergy are treated as nationally symbolic persons. Its parish system encompasses the entire country and gives special standing to its incumbents.

In contrast, the diaconal church cannot accept privileges and patronage bestowed on it by the state because these call in question the church's freedom to fulfil its mission as the servant of the kingdom community, a mission that may at times involve opposition to or denunciation of the state itself (as should have happened more publicly in Germany under the Third Reich). Any privilege and patronage bestowed on it by the state also undermines the diaconal church's stance of servanthood and its calling to serve the kingdom community not from a position of strength but from one of vulnerability.

Another problem has confronted established churches in recent years. They can give the impression that the church is an organization offering its services to the general public as a beneficent grandparent. Thus the relationship of the general public to an established church can mutate into an experience of what Grace Davie terms 'vicarious religion' (2002, p. 19). This term refers to the fact that 'for particular historical reasons . . . significant numbers of Europeans are content to let both [established] churches and churchgoers enact a memory on their behalf'. In this situation, people come to take the church for granted. They do not see themselves as belonging, if only nominally, to an institution, the maintenance of which in practice requires their tangible and continuing support.

If, in this situation, the state withdraws privileges and patronage from an established church and its clergy (as is gradually happening in much of Europe today), what can then be left is a church dressed in 'emperor's clothes'. Its laity will be poorly equipped to take responsibility for a church previously protected by the state from the consequences of declining support. And the general public, which has depended for so long on a vicarious religious experience, will no longer have the services of a church supported by the state on which to draw, and no experience to assist it even if they so wished. Nor will other churches, which over the years have been weakened by the existence of an established church, have anything like the same public credibility or resources to be able to step into the breach. The result is the collapse of every form of church.

The diaconal church needs to be independent of the state in order that its laity can know that they are responsible, as partners with the clergy, for its maintenance and mission. Those who are drawn to explore the meaning of Christian faith will then find, not the hollow shell of an established church abandoned by a secular state and left to fend for itself by a wider populace, but a Christian community in which all matter and each counts.

This does not mean that the diaconal church ignores the state. It means that the diaconal church seeks to enter into a genuine partnership with the state, just as it would with any other institution, and whenever possible works closely with government in order to build a more communal society.

Conclusion

A diaconal world

In Part 1 of this book we argued that the kingdom community is the epitome of all learning communities. In Part 2, we argued that God is now calling the church to be the servant of the kingdom community. We called this church 'the diaconal (or servant) church'. Its mission is concerned with creating a global community of learning communities transformed by the gifts of the kingdom community: life, liberation, love and learning. We went on to explore what the nature, collective forms, leadership and governance of the diaconal church would look like. Our thesis throughout Part 2 was that unless the mould of Christendom is broken, the diaconal church will not come into being.

Because the diaconal church is the servant of the kingdom community, the epitome of all learning communities, it becomes a model for every social collective, from the smallest group to the largest institution. This is the diaconal church's great privilege and terrifying responsibility.

Yet, God calls not only his church but also his world to manifest the gifts of the kingdom community. Therefore, the nature, collective forms, leadership and governance of all social collectives needed to create a world that manifests those gifts will be similar to the nature, collective forms, leadership and governance of the diaconal model of church. When this happens we shall be living in a diaconal world.

A diaconal world will be a global community of learning communities whose understanding of community and of learning is informed and enriched by the Christian images of the Trinity and the kingdom, and whose resources are God's universal gifts of life, liberation, love and learning.

In a diaconal world, all social collectives will embrace the spirit of servanthood.

'Lay people' will take centre stage in the life and work of every institution, their authority being enhanced and their experience, insights and skills being seen as an indispensable human resource.

Hearings, communal groups, networks, and partnerships will become key features of new diaconal institutions.

In a diaconal world, key leadership roles will be akin to the leadership roles of the diaconal church. Thus there will be 'presbyters', people whose task it will be to manage and nurture the internal life of the institution. There will be 'deacons', people who will catalyse and equip its members to accomplish its 'mission'. There will be 'bishops', those who will act as intermediaries, connecting and supporting the work of 'presbyters' and 'deacons'. In a diaconal world women and men will have equal access to positions of leadership.

Within a diaconal world the governance of every institution, including the state, will be founded on principles of democracy, subsidiarity and self-government.

Just as the diaconal church cannot come into being until it is able to break clear of the legacy of Christendom, neither can a diaconal world. In many situations, world and church continue to reflect the norms of Christendom. Both remain subject to exclusiveness and dogmatism, to diverse forms of 'proselytism' and imperialism, to the constraints of 'clericalism' and conformism, to élitism, authoritarianism and paternalism. To create community and to avoid chaos, secular as well as religious institutions will need to break free from the mould of Christendom to which they are still captive.

Though the diaconal church may be the community most aware of the God whose kingdom community it serves, its mission will not be fulfilled until every social collective manifests the gifts of the kingdom community. Therefore, neither the church nor any other institution can become fully diaconal until a fully diaconal world has come into being.

Part 3

The diaconal church in action

Introduction

Part 3 of this book consists of five case studies which offer glimpses of the diaconal church in action. They span some 30 years. All are projects in which I was personally involved and, in many cases, was instrumental in initiating. It might, therefore, be of help to the reader if I give a brief overview of how these initiatives came to be taken and, equally important, how they relate to one another. I often reflected on and wrote up these initiatives while they were happening, or very soon afterwards. References to the main publications concerned are included below.

In 1962, my first appointment as a Methodist minister was to the mining village of Woodhouse on the outskirts of Sheffield. While there, I undertook a doctorate in urban sociology with Sheffield University, focusing on the concept of community and its changing expressions within Woodhouse over the first half of the twentieth century (Clark, 1969).

Five years later, I moved to West Greenwich in London as minister of a struggling inner-city Methodist church. In 1968, we closed the Methodist church, the congregation joined forces with the nearby Presbyterian congregation of St Mark's and I became a member of what was then the first Presbyterian–Methodist team ministry in the country. My Presbyterian colleague and I worked together at St Mark's from 1968 to 1973 (Clark, 1987). During that time we were engaged in trying to develop the local church as what I would now call a diaconal church (Chapter 8). At that time, shared churches, team ministries, and a number of other ventures in which we were engaged, were very much pioneering initiatives. However, when my colleague and I moved on, our respective denominations decided not to maintain the team ministry at the heart of the project and much of the impetus was lost.

My ministry in London convinced me that the declining influence of the churches in West Greenwich was increasingly typical of much of urban life. Although I believed that the model of church we were pioneering at St Mark's was on the right lines, I began to realize that a much more radical alternative was needed if the church's growing marginalization was to be halted. As I saw it, the church now needed to be rebuilt from the foundations upwards, employing small Christian groups as the basic building blocks.

In 1971, therefore, I decided to become actively involved with the emerging Christian Community Movement (Chapter 9). In 1973, in part to be in a better position to respond to what I felt to be a calling to work with the many Christian groups involved in that movement, I opted to become a sector minister (a minister earning his living outside the institutional church). Over the succeeding 15 years, as a member of staff at Westhill College (a Free Church foundation in Birmingham), I sought to fulfil what I would now describe as a diaconal role of encouraging and connecting these groups, convening a number of congresses and setting up the National Centre for Christian Communities and Networks (NACCCAN) (Clark, 1977, 1984, 1987).

However, by the mid-1980s I felt that the Christian Community Movement had reached something of an impasse. I had hoped that the movement might have been a model for the church of the future. Yet the institutional church made little attempt to support the movement, to learn from it or to respond to it as a pointer to the shape of things to come. At the same time, the Christian Community Movement itself was finding it difficult to develop a sustainable identity. It was becoming increasingly dependent on the contribution of residential communities, while I had hoped that it could embrace a wider diversity of groups and networks operating within the mainstream of society as well as on its fringes. At the same time, I felt that after nearly two decades of close involvement with the movement, the moment had come for me to relinquish my co-ordinating role to those who were just as able as myself to continue that task. Thus, in 1988 I brought my time as Director of NACCCAN to an end.

In the 1950s as a student, I had been greatly inspired by the ministry of William Gowland, leader of Methodism's Luton Industrial Mission. In the 1960s, as part of my training for the ordained ministry of the Methodist Church, I spent a final year at the William Temple College in Rugby, a college set up to equip and resource lay people for their ministry at work, at that time under the dynamic leadership of an ex-civil servant, Mollie Batten. My experiences in Luton and Rugby convinced me that, unless the church committed itself to supporting the ministry of its lay people in daily life there was no hope of it effectively re-engaging with a secular society. Having failed to do much about this matter during my time as a Methodist minister in Sheffield and West Greenwich, my involvement with the Christian Community Movement was, at least in part, an attempt to explore how lay groups and networks might be encouraged to develop a ministry with a strong communal base. Nevertheless, I became increasingly aware that the vast majority of lay people within local congregations remained unaffirmed and ill-resourced for their responsibilities as the church in the world.

After ending my long involvement with the Christian Community Movement, therefore, I decided to do something about my strengthening conviction that the future of the church lay in the hands of its laity. In 1992, with the support of my college, Westhill in Birmingham, I set up the Christians in Public Life Programme (Chapter 10). This programme was intended to draw up an agenda for the church in the public arena and to suggest ways in which such an agenda might be put into practice. The programme produced several hundred position papers (CIPL Position papers; Clark, 1997) and mounted a number of conferences to discuss these papers. It also sought to create a network of contact people across the country committed to promoting the programme in their own areas. The programme ran for ten years. It aroused considerable interest. In the end, however, we failed to find a way of integrating the programme into the life and work of the mainstream denominations.

Soon after launching the Christians in Public Life Programme, I recognized that position papers by themselves would never be enough to indicate what the nature and mission of the diaconal church might look like in practice. Visions had to be made a reality if they were to bear fruit. Thus, in 1994 I set up the Human City Initiative (Chapter 11). This was a project intended to explore how a vision of the kingdom community might be worked out in a major city, in this case Birmingham. The story of this ten-year project had many twists and turns and is now on hold, but I remain convinced that it still offers a highly significant model of urban mission for the church of the future (Clark, 1999, 2004).

All the initiatives described above involved me in leadership roles of a kind that I had never envisaged when ordained. The initiatives came about because, sometimes more aware of it than others, I was seeking to explore ways in which a declining church could offer the world a vision of the kingdom community and enable people to respond to its gifts of life, liberation, love and learning.

During much of this time, as a senior lecturer in community education at Westhill College, my discussions with students considerably enhanced my understanding of both community and education. My particular concern was 'schools as learning communities', about which I wrote at some length (Clark, 1996). Through that interest I became aware that for secular institutions to accomplish their 'mission' it was just as essential that they become communal institutions as it was for the church.

Reflecting on the case studies set out in this part of the book I have come to the conclusion that it is the role of 'deacon' that has most closely accorded with my own ministry, at least as the Methodist Church has of late interpreted that diaconal calling. Thus in the last case study (Chapter 12), I look at my role as a sector minister, together with that of sector ministers and industrial chaplains as a whole, and explore how far such roles might in practice be demonstrating what it really means to be a 'deacon'.

8

St Mark's, West Greenwich
The local church

Introduction

In September 1967, the Methodist Church asked me to take up an appointment as Methodist minister in West Greenwich, some five miles south-east of the centre of London on the south side of the River Thames. I worked there for six years. My 'parish' lay to the west of Greenwich Park. Although geographically not large, with a population at the 1966 census of only 15,680, West Greenwich at that time contained two major hospitals, the borough's health and welfare department, a divisional police headquarters, a theatre, two secondary schools, a shopping centre and many tourist attractions (Clark, 1968).

Socially, West Greenwich was divided into three zones. Along the river were council tenements housing some extremely poor families; further away from the river were long terraced rows housing many older residents; 'up the hill' towards Blackheath lived the professional classes in very expensive owner-occupied properties.

The churches

In 1967, the denominations active in West Greenwich were Anglicans (two churches), Methodists, Presbyterians, Baptists (two churches), Roman Catholics and a few independent religious bodies. The Methodist church was situated in 'downtown' Greenwich not far from the river. When I arrived, its official membership was 48, over half its members living over a mile away from the church. The main morning congregation consisted of a couple of dozen people; there was no evening service. The church offered very few weekday activities. Yet the members were faced with the upkeep of a building, renovated in the 1950s with war-damage funds, that could hold well over 200 people.

Although I had been appointed to serve the West Greenwich Methodist Church, I had also been asked to advise the Methodist Church at national level on a future strategy for its work in a part of London where Methodism was at a very low ebb. After a year's research, my recommendation was that the West Greenwich Methodist Church should be closed and that its congregation should unite with St Mark's, a Presbyterian church some 200 yards away on the other side of the road (Clark, 1968).

St Mark's had also been rebuilt in the 1950s with war-damage funds, but as an entirely new church. In 1967 it had a membership of 114, a good proportion being young families. It hosted a range of weekday activities in its relatively new purpose-built facilities. Its minister, a man of my own age and, like me, a recent arrival on the West Greenwich scene, was keen to support a united endeavour. After lengthy negotiations, the local Methodist church leaders agreed to close their own building and to join up with the St Mark's congregation, who warmly welcomed this initiative. The Methodist and Presbyterian Churches at national level also welcomed the setting up of the joint venture. The united endeavour was launched at Whitsuntide 1969. So came into being the first Presbyterian–Methodist church in the United Kingdom and, when the Presbyterian–Congregational unity talks came to fruition in 1972, the first United Reformed-Methodist church. The union played a significant part in furthering the Sharing of Church Buildings Act and was cited as a model by both denominations.

The vision

When our united Methodist and Presbyterian venture began, the omens for creating a local church as an example of the diaconal church in action were propitious.

In cosmopolitan London in the 1960s, the impact of a societal upheaval was everywhere in evidence, opening up the possibilities of a sea-change in traditions, conventions and social roles on every front. No church could remain impervious to this social revolution. John Robinson, of *Honest to God* fame, who was Bishop of Woolwich at this time, lived in nearby Blackheath. Pioneering team ministries were being developed just down the river in Woolwich, headed up by Nicholas Stacey, and for Methodism on the other side of London in Notting Hill (Mason, 1967). In 1968 Methodism was devising plans to relaunch 'sector' ministry (Chapter 12). 'Conversations' about unity between the Anglican and Methodist Churches were reaching decision time, and unity talks between the Presbyterian and Congregational Churches were in full swing. In the Roman Catholic Church, the aftermath of Vatican II was causing something of a revolution in attitudes and ecumenical relationships.

Many of the features characterizing these changes accorded with my own understanding of the church as an inclusive and open learning community. They were features also reflected in the plans to bring together our two West Greenwich congregations. Two major denominations, the Methodist and Presbyterian Churches, had agreed to help fund a team ministry to lead the joint initiative. Two Christian communities, albeit small in number, had opted to undertake a bold new venture in church life. Furthermore, both churches had supported my recommendations to Methodism that 'Christian education' should be a top priority for the united venture (Clark, 1968, pp. 33–6). These 'educational' proposals focused on the need for a united church to develop new ways of communicating 'what it means to be Christian people in contemporary society', and especially on the need to engage in creative partnerships with religious and social education teachers in local schools.

My Presbyterian colleague and I were also convinced that for our vision of a new way of being church to succeed, St Mark's needed to become actively engaged with the world beyond its doors. This meant active involvement with organizations situated within the local neighbourhood, with public services, with the borough council and, in particular, with other churches in the vicinity.

St Mark's in action

Worship

St Mark's steadily built up a reputation for the liveliness of its Sunday worship, some 50 to 60 people regularly assembling from near and far. My Presbyterian colleague and I tried to make these services as participatory as possible, through dialogue sermons, 'panels' of speakers who presented their views on current issues, the congregation's involvement in prayers and readings, a new hymn book containing modern hymns and music, and presentations to the congregation by the children of projects undertaken in Sunday School. Drama arranged by church members linked to the Greenwich Theatre was a notable feature of worship. From time to time speakers of national repute came to lead or speak at our services. Every month a family service was held that involved the young people through activities such as singing, acting, puppet plays, interviewing the congregation, or, as noted, presentations of their work done over previous weeks. Although many such initiatives are now a common occurrence, at the time they were ground-breaking ventures.

Learning

The united church opened up opportunities to experiment with a new form of 'Sunday School', regularly attracting some three dozen children (NACCCAN, *Community*, 7, Winter 1973, pp. 15–16). The Sunday School programme lasted two hours and consisted of a welcome and social gathering with games, introducing the theme for the week, a break with drinks, practical activities related to the theme and, finally, joining the adults in worship.

A 'Ten (O'Clock) Club' for teenagers followed a programme of its own design. Themes were often introduced through a multi-media approach. Practical work included creating collages and posters, making articles to sell for charity, 'games with a purpose', discussions, quizzes and 'scientific experiments'. The group sometimes went off church premises to visit places such as Westminster Abbey, the Dietrich Bonhoeffer Church, a Methodist International House and a local children's home. The young people sometimes attended services in other churches. They interviewed adults in their homes about their Christian beliefs. They set up biscuits and cheese lunches for Christian Aid. They visited elderly people in a local hospital and residents in local almshouses. On one occasion, mentally handicapped children from a nearby hostel were entertained by the young people. They also twinned with a Sunday School in Sevenoaks and exchanged visits.

Adult education was integral to the life of St Mark's. One group of particular note consisted of 15 to 20 adults who met on a Sunday evening once a month at the manse. It was known as 'The Link Group', members coming from a number of churches besides St Mark's. As one person commented (Patricia Warden, in NACCCAN, *Community*, 1, Autumn 1971), the members felt 'a deep need for enduring support and the sharing of common concerns which [many] local congregations are failing to meet at present'. An informal meal was followed by a short introduction to a theme chosen by the speaker, always leading to a lively discussion.

For some time, a group of teachers who worshipped at St Mark's met together to talk over the relation of their Christian faith to their professional concerns. It was a well-informed meeting that raised challenging questions and worked hard at sharing their experiences and insights.

However, a move to promote a social education programme based on St Mark's premises and involving pupils from local schools proved unsuccessful. The model here was a social education programme then being run by the London East End Methodist Mission, where the church provided a physical base and helped design an imaginative social curriculum for pupils from local schools. In 1971 we attempted something similar at St Mark's. Contacts were made with the local girls' grammar school and their pupils invited to meet at the church from time to time for current affairs discussions. However, our lack of any track record in the state educational field worked against us and the initiative failed to bear fruit.

Ecumenical initiatives

St Mark's, as a united church itself, was fully committed to working closely with other churches in the area. Many members of St Mark's were involved in the activities of the West Greenwich Group of Churches ('Council of Churches' was felt to be too formal a title). This was a very active association with enthusiasm for new initiatives. The Roman Catholic priest was passionate about the reforms instigated by Vatican II. The two Anglican priests were also keen to further co-operation with other churches. Thus the West Greenwich Group of Churches flourished. Ventures included shared bi-monthly services as well as those held at the main Christian festivals, joint Lent house groups, joint Christian Aid lunches and an annual ecumenical weekend away from Greenwich, usually held at a Roman Catholic retreat centre.

In 1970 the West Greenwich churches played an active part in what was called 'Operation Meeting Point', an ecumenical project initiated by St Mark's. Thirty-six students from Leeds University came to research the area and, in the light of their conversations, to suggest 'an agenda for the churches'. The venture produced an intense week of encounters that helped to strengthen ties between the West Greenwich congregations, as well as between the congregations and secular agencies operating in the area. As a result of this project, the churches became involved in a Community Care Scheme (see below) and new work with young children. The project also gave fresh impetus to a professional workers' lunch held once a month.

Beyond West Greenwich, St Mark's, as formerly a Presbyterian church, had strong links with the Iona Community in Scotland. Members of the congregation visited the island of Iona on frequent occasions. I myself led a week's course there one summer. An Iona group of St Mark's members met locally. It was a link that enabled the church to be in close touch with a visionary and socially active model of community (Chapter 9).

The local neighbourhood

Soon after the launch of the united church, the frontage of St Mark's, which faced onto the main road linking Greenwich and Lewisham, was cleared of bushes and undergrowth. A large and impressive noticeboard was erected that over the following years was used very effectively to communicate to the passing public what the church stood for and the activities in which it was involved. The 'wayside pulpit' that appeared on the noticeboard was carefully thought out and avoided the glib messages sometimes associated with this mode of 'advertising'. St Mark's premises were used widely by local organizations, one of the most successful ventures being a playgroup run by church members.

St Mark's published an attractive broadsheet entitled *The Link*. Two hundred copies were printed bi-monthly and circulated among church members and well beyond. In addition to church news, the broadsheet included articles about local concerns written by those working in the neighbourhood: for example, about the Greenwich Theatre, road proposals, the new district hospital and local welfare associations.

St Mark's took the lead in involving other West Greenwich churches in a number of schemes to enhance the quality of local neighbourhood life. One of these, as noted, was a monthly lunch for professionals working in the area when they could come together to hear a short talk and, more important, to meet and chat. Another, also mentioned above, was an innovative 'Community Care Scheme' in which church members volunteered their time and skills to give back-up support to the local Social Services when needed. A further venture was organizing and staffing an annual fortnight's summer play scheme held in Greenwich Park.

A team ministry

My Presbyterian colleague and I formed the nucleus of a small and close-knit team ministry based on St Mark's. From time to time a URC chaplain working with the South London Industrial Mission and who worshipped at St Mark's, lay officers from the church and an Anglican deaconess who undertook pastoral work throughout the area attended our team meetings. The team ministry lasted from 1969 till 1973, when both of us moved to new posts.

Each minister was responsible for the pastoral oversight of his own church members. My Presbyterian colleague gave priority to the organizing and conduct of the worship, including the music, as well as to pastoral work and church-based activities such as the uniformed organizations and playgroup. He also undertook chaplaincy responsibilities at the nearby district hospital and the Royal Naval College.

My own role lay more on the boundary of church and neighbourhood. Before the move to St Mark's, I had already been engaged in researching the life of the area to help decide the future of Methodism in West Greenwich. After the move, I took responsibility for the educational life of St Mark's, a role that brought me into close contact with outside agencies as well as with the other West Greenwich churches. From 1970 to 1971 I taught religious education part-time at Greenwich Park Girls' School, and from 1971 to 1973 worked part-time helping to set up a social education department at the then renowned Eltham Green Comprehensive School (Dawson, 1981). The Southwark diocesan lay training centre, Dartmouth House, was nearby and I helped with a number of courses there.

On a broader canvas, I worked for the Methodist Church Home Mission Department visiting churches around the country as a mission adviser and enabler. I had also been instrumental in setting up the national Methodist Sociological Group, a body that was seeking to put sociological expertise at the service of the church. It was during my time at St Mark's that I became involved with the Christian Community Movement and started the magazine *Community* (Chapter 9).

In what follows, we first identify key features of the diaconal church (Part 2) as a local church that were evident in the life of St Mark's. We then review some of the attributes of the Christendom church (also Part 2) that hindered the development of our work at St Mark's. Finally, we look at a number of other challenges that St Mark's had to face.

Breaking the mould of Christendom?

The diaconal church

St Mark's was a pioneering inner-city church. The numerous initiatives that the joint venture made possible have been replicated over recent decades, but in their day many were innovative and imaginative. How then did this venture match up to the model of the diaconal church as we have described it in Part 2?

(Note: The headings below refer to the features of the diaconal church described in Part 2.)

Mission St Mark's was a church overtly committed to what we have described as a kingdom community-centred understanding of mission. My ministerial colleague and I sought to further this mission by trying to build St Mark's and those agencies with which it came into contact, Christian and secular, into learning communities. Our own members, and many others in the West Greenwich Group of Churches, responded positively and creatively to this task.

Culture St Mark's sought to affirm and actively engage with a secular society. We saw our task as being to discern, respond to and make known the signs of the kingdom community wherever evident in the life of West Greenwich.

Stance St Mark's saw its ministry as one of servanthood. Although it was usually the 'lead' church in innovative approaches to mission in West Greenwich, these were always undertaken in the spirit of partnership with others (see below) and a willingness to learn and to adapt. A number of initiatives, such as the playgroup, the Community Care Scheme and the summer play project were developed explicitly to serve the neighbourhood and not to win church members.

The laity Within St Mark's, lay people played a full and active role. They were involved in the choice of whether or not to set up a united church. Many lay people were enthusiastic about the initiatives described above, often giving unstintingly of their time and energy. Nonetheless, the scattered nature of the membership of St Mark's meant that the congregation was more dependent on its two ministers than we would have wished.

Hearings   A key tool for shaping the mission of St Mark's was that of dialogue. Dialogue between the ministers, panels of lay people and, sometimes, the whole congregation was a regular aspect of worship. Dialogue and debate were always evident within the monthly Link Group. Operation Meeting-Point used hearings as a major tool for involving visiting students in a range of conversations with those working and living in West Greenwich, as well as with members of the local congregations.

Communal groups   The ecumenical Link Group, in which members of St Mark's played an active part, was a good example of a communal group. One of its members wrote: 'Link's ability to survive [it had actually begun in the 1950s] leads one to think that such groups may well be revealing a great deal about . . . the shape of the church in the future' (Warden, NACCCAN, *Community*, 1, Autumn 1971). St Mark's Sunday School and especially its Ten Club were very successful in employing the communal group to enhance the bonding and learning of the young people involved.

Networks   Networking was promoted through the columns of St Mark's bi-monthly *Link* magazine (note the title). This not only kept a scattered membership in touch with events and personal news but also helped to establish and maintain important links with many of those not otherwise associated with the West Greenwich churches.

The communal institution   The organization and management of St Mark's was geared to supporting the diaconal nature of its ministry. Lay leaders and ministers worked closely together to develop new initiatives in worship and education, and in the life of West Greenwich. The renovated frontage and new noticeboard, the imaginative development of church premises for activities serving the area, and the use of church funds for social and charitable purposes were all furthered by a desire to enable St Mark's to accomplish a kingdom-focused mission.

Partnerships   The partnerships that characterized the life and work of St Mark's strongly exemplified the diaconal church. St Mark's was in itself a pioneering partnership – between Presbyterians and Methodists. It gave a further dimension to the idea of partnership through its active ecumenical participation in the West Greenwich Group of Churches. On the secular scene, it sought to build partnerships with Greenwich Council, local hospitals, the police and nearby colleges of education. It had links with local schools, though as we have seen an attempt to develop these into a more formal working arrangement did not bear fruit. Beyond the area it had close ties with the Iona Community.

Leadership The ordained leadership of St Mark's could be seen as modelling a mini team ministry typical of the diaconal church. At St Mark's, my colleague played the role of presbyter, concentrating on worship, church-related activities and pastoral care. His chaplaincy responsibilities were also presbyteral in nature. My role was more that of deacon, much of my time being given to making links with individuals and agencies working in West Greenwich and assisting the congregation to play their part in neighbourhood regeneration. Over the four years together, my colleague and I sought to develop these roles in a complementary and mutually supportive way.

The Christendom church

In 1973, both ministers moved on. My colleague was called to be minister of a large church in the Wirral, and I was appointed to a lecturing post at Westhill College in Birmingham. In the years following our departure, only one minister, either Methodist or United Reformed, was appointed to St Mark's. Though a good deal of 'the diaconal spirit' (my colleague's phrase) remained, seen in an ongoing desire to serve the neigbourhood and further redevelop the buildings to facilitate this, the congregation gradually dwindled to a small nucleus and many of the initiatives we had taken ceased. There were a number of reasons for this decline but underlying them all was the fact that, despite our high hopes for the future, the mould of Christendom, as we have described it in Part 2, remained firmly in place. As a result, St Mark's found it impossible to stay in business as a pioneering team ministry and diaconal church initiative.

St Mark's, as a united church, came into being because the local Methodist church was no longer a viable concern. Though many united churches born out of necessity do not survive or develop much further, for a while St Mark's bucked the trend. Initially, the Methodist Church at national level welcomed the joint enterprise (they had after all appointed me to assess the situation and bring forward practical proposals to address it), and the Presbyterian Church did likewise. However, within a month of the two congregations coming together at Whitsuntide 1969, the Methodist Conference's Stationing Committee informed me that I was to be moved immediately to a church in Rochdale where a sudden vacancy had occurred. No replacement was offered. The situation was only resolved by my refusing to move on the grounds that I had given my word to St Mark's, with the backing of Methodism, that I would be with them for at least another two years. However, the *unilateralism* (see Figure 3, p. 69) of the Methodist Conference's Stationing Committee showed that it had failed to grasp the vision for St Mark's that my colleague and I had been at pains to communicate to our respective denominations from the outset.

During the time my colleague and I were ministers of St Mark's, the national leadership of the Methodist Church, and to a lesser extent of the Presbyterian Church, rarely enquired as to how the project was developing, despite the fact that we reported on progress frequently and always mailed them copies of the *Link* magazine. St Mark's appeared to have absentee landlords.

Nor were the denominations at national level our only problem. In 1971 the dynamic Roman Catholic priest, who had put his church at the heart of the West Greenwich Group of Churches and enthusiastically supported a range of initiatives, was moved to a new appointment. Despite numerous letters and appeals to his diocesan bishop from all the churches in the area (including his own), he was replaced by a highly conservative successor who took little interest in matters ecumenical. Vatican II seemed to be losing its impetus and the Christendom attributes of *unilateralism* and denominational *separatism* were once more impinging on us.

When my colleague decided that the time had come for him to look for another appointment, my initial intention was to stay on at St Mark's to help build the foundations of a new team with his successor. However, the Methodist Church demonstrated its lack of commitment to sustaining a diaconal model of church by making it clear that the continuation of the team ministry was no longer an option. It was a decision that might well have been argued on financial grounds. However, the West Greenwich Methodist Church had at that point just been sold for many thousands of pounds and a Methodist minister, based on St Mark's as part of a team ministry, could have been funded for a good while to come if only part of that sum had been invested for the purpose. The Christendom church's attributes of *conservatism* and *centralism* seemed to be firmly in place.

Other challenges

It would be naive and unfair to suppose that the future of St Mark's did not face formidable obstacles other than the dead hand of Christendom. It was, for one thing, operating within what Harvey Cox had termed 'the secular city' (1965). Its attempts to develop a new way of being church could not be expected to impact on the local population unless it was allowed to develop this model over a good number of years. The time we had was just too short to demonstrate to a wider public that anything very different was happening.

The congregation, even of the united church, was relatively small and very scattered. Nearly half the members lived outside West Greenwich itself and travelled in to worship on Sundays. This meant that St Mark's had great difficulty in gathering a critical mass large enough to give it communal staying power. Thus responsibility for pursuing the diaconal church model fell heavily on the shoulders of the two ministers and, despite every effort to disperse leadership, an unintended *clericalism* remained an Achilles heel. When we departed, the laity at St Mark's had not been well enough prepared to build on the kind of ministry that we had initiated.

In hindsight, I also recognized that I had failed to develop the role of deacon as fully as I should have. My endeavours had been largely confined to West Greenwich as a geographical area, and to those living or working there. Apart from one attempt to bring together members of St Mark's who were teachers, I had given little attention to supporting the ministry of our lay people working outside the area, not a few of whom carried important responsibilities in the wider life of London.

Conclusion

St Mark's demonstrates how easy it is for little lights to be snuffed out by a national church still operating in Christendom mode, and consequently unprepared or unable to nurture the seeds of renewal. Within Christendom, the church takes precedence over the kingdom, centralization over subsidiarity and preservation over transformation. It is a scenario that has since repeated itself on many occasions in my own ministry, as the subsequent case studies will illustrate.

St Mark's was never a headline-grabbing venture. The time that my colleague and I spent there was relatively short. Nevertheless, St Mark's during those years offers us a brief but intriguing glimpse of a diaconal church in action. I believe that three diaconal features of its life remain of particular note.

The first is its wholehearted commitment to partnership: between two congregations and their visions of 'one church renewed for mission'; between two ministers and their readiness to work together to make visions a reality; between St Mark's and the other West Greenwich churches in a range of innovative common endeavours; and between St Mark's and secular agencies serving the local neighbourhood.

Second is the way in which St Mark's actively involved its lay people in the ministry and mission of the church, and in decisions about the many changes and innovations that characterized that phase of its life. It also sought to foster dialogue and discussion in every aspect of church life, be that in worship, small groups or through its wider ministry.

Third is the nature of the ecumenical team ministry and the division of labour that it made possible. St Mark's became a local church served by two ministers seeking to use their different backgrounds, experiences and skills to create a team ministry reflecting a division of labour that typifies the diaconal church. My colleague undertook the role of presbyter, with major responsibilities for St Mark's as a gathered church, while I sought to develop the role of deacon, nurturing the life and work of St Mark's as a dispersed church.

Although none of us at St Mark's was then aware of the model of church to which we were working, some 30 years on my Presbyterian colleague and I believe that it still remains a seminal example of the local church as the diaconal church in action.

9

'The Christian Community Movement'
Groups and networks

Introduction

Groups and networks (the latter in practice, if not in name) have played a pivotal role in the life of the Christian church throughout its history. In New Testament times, a small group of twelve people launched the early church into the unknown. From then on, whenever the church became grounded on the sands of institutionalism, it was small groups, usually as part of a much larger network, that usually laid the foundations for the emergence of new forms of church.

During the twentieth century, Christian groups and networks have continued to fulfil this function in much the same way as they have always done. Between the two world wars, many such groups and networks were concerned with issues of peace, as well as with developing micro social and economic communities that might offer an alternative way of life to a world heading towards a second cataclysmic war (Armytage, 1961, pp. 402–19).

One of the best known of such groups was the Iona Community, founded in 1938 by George MacLeod, a minister of the Church of Scotland, who took unemployed men from the slums of Govan in Glasgow to rebuild the abbey on the island of Iona. This project not only developed the men's skills, but also enabled them to gain a new understanding of the meaning of community. As the Iona Community developed, and especially after the rebuilding of the abbey, new members were attracted from far and wide. They committed themselves to a rule of life, with a particular concern for peace and justice, and to gather annually on Iona.

World War Two and its immediate aftermath saw new Christian groups and networks emerging across all denominations. Many of these were motivated by a desire to rebuild a war-torn world, like Taena (1941), originally a left-wing pacifist community in the Forest of Dean, Pax Christi

(1946), set up in France to promote reconciliation but with a large British membership, Othona (1946), a community based in Essex and concerned to strengthen international relations, and Servas (1949), known as the 'Peace Builders', another worldwide network with a strong British contingent.

If the 1950s brought something of a lull in the emergence of such groups, the 1960s was a decade for the breaking of moulds in no uncertain manner. A post-war generation had now emerged that radically questioned the lifestyle of its parents. A youth-oriented culture, given a public voice by the growing influence of the media, broke with past symbolic universes and cast aside traditional mores. The Beatles became the icons of a new world of music, fashion and art. And a revolution in birth control gave impetus to the emergence of the so-called 'permissive society'.

On a wider canvas, America's disastrous involvement in Vietnam led to massive anti-war protests across the United States, with young people in the vanguard. The civil rights movement, inspired by Martin Luther King, rocked the USA as well as giving birth to civil rights movements elsewhere, notably in Northern Ireland. Institutionalism, secular and religious, was everywhere called into question, as witnessed by student riots on both sides of the Atlantic. In this search for 'an alternative society' and 'a brave new world' few stones were left unturned.

One expression of the quest for 'an alternative society' was the emergence of the so-called 'Communes Movement' (Rigby, 1974). The concept of the commune as a microcosm of a utopian society goes back many centuries (Armytage, 1961). But in the 1960s, a fresh wave of communal experiments swept the United States and Europe, spreading as far afield as Japan (Rigby, 1974, p. 4). These initiatives were highly diverse in purpose and character (p. 8). Some communes were avowedly secular in nature; others were driven by religious ideals. One common denominator, however, was the search for small familial collectives through which self-fulfilment and a sense of belonging could be found. By the early 1970s, there were some 50 communes in existence in the UK, many of which were linked into a Communes Movement, with a formal membership of some 300, and which published a bi-monthly magazine with sales of over 2,000 (Rigby, 1974, p. 4). The Communes Movement was influential in giving impetus to what we call in this chapter 'the Christian Community Movement', a movement that came into its own in the 1970s and 1980s.

Beginnings (1971–80)

In 1962 I had visited Taizé, a post-war Christian community near Lyon. Taizé was a community of lay brothers, led by Roger Schutz, set up to pioneer a contemporary form of monastic life. Its purpose was international reconciliation, with a particular ministry to young people. My visit gave me for the first time an appreciation of the potential of the small group for the renewal of church and society.

In 1967, as a minister at St Mark's in West Greenwich, London (Chapter 8), I was in the capital when the British Communes Movement took off. In the summer of 1970, I went out of sheer curiosity to a 'Festival of Communes', a hippie gathering at the Roundhouse in London. I was fascinated as well as impressed by the idealism and energy of those who attended that event, even though certain aspects of the gathering seemed eccentric and libertarian. Here were groups of young people, including young families, prepared to launch out into the unknown in search of new ways of living and working together. Many of them were setting aside promising careers and material security for a lifestyle that, though physically very tough, lacking the luxuries of modern life and extremely demanding in terms of relationship building, furthered their vision of what an inclusive and open society should be all about.

What drew me to take a growing interest in the Communes Movement was a conviction that a Christian community movement, reflecting some of the vision and commitment of its secular counterpart, might make a major contribution to the renewal of a church struggling to engage with a post-war world. In 1971, therefore, while still a Methodist minister in West Greenwich, I teamed up with a Roman Catholic Franciscan priest and a Congregational layman to launch the magazine *Community*. For the next 30 years this became the Christian Community Movement's regular bulletin. *Community* was a 16-page broadsheet, usually published three times a year, that carried stories about groups and networks involved in a wide diversity of Christian ministries. *Community* had an important 'Switch-Board' section in which groups could publicize their needs or advertise the services they offered. *Community* never reached a circulation of more than about 750. However, it served the important function of enabling Christian groups that were often small and isolated to share their stories, ideas and concerns, as well as informing a wider readership about the movement in a way that could otherwise never have been achieved before the arrival of the Internet.

In 1973 I moved to take up a lectureship at Westhill College, Birmingham. This gave me more freedom to assist in the networking of groups involved in the Christian Community Movement. In the summer of 1974 I was able to visit groups based in Scotland, in 1975 I toured the south-west of England and went to Northern Ireland, while 1976 took me to the United States to observe similar communal initiatives there. These visits not only enhanced my own knowledge and understanding of the movement in this country, but enabled me to help the groups I visited to be better informed about one another.

In 1977 my first book on the Christian Community Movement, entitled *Basic Communities – Towards an Alternative Society* (Clark, 1977) was published. I wrote the book in an attempt to introduce the diverse range of Christian groups and networks making up the Christian Community Movement to a wider audience. An annotated list of well over 150 communities and communal associations appeared at the end of the book, all of which had come into being between the 1940s and the mid 1970s. In *Basic Communities* I argued that all those involved in the Christian Community Movement were, in some shape or form, engaged in seeking out and living out a new and richer understanding of community. In the book I placed the groups described under six headings: 'intentional communities' (those concerned with communal living); 'spirituality' (those in search of a new awareness of the presence of God); 'environmental and economic aspects of community'; 'communities of learning'; 'caring communities'; and 'neighbourhood' (those groups involved in neighbourhood regeneration). A further chapter focused on the 'networks' that linked many of the groups and individuals involved in community building.

During the 1970s the Christian Community Movement in the UK was given further impetus by the proliferation of 'basic ecclesial communities' (BECs) in Latin America (see also Chapter 13). Because of their Roman Catholic pedigree, BECs were informed by a Roman Catholic ecclesiology and theology (Clark, 1984, pp. 77–82). In 1968, the Roman Catholic bishops from the whole of Latin America met at Medellín and offered their support to BECs. A first congress of representatives of the Brazilian communities was held at Vitoria in 1975. A useful typology of BECs is provided by Kate Pravera (1981, p. 251) who distinguishes three forces that brought them into being: '(a) Efforts towards parish revitalization (organized from above); (b) Efforts based on discontent with the institutional church (organized from below, or from outside the institution); (c) Efforts centred on a collective experience of oppression.' In the Latin American situation, it was the first and third of these reasons for the emergence of ecclesial community that were largely in evidence. At the same time, BECs of various kinds were appearing in other continents (Fraser, 1975).

BECs were, in practice, very different from the groups and networks appearing in the UK, and indeed elsewhere in Europe, at this time. (See the chart comparing BECs and groups linked to the Christian Community Movement in Clark, 1984, pp. 188–91). BECs were Roman Catholic, they attracted those seriously underprivileged, they were lay led, because of a chronic shortage of priests, and they combined 'the people's religion with the theology of liberation' (Clark, 1984, p. 189). The Christian Community Movement, on the other hand, encompassed groups from every denomination, was in general middle class, saw ordained as well as lay people in leadership positions and covered a wide spectrum of ecclesiological and theological viewpoints. Nonetheless, the basic ecclesial community movement of Latin America, especially its grass-roots nature and burgeoning theology of liberation, inspired and energized many on the British scene.

In 1975 I was able to convene a first gathering of groups and networks associated with the UK Christian Community Movement at Harborne Hall in Birmingham. Two years later a second gathering was held at Hengrave Hall in Suffolk, a very significant development being the attendance of representatives from the Roman Catholic and Anglican religious orders. Following Vatican II, a number of religious orders were now keen to offer newly emerging Christian groups the benefit of their long experience and at the same time to gain new insights from working alongside them.

In September 1980 a small team of us was able to convene the first ever 'Community Congress' in Birmingham (Clark, 1984, pp. 121–2). This lasted five days and was attended by over 250 people representing 106 Christian groups and networks, as well as 42 religious orders (13 Anglican and 29 Roman Catholic). There were three keynote speakers: Jean Vanier (the founder of l'Arche), Jim Wallis (the leader of the Sojourners community in Washington DC) and Rosemary Haughton (an author and member of the Lothlorien community in Dumfries). The congress gave a unique opportunity to members of a wide variety of groups, most of which had never met before, to share their experiences and hopes at some depth. Three comments from participants give the feel of the event (NACCCAN, 1981, pp. 90, 92, 94):

An incredible, challenging, expanding, encouraging time; a time to hear, to touch, to know others – their hopes, their faith, their struggles, their pain, their past, their present – and our future.

The Congress opened my eyes to the extent of what I would call the alternative church. It is most encouraging to know just how many Christians are being called to valid ministry outside the parish.

Loved meeting all the 'rainbow' of different Christian communities and individuals. Longing for something more 'concrete' to emerge . . . This network is helping to bring in God's kingdom and root it here on earth.

The National Centre for Christian Communities and Networks (NACCCAN) (1981–88)

In 1977 a modest 'Community Resources Centre' was established in Birmingham. This began to gather and store information about the groups and networks that were linked with the Christian Community Movement across the whole of the UK. It was initially housed in the living room of a family themselves living out the community ideal. In 1980, with the support of the Congress held that year, the centre was moved to Westhill College and became the National Centre for Christian Communities and Networks, or NACCCAN as it was widely known.

NACCCAN was a registered charity accountable to a small group of trustees and a large management committee. The latter represented some 30 groups and networks from across the denominational spectrum including the Iona Community, l'Arche, USPG Root Groups, Woodbrooke Quaker Study Centre, Ammerdown, One for Christian Renewal, Christian CND, Toc H, the William Temple Foundation, Salford Community Church, the Evangelical Coalition for Urban Mission, as well as the Communities Consultative Council (Anglican), the Conference of Major Religious Superiors (RC) and the British Council of Churches. The committee was chaired by the then Bishop of Birmingham, Hugh Montefiore.

NACCCAN continued to publish the *Community* magazine, majoring on case studies of Christian renewal and its 'Switch-Board' section for the exchange of news. From 1980 and at varying intervals thereafter, NACCCAN also published a *Directory of Christian Groups, Communities and Networks*. The early editions of the *Directory* included entries for some 250 recently established groups and 200 religious orders.

In the early 1980s I edited a series of booklets for NACCCAN entitled *New Christian Initiatives*. These covered themes such as 'The Family in Transition', 'Theology in the Making', 'Christian Initiatives in Community Education', 'Christian Initiatives in Peacemaking', 'Christian Community and Cultural Diversity' and 'Christian Voluntary Organizations in a Secular Society – Where Next?' The booklets sought to share with a wider public the experiences of Christian groups and networks that were working to address these issues.

The early 1980s also saw NACCCAN setting up a series of day events, as well as two further congresses, both held in Birmingham. The 1984 congress again brought together some 250 people, and the 1987 congress around 200 participants. Both congresses were lively and creative gatherings.

In 1981 I took on the role of Director of NACCCAN, first voluntarily and then, from 1984 to 1987, on a half-time paid basis. My role was many faceted. I was responsible for the work of the centre, which now had a full-time Administrator and a part-time Resources Officer, and was dealing with many requests for information about groups and networks across the country. I continued my travels and the all-important task of promoting networking throughout the movement. In the process, the *Community* magazine and the *Directory*, both of which I continued to edit, played a key role.

My role as Director involved making the work of NACCCAN widely known, as well as its day-to-day management. The latter task required keeping a large and disparate management committee interested and involved in the development of the centre. There was also the time-consuming job of raising funds to sustain the centre's work.

I saw part of my task as trying to persuade national church leaders that the Christian Community Movement was highly significant for the church's future, and that because of this it would be more than worth their while to invest some funds in helping to maintain the centre. I was only marginally successful in such endeavours. The founding of NACCCAN was warmly welcomed in letters from church leaders such as the then Archbishop of Canterbury, Robert Runcie, the Archbishop of Westminster, Basil Hume, and the President of the Methodist Conference (Clark, 1985). In 1985, the (Anglican) House of Bishops gave formal recognition to the National Centre (Clark, 1985, p. 16). However, no financial assistance was ever offered.

In 1987, although insufficient funding had been found to maintain my half-time post as Director, I agreed to stay on for a further year in a voluntary capacity to enable NACCCAN to move from being just a centre to becoming an association. The association came into existence in 1988, the National Centre for Christian Communities and Networks (NACCCAN with three 'C's) becoming the National *Association* of Christian Communities and Networks (NACCAN with two 'C's). A new body of trustees and a new management committee were appointed. In the same year the centre moved to Woodbrooke Quaker Study Centre, a Quaker foundation and, like Westhill College, a member of the Selly Oak Colleges Federation. (For the sake of simplicity the original acronym, NACCCAN, is retained throughout this chapter.)

In the mid 1980s, I wrote two more books on the Christian Community Movement: *The Liberation of the Church: The role of basic christian groups in a new re-formation* (Clark, 1984) and *Yes to Life: In search of the Kingdom Community* (Clark, 1987). The first was a sociological and ecclesiological analysis of the growth of the movement and its potential contribution to the church of the future. The second was a more biographical account of my own search for 'the kingdom community', and how the Christian Community Movement had become an integral part of that quest.

The National Association of Christian Communities and Networks (1988–2003)

Over the next 15 years some big changes occurred in NACCCAN's constituency and mode of operation. Though the numbers involved remained significant (in 2003 there were still some 100 groups and 30 religious orders who were members), the movement became increasingly dependent on the support of residential communities, though it continued to attract many individuals as well. Groups and networks of a non-residential kind, often actively pursuing a social or political agenda, which had linked up with NACCCAN in the early years, gradually fell away.

The magazine *Community* and the *Directory* continued to be published. However in 1993, reflecting a somewhat narrower focus than I had originally intended, and to stress the movement's Christian identity more explicitly, *Community* was renamed *Christian Community*. Assemblies were held once a year, but only attended by some 50 people. Regional groups, usually consisting of some two dozen members, met from time to time. In 1998 the centre moved again, this time to Newport in Gwent.

The post of Director of NACCCAN was not taken up again after I resigned. Instead, a new role of Moderator, voluntary in nature, was instigated. For a while there was sufficient funding available to retain a centre Administrator. However, as finance became an ever-increasing problem, this role too was undertaken on a voluntary basis.

By the turn of the millennium, discussions were well under way as to the future of NACCCAN. A further change in its title had occurred, with the word 'national' being dropped, though the same acronym was retained for historical reasons. In 2001 a new constitution removed unelected trustees and made those now called 'members' responsible for the organization. However, though the number of members remained steady, it was becoming increasingly difficult to recruit trustees and members of the management committee, to fill the role of Moderator and to find people to edit and produce Christian Community. In 2003, therefore, it was decided to bring the work of NACCCAN to a formal and honourable end, with the final editions of Christian Community given over to celebrating its past achievements.

NACCCAN's departure from the scene has not been the end of the affair, however. In response to the continuing interest of many groups originally linked to NACCCAN, the Neighbours Community, based in Northampton, undertook to handle enquiries, to publish an occasional newsletter entitled Touching Place (commencing in May 2003), and to set up a web site (see Bibliography). Scargill House, in the Yorkshire Dales, and Lee Abbey, in Devon, have also hosted gatherings of Christian communities. Likewise helping to sustain an interest in the movement, a group called 'New Way of Being Church', associated with the United Society for the Propagation of the Gospel, came into being in 1992 (see Bibliography). This offers guidance, materials and conferences to assist those involved in Christian communities of one kind or another.

In what follows, we first identify features of the diaconal church (Part 2), evident within the groups and networks associated with the Christian Community Movement. We then note those features of the Christendom church (see Part 2) that hindered the movement's development. Finally, we look at other challenges with which the Christian Community Movement had to deal.

(Note: Publications and documents covering the whole of NACCCAN's history are now lodged with Birmingham University – see NACCCAN's Archives in the Bibliography.)

Breaking the mould of Christendom?

The diaconal church

Mission The Christian Community Movement, as its name infers, was a kingdom community-centred movement. The groups and networks associated with it pursued their various concerns as inclusive and open communities trying to manifest the gifts of the kingdom community in what they did and how they lived.

The movement's mission was to create and foster small dynamic signs of the kingdom community that would pave the way for the transformation of church and world. It was a movement committed to 'the liberation of the church' from the grip of Christendom and to 'the role of basic Christian groups in a new re-formation' (Clark, 1984). It was inspired by a vision of its diverse groups achieving enough impetus and cohesion to become a self-sustaining movement able to lay the foundations of a diaconal church.

The Christian Community Movement also shared a vision of 'an alternative society', a radically new kind of world in which the horrendous evils of the twentieth century were done away with and justice and peace established in their place. The formidable task the movement faced was to turn these visions into realities.

Culture The Christian Community Movement believed a secular society was God's creation, though it challenged a market culture that condoned great wealth on the one hand and extreme poverty on the other. This led some groups to become directly involved in social and political issues. Others protested by living and working by communal values on the margins of society.

Stance The movement was inspired by the concept of the servant church. The kingdom community's gifts of life, liberation, love and learning were offered through deeds rather than words: serving the neighbourhood, caring for mothers at risk, helping the homeless or unemployed, ministering to the drug dependent, offering counselling and pastoral support, farming the land in an ecologically friendly way, being involved in creative forms of arts and crafts, working for justice, reconciliation and peace, seeking new forms of spirituality, or simply living in community.

This was no easy servant ministry. In many cases, and especially for residential communities, economic survival was always a struggle. Some groups lived in old and dilapidated country houses where tilling the land and maintaining the property were major preoccupations. Others were based in some of the most deprived neighbourhoods of towns and cities. Rarely, however, did this seem to destroy the movement's zest for life. Indeed, having abandoned what many saw as 'the rat race', most groups regarded material concerns as of secondary importance.

The laity　The diaconal nature of the Christian Community Movement was clear in its predominantly lay constituency. Lay people operated autonomously with no sense of dependency on the clergy even where the latter were in leadership positions. Those associated with the movement had skills in social work, counselling, teaching, nursing, accountancy, law, engineering, building, arts and crafts, music and the husbandry of the land and farming, to name but a few, all of which they readily placed at the service of the groups to which they belonged.

Hearings　Hearings of various kinds took place throughout the movement. These often took the form of regular community meetings in which the hopes and concerns of group members were aired. The three Community Congresses were, in reality, large national hearings, that in 1984 carrying the slogan 'Live Your Vision', and that in 1987 having the slogan 'Share Your Vision'. Subsequent assemblies and regional gatherings continued this visioning through debate and discussion. The *Community* magazine created a 'virtual hearing' country-wide by carrying stories and news offered by the groups and networks making up the movement.

Communal groups　As noted above, the Christian Community Movement believed that the communal group would be the catalyst for bringing about a 'new re-formation' and the transformation of society. The movement itself was made up of hundreds of communal groups. These were in the main communities of interest, their ministries being related to a diversity of spiritual, physical, social, economic and political concerns. Some groups saw the renewal of the church as a priority. Some saw a more just and caring society as their priority.

Other groups focused on concerns that were literally closer to 'home'. For example, many were committed to creating new forms of family life that might manifest the kingdom community's gifts of life, liberation, love and learning. NACCCAN's booklet *The Family in Transition* (1982) covered a range of case studies about Christian initiatives of this kind, including 'A family for the mentally handicapped', 'A joint family', 'A shared home', 'A church family', 'A circle of families' and 'A lifestyle community'.

For some groups, community of place was particularly important. Here nature and history sometimes combined together to create a sense of community reinforced by 'symbolic place'. For example, the Island of Iona, St Columba's landing place for the evangelization of Britain, was not only the Iona Community's home base but also a place of pilgrimage to which many thousands flocked each year. Lindisfarne in the north-east, Glastonbury in the south-west and Corrymeela in Northern Ireland were also symbolic places offering communal enrichment to many.

Networks   One of the major contributions of NACCCAN was to mitigate the obvious danger of groups turning in on themselves and thereby falling victim to exclusiveness and 'the communal dilemma' (Chapter 2). NACCCAN's achievement in establishing a network of communities and groups across the UK was crucial in helping a loose-knit and dispersed expression of diaconal church to take on the shape of a movement. Here, the *Community* magazine and the *Directory* played a vital role, together with the congresses and consultations NACCCAN organized. My own itinerant ministry also helped to link group with group. In addition, many groups had their own networks of associates, supporters and friends.

The communal institution   The Christian Community Movement never intended to become an institution. Yet though its members were divided as to what its relationship to the institutional church should be, most recognized that a positive relationship with the church was necessary if the movement was to survive over the long term. However, because the institutional church never offered to play the role of an intermediary agency on the community movement scene, NACCCAN, through its centre staff, trustees and management committee, assumed that task. It attempted, as far as resources allowed, to 'connect and combine' the groups and networks that made up the movement, and to set up the Community Congresses as major symbolic events. Its resources unit also fulfilled an intermediary role by collecting and collating data, responding to enquiries, producing information about the movement and encouraging research and reflection.

Partnerships   The Christian Community Movement was an ecumenical phenomenon. Groups and networks were associated with every kind of

'church', from the Quakers to the Roman Catholics. Different denominational allegiances actually added a breadth and depth to the movement, and
were rarely experienced as divisive. What some described as 'an easy
ecumenism' permeated the whole movement, an open acceptance of one
another's denominational loyalties. The active participation of many
religious orders, Anglican and Catholic, also resulted in a creative partnership between themselves and the newer communities, as well as between
their own co-ordinating bodies.

From 1980 onwards, NACCCAN tried hard to establish closer links with
the institutional church. This proved an uphill task and eventually failed. At
the same time, few partnerships were established between the groups
involved in the movement and secular institutions, the latter generally failing to recognize the efforts of fragile Christian groups, often situated on the
margins of society, as worthy of attention.

Leadership   The leadership of the Christian Community Movement was
diaconal in character and largely lay. One or two lay leaders came to be seen
as symbolic figures of international standing, including Jean Vanier, Jim
Wallis and Rosemary Haughton, the three keynote speakers at the 1980
Community Congress. A number of Roman Catholic religious superiors,
mainly women, were active in the leadership of the movement. Some
ordained ministers were also in leadership roles, for example heading up
the Iona Community in Scotland and the Corrymeela Community in
Northern Ireland.

The style of leadership most clearly in evidence throughout the movement was that of servant leader. The movement's leaders were in the main
dedicated community educators seeking to encourage and equip their
members to build their own and other communities in a way that manifested the gifts of the kingdom community. To this end, the leaders of
groups and networks acted as catalysts, enablers, intermediaries and
resource persons, rarely as directors or chief executives. Many leaders were
members of wider communal networks, connections that not only enabled
them to inform and guide the work of their own groups but helped knit the
Community Movement together.

Governance   Because the Christian Community Movement remained
loose-knit, issues of governance were not a major issue. The trustees and
management committee of NACCCAN, first as a freelance centre and later
as an association, sought to make informed and creative decisions on

behalf of the movement. However, they were not formally accountable to the latter until very late on in NACCCAN's life. Even so, the views of participants were generally well known and always taken into account. The movement sought to work on the principle of subsidiarity by encouraging the formation of regional groupings across the UK.

My role within the Christian Community Movement

I would now interpret the role that I was able to play within the Christian Community Movement over nearly two decades as that of deacon (Chapter 7). First informally, and later as Director (I always preferred the title 'Co-ordinator') of NACCCAN, I saw myself as a community educator, helping the movement to clarify and own its vision of what community building was all about, and to find ways of making its vision a reality. I felt myself to be the servant of a movement that was 'leader-full' not leaderless. It already had its prophets. It already had its experienced practitioners. What it lacked, and what I was able to offer, was a person who had the time to meet with, encourage and link up dispersed and disparate groups, to help them find an overall identity and purpose and to assist them in reflecting on and communicating their vision to a wider constituency.

I discovered very early on that any diverse and dispersed movement was liable to produce insular relationships and closed thinking. Thus my role as a community educator had to be that of a catalyst, trying to persuade the groups concerned to share their stories (through the *Community* magazine, as well as via myself as an intermediary) and challenging exclusiveness and closed thinking. This involved me questioning communal visions that were inward-looking, prompting groups to be open to learning from one another, and persuading some groups to stay in touch with the institutional church rather than turn their backs on it.

My role as an enabler was played out in two main ways. The first was seeking to promote a greater awareness across the whole movement of what each group had to offer the rest. This task was at the heart of my reason for travelling the country and meeting scores of groups over the years, and the reason for my commissioning the stories published in *Community*. The second aspect of this enabling role was helping groups and networks to recognize that they were part of a national, and indeed international movement, with the potential to transform church and society. This part of my role overlapped with that of being a resource person, a function made possible because of the knowledge of the movement I accumulated over many years.

One other role I played in my capacity as a community educator was that of an intermediary. Many groups and networks within the Christian Community Movement were pioneering new forms of diaconal church, with little support from established church agencies, meagre resources and in very isolated situations. Thus my job was to affirm them as people with a vision, to listen to their stories and concerns and to link them up in ways that enabled the whole to become greater than the sum of the parts. It was a role that saw me trying to connect people in ways that would open their eyes to new ways of community building and to untapped resources.

In 1988, after nearly 20 years of involvement, I withdrew from the leadership of NACCCAN. For reasons already noted, I felt that it was time to move on. That NACCCAN remained in business for another 15 years and that its work continues in one form or another is, I think, evidence of the continuing tenacity of the Christian Community Movement.

The Christendom church

Though the story of the Christian Community Movement in the UK is ongoing, the hopes of those who believed that it might bring about 'a new reformation' and 'a brave new world' have not yet been realized. One reason for this is the legacy of Christendom that continues to restrict the vision of the institutional church.

By the end of the 1980s, it was clear to me that the movement was losing some of its initial impetus. There were various reasons for this. On the world stage, the euphoria of the 1960s that had led to dreams of 'an alternative society', and phenomena such as the civil rights movement and the communes movement had long since spent their force. The renewed *institutionalism* of the 1970s, with the beginning of the Thatcher era, created a very different mood. The concept of 'community' came to be seen as 'wet', and irrelevant to the needs of a market-driven society. The doors opened by Vatican II were closing, and the ecumenical vision of 'one church united for mission' had all but been dashed. With the rapid decline in church attendance, the mood was more one of retrenchment than re-engagement. Religion was becoming increasingly an individual and personal matter, with the charismatic movement, 'the house churches' and a growing evangelical constituency now regarded as the main hopes for the future.

It was not surprising, therefore, that the Christian Community Movement encountered an institutional church that failed to recognize that the host of emerging groups and networks might add a new dimension and impetus to its mission. The leading denominational bodies that had welcomed the setting up of NACCCAN failed to follow up that welcome with any real interest or tangible support. As one long-standing member of NACCCAN notes, such aloofness was a demonstration of 'how reluctant the churches were to see as serious partners those outside their control, and how their hierarchical approach to leadership made for a real culture-clash with the community movement' (Chris Lawson in correspondence, 29 December 2004). NACCCAN was eventually accepted as a 'Body in Association' with the emerging CTBI (Churches Together in Britain and Ireland). Yet, as Lawson again comments, 'The "Bodies in Association" solution left the alternative ecumenical movement (the one really getting on with being ecumenical!) safely on the margins of the main church structures.' The Christendom church's propensity for *centralism* and *élitism* still held sway.

This lack of support 'from above' was in part responsible for the fact that, apart from a few well-known communities such as Iona, Corrymeela and l'Arche, the 'men and women in the pew' remained largely ignorant of the Christian Community Movement. News of historic gatherings, such as the first Community Congress in 1980 and the establishment of NACCCAN a year later, were not reported by the Christian media. Church historians of the era, such as Adrian Hastings (1991) and Grace Davie (1994), make no mention of the Christian Community Movement. *The Liberation of the Church* (Clark, 1984), in which I attempted a detailed analysis of the movement and discussed its significance for the future, a book that some have informed me has been a major contribution to their thinking about the future of the church, was the only book I have written for which I was unable to find a recognized religious publisher. In the end it was published by NACCCAN at its own expense.

Such lack of recognition of the Christian Community Movement was also a consequence of the legacy of a Christendom model of church dominated by *parochialism* and *sacralism*. The neighbourhood congregation, rooted in community of place, was regarded as the 'real' church. Christian groups that formed beyond its boundaries seemed to those in the mainstream unconnected with and remote from what the church should be about. It was as if the church as an institution and the church as a movement were living in two separate worlds, with two quite different understandings of 'mission' and speaking two quite different languages. There was no 'fit' and few bridges linked them.

At the same time, what the Christendom church saw in the Christian Community Movement caused it some disquiet. The *conservatism* that typified the decades following the social upheavals of the 1960s led to some of the groups involved in the movement being labelled as 'way out'. Who would ever want to choose the uncertainties and stresses of living in an intentional community? And were not some of the causes espoused by those associated with the movement 'Marxist' or even 'anarchic'? A church built on a Christendom model of preservation not transformation was thus very wary of a movement that appeared to it as over-idealistic, over-enthusiastic and accountable to nobody.

The aftermath of Vatican II and the disillusionment following the ecumenical initiatives of the 1960s also witnessed the re-emergence of denominational *separatism*. Some religious orders remained supportive of NACCCAN to the very end of its life. However, there was a waning of commitment to the Christian Community Movement within many religious orders that had played a prominent role up to the time of the 1980 Community Congress and had warmly supported the establishment of NACCCAN. Forward-looking leaders of religious orders, notably women, were replaced by more cautious provincials who regarded any talk of 'a new re-formation' as dangerous, if not subversive.

The loss of the active support of the religious orders weakened an arm of the Christian Community Movement that might have proved its hope of salvation. Many religious orders were materially very well endowed, while the funding required by NACCCAN to maintain its work was very modest. With their numbers dwindling and their future becoming increasingly uncertain, one way in which the religious orders might have been faithful to the vision that had originally brought them into being would have been to have offered some financial support to NACCCAN. But the moment passed, the conservatism and denominationalism typical of the Christendom church reasserted its hold and no tangible help was forthcoming.

Other challenges

There were, of course, other factors, not directly attributable to the legacy of a Christendom model of church, that presented the Christian Community Movement with problems. The movement embraced groups and networks with very diverse agendas. Thus it had always been difficult for the movement to find a common purpose and a shared identity that would make being part of a larger whole worthwhile and sustainable. The enthusiasm that enabled the movement to cohere up to the time of the 1980 Community Congress slowly dissipated. Economically fragile groups and networks struggled not only to hold on to their vision of the church as a reflection of the kingdom community but to survive in the process. The result was that the links between the plethora of groups that had initially been eager to work together within the broad framework that NACCCAN provided became increasingly tenuous.

At the same time, the movement faced genuine differences of opinion about the nature of its engagement with both church and world. There was disagreement between those who wanted rapid and radical change (many of whom looked to the example of basic ecclesial communities in Latin America and to the theology of liberation to which they had given birth) and those, no less committed, who wanted a more gradualist approach. There were groups that espoused a 'doing' agenda, seeing practical action as a priority, and those that opted for a 'being' agenda, seeing a renewed Christian spirituality as of greater importance.

Also significant for the future was a divide that appeared between those who believed that the movement should concern itself primarily with new forms of living together in community (intentional communities), and those who felt that the movement should embrace all those committed to community building, whether living together or not. After NACCCAN became an association in 1988, it became increasingly dependent on the support of those from intentional communities, while other groups tended to go their separate ways. Living in community was a very important aspect of the movement's contribution to the wider church. However, focusing more on how to build intentional Christian communities than how to build neighbourhoods, cities and society as a whole to reflect the gifts of the kingdom community blunted the movement's cutting edge and weakened it as a model of the diaconal church in action.

Diversity and disagreements also presented problems for those seeking to 'manage' the movement as a corporate body. Any form of governance needed to avoid centralism, but there was never enough time to find a sustainable democratic alternative. What was required was a means by which the groups and networks involved could retain their identity as a movement, yet work in partnership with an inclusive and open institutional church. Such a partnership never materialized.

One other reason for the decline of the Christian Community Movement was the reluctance of a secular society to see the Christian initiatives being taken as worthy of public funding. Many of the groups and networks associated with the movement were making a pioneering contribution to people in deep need, irrespective of class, colour or religion. The l'Arche communities working with the mentally handicapped, the Cyrenians with the single homeless, Centrepoint in London with young people at risk, the Compassionate Friends with bereaved parents and Pilsdon with ex-prisoners were but a handful of examples. Yet many such groups found it impossible to attract the financial support of grant-making bodies, including government, which often undervalued their endeavours or suspected that such Christian initiatives might have a hidden agenda.

Conclusion

The Christian Community Movement offers some highly significant pointers to the diaconal church in action. Its groups and networks were passionate about community building in a world that has to become a global community or face chaos. Its members believed that the way to fulfil that calling was through servanthood not coercion. It was predominantly a lay movement enriched by an immense amount of peer support and encouragement.

The Christian Community Movement was made up primarily of a host of groups and networks that themselves exemplified the meaning of community. They were eager to learn and to share one another's experiences. They respected denominational allegiances, treating these as a resource and not a barrier to fulfilling their calling. The movement's leaders demonstrated what it meant to be community educators, with the roles of catalyst, enabler and intermediary being to the fore.

The Christian Community Movement gave birth to NACCCAN, an intermediary agency of paramount importance in giving the movement an identity and sense of purpose. This it did through its publications, its congresses, its conferences, its regional contacts and the travels undertaken by its staff. Although NACCCAN had little success in winning support for its endeavours from an institutional church still operating in Christendom mode, it was able to continue as an advocate for the movement for some 20 years. A range of factors led to the movement's decline and eventually brought the work of NACCAN to an end, but the endeavours of many of the groups and networks associated with the movement are ongoing. The Christian Community Movement's great accomplishment was that it blazed a trail by exemplifying many aspects of the diaconal church in action.

10

'Christians in Public Life'

The laity

Introduction

Despite the clericalism and conformism that permeated the Christendom church, many lay Christians openly witnessed to their faith in daily life. However, as the influence of Christendom and the clergy slowly declined, lay people came increasingly to the fore as the representatives of the church in the world. From the nineteenth century onwards, lay people became ever more prominent within the trades union movement, health and welfare services (where women were especially active), education and business, as well as within local and national government.

In this liberation of the laity, Nonconformity played a key role. During the latter half of the nineteenth century, 'Nonconformists had for the first time assumed municipal office on a large scale, had entered the world of Parliament and Cabinet, had studied and taken degrees at the ancient universities, and had won public recognition as "the backbone of British Liberalism"' (Gilbert, 1976, p. 181). In addition, a host of business enterprises, still household names today, were the result of the Christian commitment and industriousness of many from Nonconformist and Quaker backgrounds (Munson, 1991).

In the twentieth century, two devastating wars brought home the need for national reconstruction and saw the British churches giving increased recognition to the role of the laity in this task. The Industrial Christian Fellowship had been founded in 1877, but refocused its work during World War One when it was developed by Studdert Kennedy to enable 'God to be heard at work'. In 1924, 1,400 delegates, the majority lay people, came together for a national Conference on Christian Politics, Economics and Citizenship (COPEC) presided over by William Temple, then Bishop of Manchester. The conference did not at the time lead to any radical social changes. Nevertheless, it was part of 'a longer process of adult education whereby the leadership . . . of the church was being weaned from high Tory attitudes to an acceptance of the Christian case for . . . the development of the welfare state' (Hastings, 1991, p. 179). In 1937, with the spectre of war again looming, the Oxford 'Life and Work' Conference was held, and four years later, chaired by William Temple, the Malvern Conference met. Both events were set up to explore the future of British society and, just as important, in both events lay people played a leading part.

The death of William Temple in 1944, having been Archbishop of Canterbury for only two years, was a major setback to the emergence of a church that was increasingly turning to its lay people to lead the way in reshaping the life of society. Despite the publication of ground-breaking books on the laity by Yves Congar (1957, and Lakeland, 2003, pp. 49–77), a French Dominican, and the Dutch theologian Hendrik Kraemer (1958), an 'ecclesiastical social conservatism' pervaded the church scene in Britain until the 1960s (Hastings, 1991, p. 423). Even so, a number of initiatives were taken at this time to encourage and equip lay people to exercise their ministry in the world. These included the setting up of the Sheffield Industrial Mission by Bishop Hunter in 1944 (see Wickham, 1957, and Chapter 12), the establishment of the William Temple College in Hawarden in 1947 (it moved to Rugby in 1954) (see also Chapter 14), and the opening of Methodism's Luton Industrial College in 1955. However, though these endeavours were inspired by visionary individuals, they remained loosely linked to the mainstream of church life.

The 1960s witnessed renewed activity to reaffirm and reinstate the laity at the heart of the church's mission. From Vatican II came three key documents embracing the diaconal image of the church as 'the people of God in the world': Lumen Gentium, Apostilicam Actuositatem, and Gaudium et Spes (Lakeland, 1003, pp. 87–100). The Anglican–Methodist Conversations reflected a growing conviction that there should be 'one church united for mission', these 'conversations' involving the laity as never before in deciding a matter of such profound importance to both churches.

In the early 1960s, talks got under way to establish a European Association of Academies and Laity Centres, a significant number of which were to be found in the UK and as an integral part of their programmes ran consultations and courses on the relation of Christian faith to public life. In 1966 St George's House, Windsor, was opened as a centre where leading figures in church and society could meet together to debate issues of public concern. In 1968 the Christian Association of Business Executives, set up as a Roman Catholic managers' association in 1938 'to bring Christian values and moral principles to the world of work', went ecumenical. Also during this period, the Methodist Church set up a Board of Lay Training and the Methodist Laymen's Movement was very active (Turner, 1998, p. 26).

The 1960s saw the publication of Mark Gibbs and Ralph Morton's ground-breaking book *God's Frozen People* (1964) followed in 1971 by their *God's Lively People*, both titles indicative of their authors' concerns. Mark Gibbs himself took a leading role in the setting up of the Audenshaw Foundation in 1964, a project which through the *Audenshaw Papers* that he edited sought to raise awareness to the key part that the laity should be playing in the public arena.

Sadly, the high hopes of the 1960s soon waned. The Anglican–Methodist unity scheme failed and the vision inspired by Vatican II gradually faded. As church membership plummeted, retrenchment became the name of the game. Clericalism reasserted itself and the laity were again left to fend largely for themselves.

Over subsequent decades, the fortunes of new initiatives concerned with the ministry of the laity in the world were mixed. In 1971 the William Temple College proved to be no longer a viable enterprise and closed its Rugby base of operations, a sad outcome for one of the most imaginative ventures in the field of lay education since the war. It relocated to Manchester to become the William Temple Foundation, with a much reduced staff and more limited brief.

In 1982 John Stott founded the London Institute for Contemporary Christianity in London; in 1987 the Roman Catholic Von Hügel Institute (for the interdisciplinary study of church and society) was established at St Edmund's College, Cambridge; and in 1989 the 'God on Monday' project (later to become the Ridley Hall Foundation's 'Faith in Business' programme) began at Ridley Hall, Cambridge. In 1993, the organization MODEM was launched, focusing on developing forms of leadership within church and society that were informed by Christian faith and values.

Yet, in 1996 there was another reminder of the church's inability to sustain work in this field, with the closure of Methodism's Luton Industrial College. Not until the turn of the millennium, with the founding of the Quakers and Business Group, and in 2002 with the setting up by St Paul's Cathedral of the St Paul's Institute, 'A forum for 21st century ethics', were any major new initiatives taken to further the engagement of lay people in the life of society.

(Note: The web site addresses of most of the organizations mentioned here appear in the Bibliography under the heading 'Lay ministry organizations'.)

Towards the end of the 1980s, a number of churches set up working parties to explore the role of the laity as the church dispersed in the world. In 1985 the Church of England produced a report entitled *All are Called – Towards a Theology of the Laity*, and two years later a report *Called to be Adult Disciples*, both documents relating to the ministry of the laity in society. In 1987 the Synod of Roman Catholic Bishops in Rome published *Christifideles Laici*, an apostolic exhortation concerning 'the vocation and mission of the lay faithful in the church and in the world'. In 1990 the British Methodist Conference approved a report on *The Ministry of the People of God in the World* and recommended it to its districts for study. However, it was not long before these documents were gathering dust on ecclesiastical bookshelves.

A number of national conferences focusing on the ministry of the laity were mounted during this period. In 1980, 2,000 people gathered for the Roman Catholic Church's National Pastoral Congress in Liverpool (Clark, 1984, pp. 66–71). In 1991 another significant gathering, the Rerum Novarum Conference, was held to celebrate the Pope's encyclical letter of a century before on *The Conditions of Labour*, the first real protest by the Roman Catholic Church at the inhuman conditions experienced by working people during the latter part of the nineteenth century. Also in 1991, the Malvern Conference was held, a major ecumenical event to celebrate the first Malvern Conference 50 years before. And in 1999, at the 'Catholics in Public Life Conference' in Liverpool, 'for the first time ever, over three hundred Catholics and a sprinkling of invited guests ... came together ... to discuss being a Catholic in public life' (CIPL, Theresa Byrne, F15, 1999). These events were an inspiration to the many hundreds of lay people and those church leaders who attended them. Yet again, however, their impact soon waned and the clericalism and conformism of a Christendom model of church reasserted itself. It was as if the institutional church was salving a guilty conscience by publishing such documents and mounting such conferences, but then settling back with a sigh of relief to attend to business as before; except that, with a church in decline, 'before' was no longer an option.

(Note: One other constituency within the life of the church, evangelical in theology and with a strong Anglican constituency, has been prominent in promoting the ministry of lay people in society, particularly through the development of Christian groups in the workplace. In more recent years these endeavours have gathered some momentum. However, it is a movement that has stood somewhat apart from most of the initiatives described above. Thus rather than attempt to describe and evaluate this movement here, we return to it in Chapter 13, page 254.)

The 'Christians in Public Life' Programme (CIPL)

In the early 1990s, having ended my time as Director of the National Centre for Christian Communities and Networks (Chapter 9), I was in a position to give more attention to my lifelong conviction that the ministry of lay people in daily life was of fundamental importance for the church's future. The seeds of this conviction had been sown through my visits as a student to the Luton Industrial College, and during a final year of preparation for the Methodist ministry spent at the William Temple College in Rugby. It was a conviction that had in part inspired my interest in the Christian Community Movement. As my involvement with that movement diminished, therefore, my thoughts turned to how I might make some further contribution to equipping lay people to serve the kingdom community in the world.

The project that emerged was called the Christians in Public Life Programme (CIPL as it was generally known), and was based at Westhill College, Birmingham, where I worked. CIPL was formally launched in March 1992 when George Carey, then Archbishop of Canterbury, visited the Selly Oak Federation of Colleges, of which Westhill was a member. The declared aim of CIPL was: 'To achieve a new quality of public life by enabling Christians to engage, share and work together with others in addressing fundamental questions of common concern.' (The term 'public life', as used in the USA, was deliberately chosen to encompass the life of society beyond the realm of the private and personal.)

CIPL was born at a time of a growing conflict between two very different value systems. On the one hand, the ideology of the market was increasingly dominating the political, economic and social agenda. Profit, from the point of view of the producer, and 'value for money', from the point of view of the consumer, were 'the bottom line' in the private, public and, increasingly, voluntary sector. The purpose of daily work was seen, first and foremost, as meeting the demands of a market economy. Anything else that occurred by way of personal or communal fulfilment was an optional extra and dispensable. People at work were increasingly treated as the means to market economy ends. On the other hand, and not least among many Christians, there was deep unease about the power of an all-pervasive market culture and the way in which 'value for money' was ousting 'value for people'. There was a growing feeling that the churches urgently needed to offer an alternative model to that dominating the life of society, one founded on the values of the kingdom community.

In September 1991 I convened a consultation at Westhill College to address the need for a fresh agenda for a church engaged with contemporary society, and for the setting up of a national 'support system for Christians in public life'. The gathering was attended by some 60 people including non-stipendiary and sector ministers, those involved in industrial mission, members of the religious orders, people working for Christian voluntary organizations, adult educators, those engaged in special projects and from higher education and interested parish clergy. Some of these were lay people. The consultation supported the idea of a 'Christians in Public Life Programme' (CIPL) with myself as its Co-ordinator.

I was able to draw together a strong Steering Committee representing Anglicans, Roman Catholics, Methodists, Baptists, the United Reformed Church and Quakers. An Anglican and a Roman Catholic bishop (the latter had been designated by his church to have responsibility for public life issues), a Methodist Chairman of District, Moderators of the United Reformed and Baptist Churches in the West Midlands and the President of the Selly Oak Colleges, as well as a number of experienced lay people, were among the committee's members.

The work of CIPL developed in five main ways: position papers, research, meetings and conferences, 'development workers' and projects.

Position papers

From 1992 to 2001, well over 200 position papers were published under the auspices of the programme. The intention was to set an agenda for the church in the public arena since no such agenda appeared to be in evidence. Other aims of the position papers were to draw on the ideas and insights of leading thinkers in this field, to be a catalyst in prompting the churches to take new initiatives in public life, to affirm and learn from the endeavours of lay people at work and to provide resources for church leaders seeking to support them.

Each position paper was some 1,500 words in length (two printed sides of A4), a batch of five or six papers being produced three times a year. Their subject matter covered a possible agenda for the church in public life and reflections on what was needed to put such an agenda into practice. An Index of the papers published was produced annually. The Index's first heading was 'Overview and Analysis' and included papers relating to theology and mission in public life. Other headings were: 'Ethics and Issues' (including politics, economics and citizenship); 'People' (in which lay people wrote about their experiences of relating faith and work); 'Sectors' (Christian faith in relation to education, health, welfare, business, etc.); 'The Church in Public Life' (including leadership, organization, education, pastoral care, spirituality, etc.); and 'Resources' (materials and projects supporting endeavours in this field). The authors of the position papers came from all denominations, and included prominent as well as little-known names, lay and clerical. Although nobody received a fee for producing the papers, there was little problem in getting authors to write for the programme.

Many of the papers were visionary and inspirational; others were challenging and practical. They showed quite clearly that there were insights, experiences and resources in abundance on which any church that was concerned to be the servant of the kingdom community could draw. By the time the programme ended in 2001, the papers had not only set out a comprehensive agenda for the churches in the public arena, but had offered a host of ways and means of putting that agenda into practice. In 1997 I edited a selection of the most significant of the papers that had been written up to the summer of 1996. These were published under the title *Changing World, Unchanging Church?* (Clark, 1997).

Those subscribing to the papers were called 'Associates'. The number never rose to more than about 250 in any single year, but over the ten years of its life the programme attracted some 1,000 Associates. The position papers also found an audience well beyond CIPL's Associates, many being passed on to their colleagues, used by denominational committees engaged in this field, read by students in theological colleges or used as discussion starters by local churches. A regular *Newsletter* went to all Associates as well as to a mailing list of 'non-Associates' who had at one time or another shown interest in the programme.

Research

In 1993 CIPL published *A survey of Christians at Work and its implications for the Churches* (Clark, 1993). The aim of the research was to discover how lay people related their faith to their work, and what support they got from their local churches in this aspect of their ministry. Nearly 400 people, of whom all but 31 were lay people, responded. Respondents represented all denominations and age groups; many held office in their local churches. The positive findings were that nearly all respondents were deeply concerned to give meaningful expression to their faith at work and were willing to give more time to meeting with others to explore faith and work concerns. The negative findings were that most felt their working lives and their church lives failed to connect. Worship offered a majority of those replying only 'moderate' help, pastoral care gave them 'little' help and Christian education offered 'very little' help. Only a third of clergy and ministers were seen to be giving real support to them in their calling to be Christians at work.

Meetings and conferences

CIPL set up a number of day events, as well as two residential conferences, all held in Birmingham. Themes for the day events included 'The Two Cultures – Bridging the Great Divide', 'The Local Church and the World of Work', 'Bringing Faith to Life', 'Conscience at Work', 'Spirituality at Work', and 'Connecting Worship and Daily Work'. The two residential conferences were entitled 'Who Counts? – Public Accountability and Christian Faith' (1993) and 'Faith in Society – Setting the Future Agenda' (1995).

Development workers

CIPL made a real attempt to involve lay people directly in the programme through the endeavours of some two dozen development workers across the country. These were people professionally employed by the churches to engage with faith and work issues (such as industrial chaplains, diocesan staff and laity centre directors) and who were enthusiastic about the programme. The development workers met two or three times a year in Birmingham for the first four or five years of the programme. However, it was a network that proved difficult to sustain (see below).

Projects

A major concern of CIPL was to avoid becoming an organization that was simply concerned with visions and agendas and did nothing to test out the reality and feasibility of the ideas generated. Over time, the programme gave birth to two projects that sought to put into practice some of the more imaginative ideas that had been suggested in its position papers.

By far the most comprehensive of these projects was the Human City Initiative (Chapter 11). From the end of 1994, a number of CIPL's position papers had begun to explore the issue of what makes a city human. As a result, early in 1995 I set up the Human City Initiative, a project attempting to find ways of enabling Birmingham to become a more human city. The project became a major undertaking. In 1997 a Human City Institute was established, with its own staff and an annual turnover of over half a million pounds.

The second project was much more modest in scope but, as a venture that could be replicated in any local church, was an important diaconal initiative. Over the years, CIPL had published a number of position papers describing how local churches might more fully affirm the ministry of their lay people in the world and better equip them for this ministry (see Wolff and College in Clark, 1997, pp. 106–12, 119–21). One or two of CIPL's day consultations also majored on this theme. Early in 2001 I was asked by Selly Oak Methodist Church, a large church that served Birmingham University and the Selly Oak Colleges, as well as its local neighbourhood, to set up a project called 'Selly Oak Methodist Church at Work'.

This project had a number of interesting features, some inspired by the position papers noted above (see also Chapter 14). All members of the congregation were invited to fill in cards giving brief details of their daily work – paid or voluntary. The names of university students worshipping at the church and the courses they were taking were also included. This information was published in a brochure that suggested four uses for the list – to make the congregation aware of the wide diversity of work in which its members were involved, to facilitate the sharing of experiences and insights concerning 'faith at work', to aid reflection on this ministry in worship and class meetings (small groups in which Methodist members met regularly), and to enable the congregation to give prayerful support to their fellow members at work. An updated version of the brochure has been published annually since then.

The project also led to a number of Sunday services being arranged that focused on 'the church at work' and in which lay people led worship and spoke, often very perceptively and movingly, about their experiences. Occasional house groups were convened to enable members to reflect on their faith and work and to undertake this ministry with greater skill and commitment. Articles appeared in the church's monthly magazine on the theme of 'Selly Oak at Work' and a mosaic of logos from people's places of work was displayed for several weeks. Since its inception, the project has become an integral part of the church's life.

Management and organization

As Co-ordinator of CIPL, I tried to offer the programme vision and impetus. In consultation with the programme's Steering Committee, I sought a way ahead for what we hoped might become a national and ecumenical support network for lay people. I undertook the job of commissioning, editing and publishing CIPL's position papers, producing a regular news-letter, setting up consultations and conferences, undertaking the research mentioned above and supporting the network of development workers. The instigation and oversight of projects was also my responsibility. In this role, I had some much-appreciated assistance from a member of the Sisters of Notre Dame, seconded to the programme for one year, and for a couple of years after that from a member of the Sisters of the Assumption.

CIPL ran on the proverbial 'shoestring'. I gave my own time voluntarily. The funding for secretarial support, publications and an office came from Associates' subscriptions, donations and occasional small trust grants. Conferences and consultations paid for themselves. Westhill College supported the project by assisting it 'in kind'.

'The Christians in Society Forum'

The purpose of CIPL was 'to achieve a new quality of public life by enabling Christians to engage, share and work together with others in addressing fundamental questions of common concern'. From the beginning, I had been convinced that the process of 'enabling Christians to engage, share and work together with others' to achieve 'a new quality of public life' could only be maintained over the long term if a wide range of Christian agencies was involved. During the first four years of its life CIPL, through its position papers and publications, research, consultations and conferences, had attempted to set out an agenda for the churches in the public realm. However, after four years of running the programme I became convinced that the time had come to invite Christian agencies with similar concerns to work with CIPL in sustaining and developing that agenda.

It was a conviction strengthened by a number of visits I made to the United States about this time to look at how the church there was supporting lay ministries in daily life. I was particularly impressed by the work of the Coalition for Ministry in Daily Life (CMDL), an initiative that had taken off in the early 1990s (CIPL, Simmel, G23, 2001). In 1992, the Coalition gave itself a name and adopted a mission statement that affirmed 'that all Christians have been called into ministry and that for most of them their arena of ministry is in and to the world'.

The Coalition currently consists of organizations and individuals from a range of Christian traditions, mainly in the USA but also beyond. Bodies involved include campus ministries, seminaries and colleges, church departments and independent organizations concerned with ministry in daily life. The Coalition publishes a newsletter entitled *LayNet*, holds an annual conference and makes full use of its web site to link participants (see Bibliography).

The Coalition has had its ups and downs over the years, but has steadily gained momentum. In 2005 the Coalition hosted a very successful conference attended by over a hundred people at Yale Divinity School in New Haven. *LayNet* (Spring 2005) reported that for many participants the conference 'brought compelling new horizons regarding God's involvement in our ordinary places of work' and 'gave people an unusual opportunity for contact with a wide assortment of Christians sharing the same commitments and passions'. The Coalition's concerns reflect a growing movement within the USA, now being taken forward by numerous agencies and developed through a range of publications (see Hammond, 2005) concerned to affirm the ministry of the laity as key for a church seeking to re-engage with the world of the twenty-first century.

As a result of my visits to the USA in the mid 1990s, I felt that if this kind of Coalition could work in the USA, it ought to be able to work in Britain. In 1996 I persuaded CIPL's Steering Committee to back a project to establish a 'National Network for Christians in Public Life'. The aim was to secure a physical base for the project and a small paid staff. The management committee to which the project would be accountable would, by and large, be made up of representatives of the mainstream churches (from boards or divisions with responsibility for ministry in public affairs), which would make a commitment to underwrite the project financially. A formal link would also be established between the project and the public affairs desk of Churches Together in Britain and Ireland. CIPL's Steering Committee asked me to develop the details of the project more fully, and to explore its potential with other organizations operating in this field.

The process of consultation and exploration was a slow and difficult one. Over the next year the project outline was circulated to CIPL's Associates, past and present, asking for their responses. Most were enthusiastic, a minority cautious. In the light of these responses, a day event was held in February 1998 entitled 'Towards a new Christian Partnership in Public Life'. Representatives of about 20 agencies attended. The consultation was in no doubt that the creation of a network of agencies supporting Christians in public life could be very important. The problem was how to put convictions into practice.

As a start, it was agreed that 'a small working party be set up to consider the first practical steps' needed to get the project under way. The working party met in the summer of 1998 and included representatives from the Industrial Mission Association, CHRISM (Christians in Secular Ministry), MODEM (concerned with leadership issues in church and society), the Sisters of Notre Dame, the NCH, the YMCA, GFS Platform (formerly the Girls' Friendly Society) and the Saltley Trust. It was agreed that the purpose of the project should be redefined as 'enabling Christians (both as individuals and organizations) to share their visions for the transformation of society and to work together in new ways to make those visions a reality'. It was also agreed that the project should be focused on setting up what was called 'The Christians in Society Forum'.

From this stage onwards, however, the forum project stalled. Further consultations were called in November 1998 and March 1999. Each attracted some two dozen agencies, including representatives of those involved in public life ministries from the main denominations, but none felt able to commit their organizations to the endeavour. In the autumn of 1999 the forum project encountered strong and unexpected resistance from both Churches Together in England and Churches Together in Britain and Ireland (CTBI). CTBI in particular felt that CIPL's forum project might detract from its own plans (unknown to CIPL at this time) to set up a 'Church and Society Forum'. In fact the purpose of the latter – 'to share, clarify, co-ordinate and promote the response of the churches to major current political and public issues' – was quite different from CIPL's initiative. Despite its opposition to the CIPL forum, in the end CTBI's proposed forum never materialized.

Nevertheless, the Christians in Society Forum working party pressed on with tenacity, seeking to enlist the support of enough agencies to make the project viable, but with little success. Through the skills of its own members it designed and set up in 2000 a provisional 'portal' web site. This was intended to enable Christian agencies engaged in public life issues to introduce themselves to a wider public, outline the concerns of greatest importance to them, describe their current projects, list the resources they could offer and give their contact details. All to no avail. The lack of practical and financial support from Christian agencies in this field, from the mainstream denominations and from national ecumenical bodies, meant that the forum project hit the buffers. In the middle of 2001 the project was indefinitely put on hold.

CIPL bows out

Throughout the years spent trying to establish a body to put the agenda developed through CIPL's position papers into practice, the publication of these papers had continued. However, an increasing amount of my own time and energy was taken up not only with the proposal to set up a Christians in Society Forum but with the rapidly growing demands of CIPL's major progeny, the Human City Initiative (Chapter 11). With over 200 position papers published, CIPL had also achieved one of its major aims, that of exploring and setting out an agenda for the church in public life. It did not seem sensible simply to go on adding more and more position papers to those already published.

CIPL bowed out almost exactly ten years after it began. The last set of position papers was published in November 2001. One of these papers, that I wrote as an 'end piece', was entitled *Christians in Public Life: An Unfinished Task* . . . In it I briefly told the story of CIPL described above. I went on to argue that the task of implementing the agenda that the many authors of the position papers had set out remained an 'unfinished task' and a top priority for the church in the years ahead.

However, the work begun by CIPL has not ended. Discussions are currently under way for the programme to be taken into another stage by Sarum College, formerly Anglican but now describing itself as an ecumenical theological college, currently developing and diversifying its Politics and Theology Programme (see Bibliography).

Below, we first identify those features of the diaconal church (Part 2), especially concerned with the laity, that can be seen in the Christians in Public Life Programme. We then look at how a Christendom model of church hindered the work of CIPL. Finally, we look at other challenges that CIPL had to face.

Breaking the mould of Christendom?

The diaconal church

Mission   The Christians in Public Life Programme was a diaconal initiative. Its understanding of mission was kingdom community-centred not church-centred. CIPL's mission statement was 'to achieve a new quality of public life by enabling Christians to engage, share and work together with others in addressing fundamental questions of common concern'. It attempted through its position papers to set out a vision of the diaconal church as a *community*, by emphasizing 'engaging, sharing and working together'; and as a *learning* community, by developing its openness to 'addressing fundamental questions of common concern'.

Culture   CIPL sought to engage positively yet critically with a secular society in a quest to achieve 'a new quality of public life'.

Stance   CIPL regarded itself as a servant of the kingdom community. It did not attempt to prescribe or impose an agenda for the churches in public life. Rather, it invited a wide range of authors, from lay people of all denominations (see the position papers originally entitled 'Christians speaking', Clark, 1997, pp. 143–62) to bishops and archbishops (Carey and Williams, in Clark, 1997, pp. 57–9, pp. 48–50), to offer their visions and insights of a church seeking to make manifest the gifts of the kingdom community within society.

The laity   CIPL placed the ministry of the laity at the very top of its agenda. The programme challenged the culture of clericalism through position papers on the mission of the church in the world (see CIPL's papers on the theme of 'the human city'), the nature of lay vocation, and how the church might better support and equip lay people for that calling (see CIPL Resources Sheets R1–R21). In the process, CIPL sought to consult lay people widely. One example of this was its *Survey of Christians at Work* (Clark, 1993), an enquiry that encouraged lay people to question the conformism that so often permeates the life of the local church.

Hearings and networks   The concepts of hearings and networks were important features of CIPL's programme. It worked hard to connect up the writers of its position papers, their ideas and insights often being stimulated by what others had written. Networking occurred through the dissemination of position papers and the feedback received, a process that created a 'virtual' hearing among CIPL's Associates. The position papers were also used as the subject matter of actual hearings in local churches, conference centres and theological colleges. CIPL's own day events and conferences frequently took the themes explored through the position papers as the focus of their deliberations. The consultation and visioning process concerned with proposals to set up the Christians in Society Forum was a further example of the role that hearings might play in the diaconal church. Dialogue, as a tool for learning as well as mission, lay at the heart of the programme.

The communal institution and partnerships   Organizationally, CIPL was a very modest undertaking and never regarded itself as in any way an institution. However, its Steering Committee saw its role as one of 'combining and connecting' and was careful not to set rigid boundaries. The ecumenical composition of the Steering Committee reflected the nature of the whole programme, all involved being seen as partners, and denominational allegiances as a resource not a liability.

Leadership   I interpreted my own role as Co-ordinator of CIPL as a diaconal one; that of a community educator seeking to help lay people to become community builders in the public arena. This necessitated my being a catalyst, stimulating visions of the potential of a renewed laity for transforming the life of church and world; and an enabler, encouraging and equipping the laity for that mission. My role was also that of an intermediary: between the wider world and the programme, between the mainstream denominations and the programme, between the writers of the papers, and between CIPL's link persons scattered around the country. I was located on the boundary of church and society, attempting to discern the signs of the kingdom community at work and, through CIPL's papers and consultations, to bring these signs to the awareness of lay people and those seeking to support them.

The Christendom church

The Christians in Public Life Programme lasted ten years. However, the legacy of the Christendom church impinged negatively on a number of aspects of its life and work.

Sacralism, the all-embracing belief that the church is a world unto itself, was one reason that the mainstream churches took only passing interest in CIPL and its concerns. In principle, the churches acknowledged that the ministry of the laity in public life was extremely important. However, the second half of the twentieth century saw them again and again failing to turn principles into practice. CIPL was but one of numerous initiatives that here struggled to make a breakthrough.

Clericalism hindered the programme's development. As CIPL's research into 'Christians at Work' showed, presbyters for whom the task of servicing the gathered church was all-consuming had little reason to take much interest in an initiative concerned to support the laity as the dispersed church. Furthermore, clergy who worked in the public arena, as sector ministers or chaplains, generally construed their role in presbyteral rather than diaconal terms (Chapter 12). Thus few clergy saw the need to introduce lay people to the programme.

The problem of clericalism was further compounded by *conformism*, the dependency of the laity on the clergy. Over the years, this has resulted in very few lay people being challenged to look seriously at their vocation to be the people of God in the world. Thus CIPL, like numerous ventures over the half-century before it, was faced with trying to engage with *God's Frozen People* (Gibbs and Morton, 1964) still in the grip of an ice age.

In addition to these attributes of the Christendom model of church ranged against it, CIPL encountered denominational *separatism*. CIPL, and not least its proposals to set up the Christians in Society Forum, depended on the synergy of 'one church united for mission' being stronger than the drag of denominationalism. However, CIPL was unable to overcome a separatism that prevented enough Christian organizations working in this field coming together to create a partnership strong enough to take forward the agenda set by the programme's position papers.

The problems posed by denominationalism were not made any easier to deal with in an ecclesiastical culture where *unilateralism* was also an issue. A significant setback for CIPL was the hostility of the leadership of Churches Together in Britain and Ireland, as well as of Churches Together in England, to its proposals to set up the Christians in Society Forum. Both national ecumenical bodies had from the outset been kept informed of CIPL's proposals to set up such a forum. However, rather than opening the way for a discussion of how best a common concern might be progressed, the 'ecumenical' response at national level was negative and autocratic. Bodies that in principle were set up to encourage and nurture ecumenical initiatives in this instance blocked them.

Other challenges

The Christians in Public Life Programme faced other difficulties that could not be attributed, at least directly, to a lack of 'fit' with a Christendom culture. CIPL's programme did not have the standing of projects set up by the mainstream churches, though few new endeavours in this field of mission had been made by the latter after the publication of their reports on the role of the laity in the late 1980s. Though CIPL benefited from the support and guidance of an influential ecumenical Steering Committee, this was an invited group and did not carry the imprimatur of the wider church.

In retrospect, CIPL was perhaps overambitious to attempt to move from a relatively modest programme to setting up a formally constituted umbrella body, the Christians in Society Forum. To try and build a national forum maintained by the wide diversity of Christian organizations operating in the public arena, few of which had worked closely together before, was moving too fast too soon. Nor did the alternative plan of setting up the forum as a web site provide a strong enough reason for them to commit themselves to a joint enterprise. Thus the collective support and resources needed to sustain the agenda set by CIPL failed to materialize.

Conclusion

The Christians in Public Life Programme, even though relatively small-scale and limited in scope, was an important diaconal initiative. Its vision was that of an informed and empowered laity, community building in their places of work as servants of the kingdom community. Through its couple of hundred position papers, CIPL set out a comprehensive agenda for a diaconal church operating in the public arena. The papers drew on the work of a wide range of imaginative and articulate writers and created a 'virtual' hearing for those who read them regularly or attended CIPL's gatherings. CIPL also provided a model of how informal networking could harness the experiences, insights and resources of those called to lay ministry in public life, even when constrained by the culture of a Christendom church. My own leadership, diaconal in nature, was a means of catalysing and enabling a broad range of people, lay and ordained, to grasp what the ministry of a church committed to serving the kingdom community in public life might look like.

CIPL's two main projects offered important models of the diaconal church in action. The Human City Initiative will be considered in the next chapter. The Selly Oak at Work Project, though a drop in the ocean in the context of the church as a whole, nonetheless remains an illustration of how a local church can begin to raise the awareness of its lay people to their missionary calling. If it were to be multiplied many times over, the change of culture that it would engender could play a vital part in breaking the mould of Christendom.

11

'The Human City Initiative' (HCI)

Mission

Introduction

'There never really was a "golden age" for the Church of England in the city.'
So comments *Faith in the City*, the Report of the Archbishop of Canterbury's
Commission on Urban Priority Areas published in 1985 (p. 31). What is true
for the Church of England is equally so for all mainstream Christian
churches.

From the onset of the rapid growth of cities in the West in the nineteenth
century, the churches put immense effort into trying to meet the spiritual
needs of a world that was now industrial as well as urban. New churches
were built and clergy imported into the heart of 'darkest England'. But the
urban masses, uprooted and freed from the dependency culture of
Christendom, were slow to respond.

Where the churches did make a real impact, and found a ready response,
was in their attempts to care for the urban poor. From the mid-nineteenth
century onwards, there was a growing awareness of the acute needs of the
inner cities caused by poverty, appalling working conditions and the lack
of a welfare system to assist those unable to work. William Booth's
Salvation Army, founded in 1865, led the way. Over the following decades,
the Settlement movement, in which the Church of England was especially
prominent, and Methodism's 'Forward Movement', which led to the building of 'central halls' in many inner-city areas, appealed to the church's
middle-class members, challenging them to address urban deprivation
financially or through personal involvement.

The twentieth century, however, saw the church losing its tenuous
foothold in disadvantaged urban areas, be these within the inner city or on
post-war estates. The secularization of society, the emergence of the
welfare state and the increasing 'suburban captivity of the churches'

(Winter, 1961) gave impetus to the decline of the settlement movement, the closure of many Methodist central halls and a steady shrinkage in the number and strength of inner-city congregations.

The Sheffield Industrial Mission and the South London Industrial Mission came into being in 1944 (Chapter 12), but such endeavours were addressed more to the world of industry than to disadvantaged areas of urban life. In the mid 1960s, Harvey Cox gave a boost to the debate about the church's ministry to the city with his seminal and relatively optimistic book *The Secular City* (1965). There followed a number of one-off initiatives, including the Urban Theology Unit set up by John Vincent in Sheffield in 1969, the Urban Ministry Project founded by Donald Reeves in south London and the Evangelical Urban Training Project. However, as Laurie Green comments, 'Despite all the excitement of these projects and others like them around the country, urban theology and mission were still not acknowledged by the mainstream church to be of critical importance to Christian life in the UK' (2003, p. 36–7).

Faith in the City

The publication of *Faith in the City* in 1985, the Report of the Archbishop of Canterbury's Commission on Urban Priority Areas, was, therefore, a milestone in raising the awareness of all the churches to their long neglect of urban mission. The Commission engaged in what, in practice, was a series of 'hearings', travelling the country and taking evidence from those living or working in areas of urban deprivation (Garner, 2004, p. 25–6). Though it is generally agreed that the Report's attempt to develop a relevant urban theology was its weakest component, the data it collected about the needs of 'urban priority areas' and its recommendations for radical change addressed to the Thatcher government (evoking open hostility from the latter) once again put urban mission on the map. As a direct result of *Faith in the City*, the Church Urban Fund was established, as well as Methodism's fund for 'Mission Alongside the Poor'. Both funds distributed grants to church initiatives seeking to improve the lot of residents living in deprived urban areas. An Archbishop of Canterbury's Urban Theology Group was also established and continued to meet and publish its reflections over subsequent years (for example, Sedgwick, 1995; Northcott, 1998).

Over the next two decades a spate of other reports, books and articles on urban mission were published. Among these were *Faith in the City of Birmingham* (1988), *Theology in the City* (Harvey, 1989), *Hope in the City?* (Farnell et al, 1994), *Staying in the City* (1995), *Church for the City* (focused on London, Blakebrough, 1995), the last three being published as reflections on urban mission ten years after *Faith in the City*. After 1995, came such books as *The Cities: A Methodist Report* (1997), *Urban Christianity and Global Order* (Davey, 2001), *Urban Ministry and the Kingdom of God* (Green, 2003) and *Facing the City – Urban Mission in the 21st Century* (Garner, 2004). In 2002, the Anglican Urban Bishop's Panel set up a Commission on Urban Life and Faith to respond 'to the need for a wider review of the Church of England's urban mission on the twentieth anniversary of *Faith in the City* in 2005', and to report at the end of that year.

During these years, government policy for addressing urban deprivation had passed through a series of major changes. Post-war efforts had gone into a massive estate building and rehousing programme to get rid of the legacy of Victorian slums. However, by the mid 1960s, the hope that this programme, allied to the 'safety net' provided by a comprehensive welfare state, could do away with urban poverty was fading fast. Targeted neighbourhood intervention, such as the Community Development Programmes initiated by the Home Office in 1969 (*Gilding the Ghetto*, 1976), was tried for some time, but this again failed to produce lasting results. From the onset of Thatcherism in 1979, the emphasis shifted to market-led economic regeneration through private ventures such as Urban Development Corporations and Enterprise Zones, with self-help and consumer choice being to the fore. When this philosophy also failed to deliver, 'approaches rooted in more inclusive partnerships embracing local authorities and community organizations' moved centre stage (*Hope in the City?*, p. 34). This partnership approach has, in broad terms, remained in place ever since, involving an attempt in more recent years to set up 'Local Strategic Partnerships' (Russell, 2001) to give strength and sustainability to grass-roots co-operation.

Beginnings of the Human City Initiative (1995–97)

The Human City Initiative (frequently referred to by its acronym HCI), the project that forms the subject matter of this chapter, began in Birmingham in 1994. The idea of setting up the Human City Initiative was sparked by my own wish to test out in practice a range of new ideas about the mission of the church in an urban society being put forward in the position papers published by the Christians in Public Life Programme (Chapter 10). The overall thrust of these papers was that the church's mission should not be focused on attempting to make people Christians, but on enabling them to become a fully human community reflecting the fullness of life offered by the kingdom community. Thus the church's task was to enable like-minded people of all faiths and convictions to share their visions of 'the human city', and to work together to make these visions a reality. A human city initiative was seen as a major step towards building a human society and a human world.

A project focused on the human city was also an attempt to respond to 'the inhuman city' where market forces were putting 'profit' and 'efficiency' before the basic needs of ordinary people. The problem was not only that deprivation, unemployment and poverty still loomed large in the experience of many city dwellers. It was that the lives of the thousands who were in work were now governed by a host of targets and outputs that had to be achieved at considerable human cost. This created a competitive and communally divisive culture across all sectors of society, public and voluntary as well as private.

Origins

In 1994 I was given the opportunity by Westhill College where I worked to explore how the suggestions made in CIPL's position papers on urban mission might be tried out in Birmingham. Another useful source of ideas was *Faith in the City of Birmingham* (1988), Birmingham's own attempt to replicate the work of the *Faith in the City* Commission at city level. Suggestions also came from many interviews I undertook during 1994 to discover how the church might more effectively engage with the city. There was general consensus that an initiative by the churches to enable Birmingham to become a more 'human' city would arouse much interest and gain considerable support.

At the end of 1994, therefore, I wrote a position paper for the Christians in Public Life Programme (CIPL, A3) that set out three observations on 'a Human City Initiative'. The first was that the image of 'the human city', a name first suggested by the Provost of Birmingham, could become a key symbolic image in stimulating people's imagination and commitment. I saw the image as representing 'a new way of being city'. I also believed the image of the human city would necessitate 'a new way of being church'; only a fully human church could be instrumental in creating a fully human city. My second observation was that new partnerships would be essential if a human city were to come into being. I saw such partnerships as bringing together the public, voluntary and private sectors; 'professionals as well as politicians'; 'those on the margins as well as those at the centre'; 'the poor as well as the wealthy'. My third observation was that the church's contribution to the task of transforming the city would only be effective if Christians worked together across denominational boundaries.

The early years

The Human City Initiative (HCI) was formally launched, in January 1995, at a packed meeting, which the Lord Mayor of Birmingham attended at his own request, held at Westhill College. HCI's first phase lasted from 1995 to 1997 and had two important features. First, during these years HCI was an explicitly Christian undertaking, with lay people providing most of the personnel and resources to take it forward. Second, these years provided an important dress rehearsal for the longer-term initiatives taken after 1997.

From 1995 to 1997, though HCI remained explicitly a Christian venture, it welcomed the contributions and suggestions of all those who wanted to be associated with it. Lay people from every denomination played an active role in HCI's development. Half a dozen people formed a small 'core group' that, among other responsibilities, produced a *Human City Bulletin*. Others acted as 'link persons' to help HCI keep well informed about important spheres of Birmingham life in which they were involved, such as education, health, the media, the arts, industry and the environment, as well as religious affairs. An Advisory Group, which met together to prepare for the establishment of the Human City Institute (see below), was made up of those enthusiastic about the idea of working together to make Birmingham a more human city.

During this period, HCI took a number of initiatives, some of which became proto-types for its future work. The *Human City Bulletin* first appeared in September 1995. Until 1997, the Christians in Public Life Programme continued to publish papers on the theme of 'the human city', but from 1999 these were superseded by what came to be known as the 'Human City *Futures Papers*'. A range of conferences and consultations was held that later paved the way for a series of human city 'hearings'. The concept of 'human circles' was coined, the forerunner of what came to be called 'human city sites' (see below). The Human City Youth Project (HCI, 1997d, 1999), which began in March 1996, brought together young adults and city leaders on a one-to-one basis to share their hopes for the future of Birmingham.

By 1996 it was clear that HCI had gathered sufficient momentum to justify its continuation beyond 1997. To take the work of HCI forward, the Advisory Group's recommendations that a Human City Institute be set up, as a company limited by guarantee and a registered charity, were accepted. The Institute was established in May 1997.

The Human City Initiative in full swing (1997–2000)

The Human City Institute

The establishment of the Human City Institute (from here on referred to as 'the Institute') was a watershed in the development of HCI. The principles on which the Institute was founded were set out in a paper that argued:

The humanity of institutional life is essential to civic renewal:
– the debate about the nature of the human city must go beyond values to embrace the convictions and commitment on which truly human institutions are founded;
– new understandings and alliances need to be created across occupational, social, religious and ethnic divides;
– civic renewal is an 'all-in' process dependent on every sector of urban life recognizing its collective responsibility for the well-being of the whole.

The Institute adopted a mission statement, which described its purpose as: 'To enable those who share a vision of the human city to work together with others to make that vision a reality.' A further mission statement adopted a little later to sum up more succinctly the nature of the human city ran: 'All matter; each counts'.

The Institute itself was made up of a Governing Council, Trustees, and a Director with a small staff. The Governing Council eventually represented nearly forty Birmingham organizations from the public, voluntary and private sectors. Four organizations were ex-officio members: the City Council, the Chamber of Commerce, the Voluntary Service Council and Birmingham Churches Together. Seven Christian bodies were represented on the Council, including the Anglican Diocese, the Methodist District and Warwickshire Monthly Meeting of the Society of Friends. The Roman

Catholic Archdiocese declined to become a member, but two religious orders came on board. The Birmingham Central Mosque, the Birmingham Hindu Council and the Council of Sikh Gudwaras also became Council members.

The make-up of the Institute's Governing Council represented a deliberate decision on the part of the Advisory Group to move HCI beyond its explicitly Christian origins to an organization with a more inclusive character. This move was an acknowledgement that, in a multicultural and multifaith city like Birmingham, it would have been a contradiction in terms to continue to pursue the vision of the human city from a purely Christian perspective. However, the Institute's constitution deliberately included a sentence to ensure that the Institute would remain representative of 'the religious aspect of life in Birmingham'.

I was appointed the first Director of the Institute. The Institute employed three administrative staff and, from 1999, three Human Neighbourhood Project workers, funding for all these posts coming largely from grants received towards the cost of the Human Neighbourhood Project (see below).

'Hearings'

In the autumn of 1997, following closely on the establishment of the Institute, HCI mounted a series of ten public 'hearings' in the Council House, Birmingham. Their purpose was threefold: to bring together a wide range of people from every sector of Birmingham life to share their visions for the future of the city; to begin to set an agenda for Birmingham as a human city; and to help make the Institute and what it stood for more widely known across the city.

The overall theme of the hearings was 'Imagine Birmingham'. Ten hearings were held in all. Their topics were: 'Imagine a Human Education System', '... Human Community Care System', '... Human Business World', '... Human Health Service', '... Human World of the Arts', '... Human Police Force', '... Human City Centre', '... Human Transport System', '... Human Media' and '... Human System of Local Government'. The hearings consisted of a short keynote address, discussion in small groups and a final plenary. The proceedings were recorded, documented and published in March 1998 (HCI, 1998). The hearings created considerable interest across the city and were attended by some 500 people.

In 2000 HCI instigated a second set of hearings. This time the aim was to encourage people to share their visions on topics that were more directly related to everyday life than the all-embracing concerns of 1997. Nineteen hearings were held. The topics included: imagine a human family, imagine a human school, a human play service, a human neighbourhood, a human health centre, a human hospital, a human college of further education, and a human university. Once again vigorous debate typified all the hearings. The findings were published in February 2001 (HCI, 2001) and disseminated widely.

The *Human City Bulletin* and *Futures Papers*

The *Human City Bulletin*, which I edited, first appeared at the end of 1995. From then on it was published three times a year. The *Bulletin* went out free to some 4,000 people across Birmingham. The expense was felt to be justified in view of the high profile it gave to HCI, the range of people it involved in reflecting on the nature of the human city, the discussion that its editorials produced and the compelling nature of the human stories which it told.

After the setting up of the Institute in 1997, the *Bulletin* dropped most of its more overtly Christian content and sought to involve any person, group, organization or institution in Birmingham interested in offering their ideas about or their experiences of trying to create the human city. There was rarely a problem in getting people to contribute articles. Many people expressed their appreciation at being challenged to explore an image of the city that was rarely given much attention in any sphere of city life, including religious life. In each issue of the *Bulletin*, a prominent figure in the life of Birmingham was asked to offer his or her views on the nature of the human city (for several years each new Lord Mayor contributed an article to the *Bulletin*). My own editorials had titles such as 'Cities are our future', 'Imagine Birmingham', 'What role for the private sector?', 'Ten signs of the human city', 'The inhuman city' and 'Citizenship'. A large number of local groups provided stories of their own human endeavours, and the private sector offered a range of viewpoints on the human business. News of events and activities associated with the theme of a human city was also provided.

From early 1999, HCI began to publish a series of what were called *Futures Papers*. Over 30 *Futures Papers* were produced on topics including: 'What makes a city human?', 'The human neighbourhood', 'The human school', 'The human business – a vision for the future', 'The human bank', 'A human transport system' and 'Policing with humanity'. One thought-provoking paper focused on 'The human church'. Though some *Futures Papers* were circulated free with the *Bulletin*, most were sent to Associates of the Institute who paid a small subscription for them. Alongside the hearings and the *Bulletin*, the *Futures Papers* were an important means of furthering HCI's mission statement of enabling people to share their visions of the human city.

'Human city sites'

The concept of 'human city sites' was set out in a paper I wrote soon after the Institute was established (HCI, 1997c). We defined a human city site as any group that believed itself to be making a practical contribution to the creation of a human city, and was at the same time prepared to associate itself publicly with the mission statement of the Institute. The philosophy behind the concept of human city sites reflected the thinking of Leonie Sandercock, who has written about cities requiring not grand schemes of regeneration but 'a thousand tiny empowerments' (Sandercock, 1998, p. 6), that is a host of small endeavours generating the synergy required for radical change.

Any group interested in being associated with the Institute as a human city site was asked to offer 'a human agenda', which would be made widely known as a means of inspiring and encouraging others. Examples of the agendas offered by the sites linking up with the Institute were:

- To provide support for existing and potential cyclists. (An environmental group)
- To increase respect for Hindu elderly people. (A Hindu association)
- To develop ways of reducing anxiety in clients when coming to our centre for the first time. (A disability centre)
- To ensure that our buildings and facilities are made available to community groups. (A church)
- To explore and share the extraordinary rich culture and history of Yemen with the citizens of Birmingham. (A Yemeni centre)
- To pioneer the principle of forgiveness as the norm in the school curriculum. (A centre for pupils at risk)
- To give women greater self-confidence through singing. (A Sikh women's choir)

- To produce a video to raise the awareness of schoolchildren to vandalism and the need to combat it. (A girls' secondary school)
- To give policing a more human face. (A police Operational Command Unit)
- To develop a Birmingham–Johannesburg community link. (A One World group)

The Institute identified, supported and linked up human city sites by entering into a 'covenant' with each of them. For its part of the covenant, the Institute offered sites a visiting consultancy service, a newsletter that carried stories of their endeavours, space to report on their work in the *Bulletin*, a page on the Institute's web site and an annual gathering at which sites could make a presentation of their work to the general public. The Institute also produced a *Sites' Handbook* consisting of guidelines to enable sites to monitor how the task of accomplishing their agenda was going. For their part of the covenant with the Institute, each site made a year's commitment to working at its chosen agenda, accepted that its agenda should be made public and agreed to link up with other human city sites to share insights, experience and resources.

Each year, the Institute set up a 'Human City Trail' for the human city sites associated with it. The word 'Trail' referred to the 'journey' of one year's duration taken by each site as it sought to accomplish its chosen agenda. Sites were invited to send representatives to monthly meetings where they could share their hopes and stories, as well as their concerns and difficulties. At the outset of the Trail, each site was awarded a 'site certificate'. This formally recognized the site's commitment to fulfilling its chosen agenda in partnership with the Institute. These certificates were often proudly displayed at the sites' home bases.

The human city sites programme soon became widely known across Birmingham, as well as further afield. In large part because of its development of the concept of human city sites and Human City Trails, HCI was twice shortlisted by the Schumacher Society for the prestigious annual Schumacher Award (1998 and 1999).

'The Human Neighbourhood Project'

1999 saw the beginning of a project that was to dominate the life and work of HCI over the next five years: 'the Human Neighbourhood Project'. In 1996 HCI had mounted a well-attended consultation entitled 'Building the

Human Neighbourhood – the Continuing Challenge'. This provided the momentum for a successful bid to the National Lottery Board for a Human Neighbourhood Project to be undertaken in three areas of Birmingham.

At the same time, HCI was exploring the possibility of setting up Human Neighbourhood Projects in two other cities, Bradford and Swindon. Bradford and Swindon were chosen because they were located north and south, had a different history and culture from Birmingham and had expressed interest in a 'human city' initiative. With the help of church leaders in both Bradford and Swindon, meetings were arranged between HCI, representatives from local government and a number of organizations already involved in neighbourhood regeneration in those cities. The successful outcome of these negotiations led to the then DETR (Department of Transport and the Regions) offering funding for Human Neighbourhood Projects in both cities to match National Lottery support for the Birmingham-based project.

HCI's purpose in promoting the Human Neighbourhood Project was to end the fragmentation and segregation of urban neighbourhoods by encouraging neighbourhoods to combine together to build the human city. The project focused on HCI working with a multiplicity of neighbourhood groups (in this case called 'human *neighbourhood* sites') to enable them to share their visions of the human neighbourhood and to work together to make these a reality. HCI believed that if the energy of such groups could be harnessed and sustained by helping them to link together within and between neighbourhoods, as well as across the three cities concerned, then there would be a new kind of synergy created to further urban regeneration.

The Human Neighbourhood Project set out to identify three neighbourhoods in each of the three cities, Birmingham, Bradford and Swindon, where there was clear evidence of deprivation and where existing efforts to address the reasons for this had met with little success. Human Neighbourhood Project workers (initially one in each city) were appointed by HCI to identify (or create) and work with at least five sites in each of the neighbourhoods. A 'host agency', an organization that was already well established in each neighbourhood, was appointed to support the project worker, to ensure continuity with the past and to be there to support the neighbourhood sites when the project worker moved on.

A cross-section of the agendas offered by the human neighbourhood sites selected was:

In Birmingham:

- To develop a mentoring service to support new tenants settle into the area. (A residents' group)
- To set up a self-advocacy group to help members develop confidence to speak up on issues of concern and interest. (A group of adults with mental health and learning difficulties)
- To develop inter-generational partnerships through music. (A music group)
- To build a tranquil, sensory garden that will be accessible to all children. (Parents of children suffering from autism and Asperger's syndrome)

In Bradford:

- To improve the communal area between three rows of houses. (A mixed age group)
- To develop a mural. (A group of 7 to 12 year olds)
- To create a facility that offers access to fresh fruit and vegetables at affordable prices. (A residents' group)
- To campaign for an accessible bus service for the estate. (An adult group)

In Swindon:

- To set up a local newsletter and consultations on the future of the area. (A neighbourhood forum)
- To develop an area of ponds and streams in the area. (An environmental group)
- To create an intergenerational singing group. (A group aged from 14 to 70+)
- To consult on the creation of recreation facilities for young people in the area. (14 and 15 year olds from a local school)

The Human Neighbourhood Project did not attempt to replicate all the features of Birmingham's Human City Trail. For example, the Trail's more formal covenant gave way to an informal agreement between human neighbourhood sites and the Institute. No certificates were awarded to human neighbourhood sites and there was no annual time limit set for accomplishing their agendas. However, the idea of sites choosing their own agendas and networking together to help achieve these remained paramount for both the Human City Trail and the Human Neigbourhood Project.

This networking process was crucial in moving the Human Neighbourhood Project from a run-of-the-mill neighbourhood development initiative to a unique venture in urban revitalization. In Bradford, the sites met together across neighbourhoods on a two-monthly basis, the venue for the forum changing each time. In Birmingham, with greater distances between the neighbourhoods, the focus was on an annual get-together. In Swindon, sites met up on a more ad hoc basis. Early in 2000, the second year of the project, Birmingham and Bradford began to produce their own *Human Neighbourhood Newssheet*, which reported on their sites' agendas and progress. By 2001 this had been upgraded to an *Intercity Newsletter* covering the activities of the sites in all three cities. Intercity gatherings were also arranged from time to time. In 2002 a major gathering was held in Birmingham for representatives of the sites from all three cities.

Such cross-city and intercity gatherings were demanding to set up, in terms of time, energy and finance. For this reason, the Human Neighbourhood Project saw information technology as vital in maintaining the networking process. Project workers made their lap-tops available to sites whenever possible. The workers also had digital cameras that could be used to transmit pictures of the sites' work within and between the three cities. The Institute's web site, launched in 1999, carried information about the Human Neighbourhood Project and many of its human neighbourhood sites, a facility that the sites themselves could use to promote their activities in any way they chose.

A change of focus and decline (2000–04)

In 2000 I retired as Director of the Institute. I was followed in this post by a lecturer seconded from the Department of Social Policy and Social Work at the University of Birmingham. She had been appointed as consultant to the Human Neighbourhood Project at its inception and had been a keen supporter of HCI throughout. The appointment could only be half-time, as core funding for the Institute, brought in by the Human Neighbourhood Project and a few other grants, remained limited.

The appointment of a new Director, whose expertise was in the field of community development, brought a change of focus. Largely because of the new Director's interests and skills, but also because it remained the major source of funding, the Human Neighbourhood Project gradually moved centre stage. Funding was obtained for the extension of the work in Birmingham, Bradford and Swindon, and additional project workers were appointed in all three cities. The project workers moved into a number of new neighbourhoods, more human neighbourhood sites were identified, and city-wide together with occasional three-city gatherings were held.

During this period, the Human Neighbourhood Project not only became the heart of HCI's work but gathered momentum. However, this meant that, with the time and energy of the Institute's staff now being given almost entirely to the Human Neighbourhood Project, other aspects of HCI's original programme were gradually lost to view. Apart from an ongoing project concerned with the human face of policing and a small pilot project on the theme of the human school, no new projects came on stream. No more hearings were held and only three more *Futures Papers* were published. The Institute's web site was developed further in an imaginative way, but the information appearing on it was largely about the Human Neighbourhood Project.

The *Human City Bulletin* continued, its style of production going more up-market. However, its content was more and more concerned with news from the Human Neighbourhood Project. Few stories appeared about human city sites in Birmingham not associated with the Human Neighbourhood Project, and no more Human City Trails were set up. The *Bulletin* no longer carried ideas and comments from Birmingham residents and its more prominent citizens were no longer invited to offer their views on what it might mean to be a human city. Thus HCI began to lose much of its Birmingham identity and its city-wide appeal.

In 2002 the Institute's second Director decided to return full-time to her work at Birmingham University. Her departure led to a rapid decline in the Institute's fortunes. A third Director, with interests and skills quite different from those of his predecessor, struggled to refocus and redevelop the work. Applications for further grants to extend the life of the Human Neighbourhood Project and other aspects of HCI's programme failed. As a result core funding suffered badly. By 2004 it was clear that HCI could unfortunately no longer continue with even its Human Neighbourhood Project, and this too came to a close. With this project gone, HCI had no ongoing means of support. All the staff departed and the work ceased.

A small group of trustees remained in post, however, and continued to work at the question of how to recapture the original vision of HCI. A major concern was how to enable HCI to become once again an advocate

for the human city, with a greater focus on Birmingham, greater prominence given to the *Bulletin* and *Futures Papers*, a readiness to set up further
hearings and less dependence for core funding on projects. At the same
time, links that had been in existence for some years between HCI and the
Trident Housing Association, an organization based in Birmingham,
began to develop into an active partnership. By 2005 plans were being
made for a relaunch of HCI in close association with Trident, the focus
being on the kind of initiatives taken by HCI before the Human Neighbourhood Project came to dominate the scene.

In our discussion below, we first identify those features of the mission of
the diaconal church (Part 2) manifest in the work of the Human City
Initiative. We then consider attributes of a Christendom model of church
(also Part 2) that hindered HCI's progress. Finally, we look at the other
challenges that HCI had to face.

Breaking the mould of Christendom?

The diaconal church

Mission   The choice of 'the human city' as the title of the Human City
Initiative was more than a pragmatic one. Those of us who set up HCI, all of
whom were Christians, were looking for a title that would encompass a
Christian vision for Birmingham as well as fire the imagination of those of
other faiths and convictions. 'The human city' was a title meant to express
our hopes for the city, not only as a community through which the fullness
of our common humanity could be realized, but also as a vision of what,
in this book, we have called the kingdom community. Thus, choosing
'the human city' as the title of HCI was for us a means of pursuing, with
others, our calling as Christians to make the kingdom community, and its
gifts of life, liberation, love and learning, manifest in the life of
Birmingham.

We saw both the human city and the kingdom community as about
visions and hopes 'made flesh'. Both were incarnational. Both were about
putting an end to inhumanity. Both were about justice and peace. Both
were about being, as well as becoming. Both were about a company of
travellers on a journey, never about a final destination. HCI sought to offer
a vision of the human city, and thus of the kingdom community, that was
clear enough to enable people to work together for its coming, but never a

blueprint that would limit possibilities and stultify growth (see 'Ten Signs of the Human City', *Bulletin*, No. 12, December 1998).

Because HCI was an initiative taken to serve the human city and thus, by implication, the kingdom community, it was engaged on a mission akin to that of the diaconal church. Like the diaconal church, HCI was committed to reshaping the city as a community of communities, and in the process paving the way for the emergence of a global community of communities. Like the diaconal church, HCI was also committed to promoting the concept of 'the learning city' (*Learning City in Europe*, 2001), that is, the idea of urban communities large and small being not only inclusive, but also open to learn from one another in their attempts to revitalize the life of the city. Therefore, despite its relatively short life (ten years), HCI can be seen as a model of how the diaconal church might engage in urban mission on a city-wide scale.

At this time, other images of the city were vying for pride of place. These images included 'the healthy city', 'the sustainable city', 'the creative city' (Landry and Bianchini, 1995; Landry, 2000), as well as that promoted by the Home Office, so-called 'safer cities'. However, those of us who set up HCI believed that the image of 'the human city' was different in kind from these other images, its shorter mission statement summing up its unique character in the words 'All matter; each counts'. The human city' was about the city as an organic whole within which all citizens affirmed their common humanity by sharing together in a quest for the common good. It was a city with which every citizen was able to identify, and to the well-being of which each could contribute, whatever their social or cultural background, their beliefs or their convictions. From our perspective as Christians, 'the human city' was an image of a community of communities transformed by the gifts of the kingdom community.

When in 1997 HCI moved on from being an explicitly Christian initiative, those of us who were Christians saw it as even more fully serving the kingdom community and as an even better model of the diaconal church in action. What was different from that time onwards was that the Christians who became involved in HCI did so on an equal footing with others, a form of mission incumbent on all Christians seeking to act as the diaconal church in the world.

Culture HCI accepted the secular city as a reality of ever-growing importance on the world scene and for the future of humankind. Yet it recognized that the secular city could just as easily dehumanize and degrade as enhance and enrich the lives of its citizen. Thus, HCI worked for the trans-formation of all urban institutions, including the church, into learning communities that reflected the gifts of the kingdom community.

Stance   HCI was set up to operate as a servant of the kingdom com-munity. That meant that it was also a servant of the human city. Its aim was to be guided by the nature of servanthood and not to coerce or control. It saw its purpose as using what influence it had not to impose its convictions on others, but to enable them to make their distinctive contribution to visioning and building Birmingham as a human city. It affirmed and encouraged all endeavours, great or small, that sought that end. Its original logo, two cupped hands holding an image of the city, was an attempt to symbolize this idea of servanthood.

The laity   HCI was predominantly a lay venture. From the outset it was largely lay Christians who helped set up the Initiative, associated them-selves with its vision and furthered its work. Some were lay people of con-siderable influence in the life of Birmingham, linked with sectors such as business, health, education, law or local government. Others were less well known but active in a wide range of grass-roots projects, often located in very disadvantaged parts of Birmingham. In a city where they had played such a prominent role in the past, members of the Society of Friends were notable supporters of HCI. Many 'lay people' associated with other faiths also made an important contribution to HCI, not least as Trustees, members of the Governing Council and through the work of human city sites.

Hearings   HCI's mission statement described one of the Initiative's main purposes as bringing together 'those who share a vision of the human city'. Through the hearings held in 1997 and 2000, HCI demonstrated the way in which visioning and dialogue could become an integral part of the mission of the diaconal church. These more structured hearings were supple-mented by lively discussions that took place at gatherings of human city sites, by the visioning that characterized the Human City *Futures Papers* and by the sharing of stories through the columns of the *Bulletin*.

    The inclusiveness and openness of the image of 'the human city' enabled Christians involved in these hearings to share their visions of what it meant to them to be human, without this being seen as any form of proselytizing. Those holding different beliefs and convictions were encouraged to do the same. Thus a faith perspective on the building of the human city was given its due place in the visioning process. In a profound way, the hearings often transformed the ground where people met into 'holy ground' (Hull, 1993) simply because they were given the space to share their understanding of what it meant to be human.

Communal groups One of the central convictions of HCI was that a host of small communal groups working together had the power to transform the inhuman city. Thus HCI sought to foster the endeavours of any group seeking to bring more humanity into urban life. This purpose was behind the creation of human city sites and of the annual Human City Trails. It also motivated the setting up of the Human Neighbourhood Project and human neighbourhood sites in disadvantaged areas of Birmingham, Bradford and Swindon. HCI supported all such communal groups wherever they were located, be that in institutions such as schools, churches and the police service, or within local neighbourhoods.

Networks A good deal of HCI's energy went into enabling human city sites to network together. Networking happened through regular staff visits to sites, as well as through HCI's *Bulletin*, web site and the sites' *Newsletter*. The city-wide and intercity gatherings arranged by the Human Neighbourhood Project gave a personal touch to this networking process. In addition to connecting such groups, HCI sought to link together individuals, groups, organizations or institutions that expressed an interest in the creation of the human city. Here HCI's *Bulletin* again played a vital role, especially in the years following the setting up of the Institute in 1997.

The communal institution and partnerships The Human City Institute was an attempt to translate HCI into institutional form. It met with limited success (we return to this matter below). However, its Governing Council was as representative of the public, private and voluntary sectors as any such body serving a city the size of Birmingham could be. This wide and diverse representation gave Council members a glimpse of the holistic nature of the human city and stimulated the sharing of ideas across occupational and professional divides. It was, too, a tribute to HCI that other intermediary agencies, such as the Birmingham Chamber of Commerce, the Voluntary Service Council and Churches Together in Birmingham were prepared to lend their support.

The Institute sought to promote 'the human city' as an image of national and international significance. Through the Human Neighbourhood Project it 'exported' the idea of the human city from Birmingham to Bradford and Swindon. Internationally, it built close links with Chicago through an organization with a similar purpose known as 'Imagine Chicago', as well as with Johannesburg (HCI, *Futures Papers*, N1–4, 1999–2000).

Leadership   The success of the Human Neighbourhood Project was in large part due to the skill and sensitivity with which the Institute's project workers went about their task. Though none of them was Christian, they espoused a diaconal style of leadership, operating as community educators to equip the members of the human neighbourhood sites to become community builders. In the process the project workers became catalysts, enablers, intermediaries and resource persons, linking and connecting human neighbourhood sites. Another demanding task was enabling groups, hitherto marginalized or isolated, to gain the self-confidence to choose and develop their own agendas, and to share their experiences and ideas with one another. The process also required the project workers to act as resource persons by offering their skills, advice and knowledge wherever needed.

My own role as Director required similar skills. I operated as a community educator seeking to assist the citizens of Birmingham to build the human city as a city-wide community of learning communities and, as I hoped it could become, a city manifesting the gifts of the kingdom community. This task involved my acting as a catalyst, inspiring people to express and share their vision of the human city and encouraging them to put their vision into practice. It involved enabling both the vulnerable and the strong to see one another as partners in community building. It saw me acting as an intermediary between a wide diversity of groups, organizations and institutions from all sectors in the life of the city.

In hindsight, I recognize that I was fulfilling the role of the deacon as pioneer (Chapter 7). I was involved in trying to help the church to discern the kingdom community at work within the life of Birmingham, often manifesting itself in very unexpected places, and to recognize the communal potential of the metropolis as a means of transforming our world into a global community. A key part of this diaconal role was trying to exemplify for lay people what it might mean to be the servants of the kingdom community in different spheres of city life.

A diaconal style of leadership typified not only the work of HCI's staff, but the organization as a whole. The Institute was itself an 'intermediary agency'. In the first phase up to 1997, HCI exercised this intermediary role as a 'Christian' agency; after 1997, as a 'human' agency. It was this transition that enabled HCI to serve an ever-widening constituency of those of all faiths and convictions. HCI's Governing Council also possessed this intermediary character. It was regarded by most people as free of the vested interests associated with other agencies, private, public and even voluntary, which often seemed to be pursuing their own relatively closed agendas.

The Christendom church

HCI received little active support from the institutional church. There was some initial curiosity about an initiative that began as a Christian endeavour, the Secretary of Birmingham Churches Together being particularly supportive. However, after 1997, when HCI moved from being an overtly Christian to becoming a 'Human' Initiative, suspicion of 'the secular city' surfaced and the Christendom church's propensity for *sacralism* and *conservatism* came to the fore. Despite numerous approaches, the Roman Catholic Archdiocese never associated itself with HCI. After offering HCI initial support, the other mainstream denominations took relatively little interest in the Initiative.

Nor did the institutional church respond to the interest and excitement that HCI created among many lay Christians involved in the life of Birmingham. A few clergy gave stalwart service to HCI over the years. However, *clericalism* still seemed to hold sway and although the *Bulletin* was mailed to all Birmingham clergy few showed much interest in the Initiative. In the first phase of HCI's work, an attempt to promote a 'human city Sunday' (when worship and prayers would be focused on the needs of the city) failed, and attempts to set up gatherings and hearings on the theme of 'the human church' met with a poor response.

HCI's move to a more explicitly open 'human' agenda after 1997 was a challenge to its Christian supporters to find ways of pursuing the mission of the church in new and untried ways. Many responded magnificently; others quickly fell away. The response to this more open-ended form of mission showed that many lay people have a long way to go before they are liberated from *conformism* and freed to fulfil their ministry as community builders in the life of the secular city.

The Christendom church in Birmingham remained at the mercy of *parochialism*. In attitude as well as organizationally, it was preoccupied with community of place and thus unable to understand or engage with HCI as a diaconal initiative that embraced communities of occupation and concern. Most clergy continued to focus their attention on the local neighbourhood and had little time to give to the needs of their lay people embedded in the life of Birmingham, and who urgently needed the church to affirm and equip them for their ministry there.

A major problem of the Christendom church in Birmingham, however, was its unwillingness, as well as inability, to operate as a partner with other institutions in community building. *Separatism* not only existed between the denominations, and the different faiths, but also characterized the relationship of the church to the city's secular institutions. The Church of England was somewhat more practised at engaging in such partnerships, but *imperialism* was evident in the way it frequently saw itself as pre-eminent among other denominations. The church as a whole seemed held fast by the mould of Christendom and unable to respond, even in a modest way, to the servant ministry of the kingdom community that HCI was trying to further.

Other challenges

The termination of HCI's ongoing work in 2004 was the result of a number of other factors that should not be laid at the door of the institutional church.

It was clear that the Human Neighbourhood Project, stretching HCI's limited resources across three cities, came to loom far too large in the life of the Initiative. In the end, a great deal of the time and energy of HCI's staff were consumed by it and the core funding of the Institute became over-dependent on it.

Even more significantly, however, the demands of the Human Neighbourhood Project led to the neglect of two other initiatives which, in the long term, could have made a significant contribution to building Birmingham as a human city: the hearings of 1997 and 2000, and the annual Human City Sites Trails of 1998 and 1999. The first of these offered a unique process for visioning and dialogue across occupational, social and cultural divides; the second, a model for a city-wide mosaic of small human endeavours which, when working together, had the potential to offer a new synergy for building the human city.

Conclusion

The Human City Initiative lasted ten years, though its vision and its work may yet be revived, as we have noted. However, from the perspective of the diaconal church, HCI's importance lies not so much in its 'success' or 'failure' as in what it can teach us about a diaconal model of mission.

The model of mission espoused by the Human City Initiative exemplified many facets of what a diaconal church's model of mission might look like. It was a model developed from principles, insights and ways of working that included the following:

- Offering a vision of 'the human city' as a means of enabling those of all faiths and convictions to work together to build communities transformed by the gifts of the kingdom community: life, liberation, love and learning.
- Taking a stance of servanthood not of control.
- Upholding the primacy of the laity and their role as community builders in the church's mission to the city.
- Recognizing the importance of hearings as a means of fostering visioning and dialogue.
- Harnessing the power of small communal groups to bring humanity to the city.
- Networking a plethora of small groups in order to create the synergy to transform the city into a human city.
- Entering into partnerships with other bodies, secular and religious, to work together to make visions of the human city a reality.
- Operating as a team of community educators to equip people to build the human city as a community of learning communities.

That the legacy of Christendom hindered the institutional church from encouraging such an imaginative and creative diaconal initiative as HCI, once again underlines how critical it is that this legacy be jettisoned.

12

Sector ministers and industrial chaplains

Leadership

Introduction

Although itinerant preachers in the early church depended on the material support of small groups of Christians to help sustain them in their ministry, many earned what they could when they could. Luke was a doctor, Paul a tent-maker. After Constantine, however, the land and wealth that steadily accrued to the Church meant that a full-time ordained ministry gradually became the norm and remained the case in all the mainstream denominations until well into the twentieth century.

Anglican ministers in secular employment

The industrial revolution and the urbanization of society ushered in a reappraisal of normative practices. 'The earliest challenge to traditional constraints on the secular employment of the clergy came from Thomas Arnold (1795–1842), headmaster of Rugby' (Vaughan, 1990, p. 26) in a pamphlet entitled *Order of Deacons*. In this he called for the repeal of all canon laws that prevented an Anglican deacon following a secular profession. His reasons for this call included not only the need to address a shortage of clergy in industrial towns, but also the desire to sanctify the world of business, a concern to bridge the false division between clergy and laity, the wish to widen the spectrum of social class from which the clergy came, and the hope that the concept of team ministry, including ordained and laity, would grow (pp. 28–30). Though no significant change came about as a result of Arnold's pamphlet, these issues were to reverberate across the church and down the years for a century and more.

In 1923 Roland Allen, an Anglican priest and missionary, now regarded as the *animateur* for the church's acceptance of ordained ministers being employed in secular occupations, published his book *Voluntary Clergy* (Vaughan, 1990, pp. 74 f.), a powerful apologetic for 'men in Full Orders, exercising their ministry but not dependent on it for their livelihood' (p. 81). Despite Allen's advocacy, however, it was not until 1960 that significant changes began to occur. In that year, the Southwark Ordination Course, a three-year part-time course, was set up to train for the priesthood men who were still in secular employment. This initiative was to pave the way for the first ordinations of 12 'non-stipendiary ministers' in the Church of England in 1970. By 1981 this figure had reached 123 per annum. Since then an average of about a hundred such ordinations per year has been maintained. In 2003 the *Church of England Year Book* recorded that the Anglican Church had 1,779 non-stipendiary ministers, 993 men and 786 women.

Most non-stipendiary ministers in the Church of England see their role as a presbyteral one. The focus of their ordained ministry is the local parish church, on whose staff they usually serve part-time. However, some 10 per cent of non-stipendiary ministers (NSMs) (the majority are priests but there are a few deacons) believe their calling is not primarily to the parish but to the world of work. They have come to be known as 'ministers in secular employment' (MSEs), and it is with their ministry, together with that of Methodist sector ministers and of industrial chaplains, that we are primarily concerned in this chapter.

In the 1970s a number of Anglican MSEs began to meet in London. They were known as the Wardrobe group (they first gathered at St Andrew's in the Wardrobe). At their instigation, the first national conference of MSEs was held in 1984 at Nottingham University with about 150 people attending. At that conference a statement on MSEs was drawn up to indicate the focus of their workplace ministry. Two years later a second conference was held in Manchester, with other conferences following at regular intervals. In 1993 a new association, CHRISM (Christians in Secular Ministry), was formed. This aimed to embrace MSEs of all denominations, as well as lay people, 'to celebrate the presence of God and the holiness of life in work, and to see and tell the Christian story there' (CIPL, R11, 1994), though, in practice, CHRISM has remained an association largely made up of Anglican clergy. In 2004 it had a paid-up membership of about 125. CHRISM currently holds an annual conference and an annual retreat. It publishes an informative quarterly journal entitled *Ministers-at-Work*.

Methodist sector ordained ministers

Background

Within Wesleyan Methodism, it was possible for ministers to obtain 'permission to serve' external organizations as far back as the nineteenth century, though most of these appointments were in Christian organizations such as the British and Foreign Bible Society (Clark, 1986). Immediately after World War Two, 40 men were granted 'permission to serve' a number of government agencies, universities, teacher training colleges and one school, though all Methodist ministers were normally expected to serve for some years full-time in circuit work before it was considered appropriate for them to seek employment outside Methodism. By 1957, 53 Methodist ministers had 'permission to serve'.

Up to the mid 1960s, however, the Methodist Conference was still reluctant to widen the list of 'permitted organizations' in which ordained ministers might be employed full-time, even refusing to allow teaching (other than religious education) and lecturing in training colleges (other than those under the authority of Methodism) to be included on the 'permitted' list. As a result, the 1960s saw a significant number of Methodist ministers relinquishing their ordained status in order to go into teaching and a number of other 'unlisted' posts.

In response to increasing disquiet about this situation, the Methodist Conference of 1967 set up a 'Commission on the Church's Ministries in the Modern World', with the brief to review the situation regarding ministers requesting 'permission to serve' external organizations. The Commission's two reports to the Methodist Conferences of 1968 and 1970 remain a milestone in the development of 'sector ministry', a term coined by the Commission, and the Methodist equivalent of the Anglican term 'ministers in secular employment'. By 'sector', the Commission meant a distinctive sphere of work in the life of society such as education, health, social welfare, law and order or industry.

The missiological stance of the Commission can be illustrated by the following quotations from its reports (Methodist Conference, 1968, 1970).

There is a growing conviction that the circuit system alone as we know it is quite inadequate if we are to fulfil our task of presenting the Gospel to our age. New patterns of ministry are needed if the church is to exercise the ministries of Christ in present-day society, and such patterns are beginning to emerge from the thinking . . . of every denomination. (1970, p. 4)

The ministry of laymen will be the principal means of Christian impact in the sectors. It is through their skills and experiences that Christian insight and understanding will be offered. The problem is that the Christians in [a particular] sector are often unrelated to each other, and their gifts and experience unco-ordinated. They often lack the opportunity to consult with those who can help them to develop Christian insights within the context of their sector. (1968, p. 2)

The church in the sector will depend largely on the skills and experience of its laymen and women. Here the minister will be the servant, bringing the gifts and skills of his own ministry and training. His coming should enable the abilities and understanding of his lay colleagues to be fully released and co-ordinated. (1968, p. 3)

The role of an ordained minister in a sector is not different from his role in a neighbourhood . . . but the way in which he fulfils this role depends on his station. [He will be] more conscious of his role as an 'enabler', a co-ordinator and a resource person, especially in biblical, theological and ethical questions. (1970, p. 3)

It is important that the minister in the sector should come to his appointment with the full authority of the [Methodist] Conference and bring with him the sense of being related to the whole church. (1968, p. 2)

One of our main intentions is to get rid of the notion that ministers who are not paid directly by the church are working outside the church. Instead we want it to be accepted that some ministers should serve where our people are working. (1968, p. 4)

We expect that the sort of ministry we envisage will, as soon as possible, be planned and fulfilled ecumenically. (1968, p. 1)

Following the recommendations of the 1967 Commission, the Methodist Conference agreed to reinstate those ministers who had been refused 'permission to serve' and who had consequently relinquished their ordained status (provided that they reaffirmed their calling to the Methodist ministry). In 1969 a Committee for Ministry in the Sectors was set up with a full-time Secretary. However, Methodist ministers were still required to serve in a circuit appointment before being allowed to move from circuit ministry into sector ministry, and a quota of the number permitted to move into the sectors was set annually. By 1976 there were 97 ministers in sector appointments, and by 1986, 135, most of these serving in education, social work or the probation service.

The Methodist Sectors Group

I had myself received permission to become a sector minister when I transferred from circuit work in London to the staff of Westhill College, Birmingham, in 1973. Over the next few years, however, I became aware that Methodism was honouring the letter and not the spirit of the 1967 Commission's recommendations. Although more ministers were taking up sector appointments, Methodism as a whole, especially its circuit ministers, remained very ambivalent about sector ministry. At the same time, contacts between ministers who were working in the sectors remained few and far between.

In 1981, therefore, I circulated a paper arguing for 'the awakening of a Christian voice and the building of Christian community within each sector and across sectors which can give continuing expression to the meaning of the Gospel for our time'. I added that 'the need is for . . . reflection and discussion (involving lay people as well as sector ministers) to be carried out in the context of the search for a Christian spirituality and Christian political awareness relevant to the modern world' (Clark, 1981). My practical suggestion was for the Methodist Church to convene a meeting of sector ministers to address this agenda.

In April 1982, as a response to my paper, a meeting of sector ministers took place in Birmingham. However, this meeting was convened not by the Methodist Church, which still remained ill at ease with the concept of sector ministry, but by sector ministers themselves. Twelve ministers attended; there were 13 apologies. An agreement was reached to meet again in June 1983 at Cliff College in Derbyshire. The Cliff College meeting attracted 21 people, including some Wesley deaconesses working in the sectors. It became a gathering of an almost cathartic nature. As one participant put it:

In the opening session each one of us spoke freely about ourselves and created an experience that could only be covered by a whole kaleidoscope of adjectives. There was hurt, the hurt of parting (from our Church) and the hurt that was a result of the things that were said and done at that parting. There is still for many a sense of isolation, for some admittedly self-inflicted but for more, stemming from a lack of understanding from others within and without the ministry, of those forms of ministry which the Church does not see as ordained. I sensed no bitterness in any of this, only sadness. (SOM, 1983)

The Cliff College weekend decided on a further gathering in the autumn of 1983, this time in Blackpool. At that meeting, a 'Statement of Intent' was drawn up that formalized the creation of a Methodist Sectors Group and, among other things, committed members to gather together residentially twice a year, to meet in regional groups, to offer one another mutual support through prayer and to explore the implications of experience in the sectors for the future of ordained Christian ministries. It was decided that the group should be open for lay people to join and a few did so. A newsletter was produced and, from September 1985, a *Sectors Newsletter* published. By 1986 there were around 50 people on the mailing list; gatherings attracted some two dozen.

In 1985 the group was given fresh impetus when the Methodist Conference set up another 'Commission on the Church's Ministries in the Modern World' to review all forms of ministry in the Methodist Church in the light of changing needs. The Sectors Group, representing as it did ministers who had felt marginalized almost from the outset of the new era promised in 1970, was eager to persuade Methodism to recognize the importance of sector ministry. In 1986 the Commission presented its initial report to the Methodist Conference, but it was asked to consult more widely, revise a number of sections and bring an amended report to the Conference in 1988.

At its autumn meeting in 1986, the Sectors Group considered at some length a paper that I had been asked to prepare that contained many recommendations to the Commission (Clark, 1986). These recommendations were debated by members of the Sectors Group throughout 1987, on one occasion with officers from the Methodist Division of Ministries who were present. In March 1988 the Sectors Group submitted its final recommendations to the Commission.

Its main concerns were for greater mutual accountability (of the church to the sectors and the sectors to the church), for sector ministers to be seen as integral members of team ministries based on local churches or circuits, and for an annual gathering of sector ministers to be convened by the Methodist Church at national level. There was strong opposition by the Sectors Group to the quota system by which the needs of the circuits always took precedence over the needs of the sectors. The group also asked if it could be allowed a representative at the Methodist Conference to speak to its recommendations, but the Division of Ministries deemed this to be unnecessary.

The Commission's final report to the Methodist Conference, entitled *The Ministry of the People of God* (1988) was, from the perspective of the Sectors Group, a damp squib. The Commission failed to include any of the Sectors Group's recommendations as firm proposals. Worse still, it confirmed the 'persistent opinion within some parts of the Methodist Church that [sector ministers] are doing a job which could equally well be done by lay people' (05 (iii)). However, it did go on to add:

> Conference has examined this viewpoint on a number of occasions and each time has reaffirmed its commitment to ministry in the Sectors. Some of the work done by those working in this area is innovative and pioneering; some arises from a deep sense of call and commitment to a particular sector; some is an indication of specific skills which some of our ministers possess or have been encouraged to acquire. Much of it brings new insights and resources into the life of the churches.

The ambivalent response of the Commission to the hard work put in by the Sectors Groups to get Methodism to give more overt and structured support to the ministries of its members took its toll on the group. A sense of rejection and powerlessness was experienced by many sector ministers involved in the discussions, and a rapid decline in the membership of the group followed. By the end of 1988, lack of numbers meant that the group's annual conference had to be cancelled. The last *Newsletter* appeared in October 1988 and from 1989 the Sectors Group ceased to meet. In 1990 the Methodist Conference's report on *The Ministry of the People of God in the World*, a follow-up to *The Ministry of the People of God*, made no reference to sector ministry as such. Although, over the next three or four years, Methodism's Division of Ministries did take the initiative in convening a number of 'voluntary' gatherings of sector ministers at Luton Industrial College, these too eventually petered out.

In the 1990s, sector ministry in the Methodist Church drifted further away from the bold vision of the late 1960s. Other than the fact that it was at last agreed that ministers could be employed in the sectors without first having to serve in a circuit appointment, sector ministry received no further consideration by the Methodist Conference. A Methodist Conference report of 2002, *On Being Ordained in Full Connexion*, expressed the view that within the Methodist Church as a whole the category of sector minister had become 'marginalized' (1.2). Apart from the church's ambivalence about this form of ministry, two other factors underlined this 'marginalization'. One was the increasing number of people offering for ordination as a second career. Those ordained out of the sectors were unlikely to want to return to the sectors. The other factor was the emergence of a new category of 'local ordained minister'. This encouraged lay people to be ordained in order to take on the role of part-time presbyter within their local church while remaining in secular employment. The Methodist Church showed far more interest in this new presbyteral category of minister than it had ever done with respect to sector ministry.

In 2002 the Methodist Conference opted to get rid of all categories of ordained minister other than those of 'presbyter' or 'deacon'. Those working in the sectors were defined, negatively, as being 'in appointments not in the control of the church' (*Minutes of the Annual Conference*, 2004, pp. 182–5). Within this broad category, there are now (2004) only 76 sector ministers, the large majority working in education. However, it is worth noting that within this category are also listed some 50 full-time chaplains, a steadily increasing number.

Industrial Mission

One other important category of work-related ordained ministry is that of chaplain. Though many chaplaincies are still funded by the church, their relationship to the world of work means that their role is relevant to this chapter. Our focus is here on Industrial Mission, as embracing a particular model of chaplaincy that appears to have many diaconal features.

There is some debate as to whether Industrial Mission originated in Scotland, south London or Sheffield (Reindorp, 2000, pp. 4–6). However, as our case study, we focus on industrial chaplaincy as developed through the pioneering endeavours of the Sheffield Industrial Mission.

The Sheffield Industrial Mission was established in 1944. It was the inspiration of the then Bishop of Sheffield, Bishop Hunter, but given impetus and shape by Ted Wickham, the Mission's first leader. Bishop Hunter's vision was for 'a "re-evangelization of Britain", through the co-operation of all Christian communities, and by means of a partnership between clergy and laity' (*Industrial Mission*, 1988, p. 37). Bagshaw (1994) sees the Sheffield Industrial Mission (SIM) passing through a number of different phases up to the mid 1990s (when his book was written).

Before 1959, SIM was very much concerned with 'new expressions of church' (Bagshaw, 1994, p. 9f.). This first phase saw chaplains working outside the existing structures of the church, making contacts with industry, visiting on an individual basis and loosely knit into a chaplaincy team. From 1955 onwards SIM sought to establish autonomous 'lay projects' whereby lay people employed by Sheffield steel firms would gather groups together to explore the meaning of Christian discipleship at work and to offer pastoral care. However, attempts to spread this form of mission met with some resistance from church authorities afraid that the lay people might be drawn away from a commitment to their local church. At the end of this period, Ted Wickham's hopes of becoming a non-territorial bishop of a national industrial mission programme came to nothing when he was 'neutralized as a political force' (p. 41) by being made Suffragan Bishop of Middleton.

The second phase, which began in the 1960s, saw SIM in some disarray. Bishop Hunter was replaced by John Taylor as Bishop of Sheffield, and Ted Wickham was replaced by Michael Jackson as the Mission's leader. The new leadership was more conservative in character than the old, the emphasis shifting from a freelance style of mission to industry based on a para-church model, to the gathering of people into more formalized groups with closer ties to the institutional church for study and reflection. As Bagshaw puts it (p. 58), throughout the period 'the underlying battle was between traditional faith and radical and dangerous innovation' seen as inspired by the 'secular theology' of the 1960s, and espoused by most SIM chaplains, as well as by Ted Wickham himself. These tensions, together with Bishop Taylor's cautious stance and Michael Jackson's autocratic style of leadership, led to a number of chaplains being asked to leave SIM (CIPL, Rowland Goodwin, E2, 1992). The involvement in SIM of a number of chaplains from denominations other than the Church of England was also called into question.

The Forder Enquiry of 1969 spelt out three future aims for a third phase in the life of SIM (Bagshaw, 1994, p. 69). These aims were to win Christian disciples, to bring Christian faith to bear on industrial society and to offer Christian pastoral care to workers. Thus the 1970s saw SIM continuing to take on a more 'churchy' approach to its work (p. 75), with less emphasis on social justice and on standing shoulder-to-shoulder with the man or woman on the shop floor over against the 'bosses'.

The 1980s, with the coming of the Thatcher era, ushered in a fourth phase for SIM. It now had to respond to a very different economic and political climate. First, there was a steep decline in the fortunes of heavy industry (including the Sheffield steel works), a move towards service industries and the growing domination of information technology. The service industries, and especially the retail sector, gradually emerged as a new focus for chaplaincy. Second, throughout the late 1970s and 1980s, came the decline of the trades unions. This strengthened the growing tendency for chaplains to identify with management rather than workers. Third, the 1980s saw a massive rise in unemployment. The emergence of the Manpower Services Commission led to a demand for industrial chaplains, who often possessed the necessary experience, to head up a range of government initiatives to alleviate unemployment. 'This placed chaplains in a new position, often a much more satisfying one, and enabled a whole string of new models of Industrial Mission to develop' (Reindorp, 2000, p. 8). However, as unemployment declined, the schemes related to it ended and this window of opportunity gradually closed.

In 1990 its fifth phase saw SIM taking on the title and stance of 'Industrial Mission in South Yorkshire', 'an ecumenical agency, serving as a link between the world of faith and the world of work' (Reindorp, 2002, p. 128). Its mission was now defined more broadly (as was the case with other industrial mission agencies: CIPL, Rowland Goodwin, E2, 1992) as that of 'developing and sustaining diverse forms of Christian presence in the world of work; sharing in the creation of Christian understandings of economic, social and political issues; working to promote God's justice . . . alongside people within and outside the church; [and] encouraging the whole church in South Yorkshire in its engagement with the world of work' (Bagshaw, 1994, p. 128).

In the late 1980s and 1990s, a shift towards the retail sector gradually brought with it a recognition that institutions concerned with serving the public needed to give greater attention to personal relationships with regard to their customers, clients or patients. This concern with 'the human factor' has been one reason for the growth of chaplaincies in sectors such as retail, the travel industry, the health service, the police service, the prison service and the fire service.

More recently, chaplains have also been required to respond to a growing interest in 'the spirituality of work' (Bagshaw, 1994, p. 112). Some employers have come to see the accessing of 'spiritual resources' as a means of addressing worker stress, rapidly on the increase because of the pressures of a competitive economy, long hours and the greater insecurity of employment as permanent contracts are phased out. Here chaplains face the difficult task of differentiating between a superficial 'consumer spirituality', and a kingdom spirituality that is about confronting inhuman practices as well as supporting those suffering as a result.

Although chaplaincy continues to develop and in some places to flourish, though often on a part-time and voluntary basis, the institutional church has steadily become less willing, as well as less able financially to support it. Thus over recent years, 'the number of full-time posts has dramatically declined and many posts have been combined with a parish base' (Reindorp, 2000, p. 10). Such posts are increasingly seen by a church struggling to survive as an optional extra to what is believed to be the primary task of maintaining the local church.

In what follows, we address the task of identifying the extent to which sector ministry and chaplaincy, particularly industrial chaplaincy, offer us examples of the diaconal church in action, especially in relation to the issue of leadership (Chapter 7). We then review those attributes of the Christendom church that have prevented such ministries fulfilling their potential. Finally, we look at other factors that limit the development of sector ministry and chaplaincy.

(In the following section, the term 'sector ministers' is taken to include both Methodist sector ministers and Church of England ministers in secular employment (MSEs).)

Breaking the mould of Christendom?

The diaconal church

Where sector ministers and industrial chaplains have adopted a diaconal approach to their ministries, they have helped to blaze a trail for the emergence of the diaconal church as a whole, and of the development of the role of deacon in particular. In what follows, our discussion focuses on what is to be learnt about the nature of the diaconal church and role of deacon from those sector ministers and industrial chaplains who have adopted a diaconal form of leadership.

Mission   'Kingdom theology has been at the heart of Industrial Mission', writes Reindorp (2000, p. 63). Many sector ministers and industrial chaplains have seen themselves as, first and foremost, 'ministers of the kingdom' (Baelz and Jacob, 1985) and 'working for the kingdom' (Fuller and Vaughan, 1986). They have interpreted their role as discerning and making known the signs of the kingdom community within the life of a secular society. Their primary concern as diaconal leaders has not been to draw those with whom they come into contact into the gathered church, but to enable them to build communities that manifest the gifts of the kingdom community wherever they work.

Culture   Sector ministers and industrial chaplains affirm that the world of work is as fully the realm of God's activity as is the church. Nevertheless, they challenge and seek to transform inhuman working practices. In more recent years, some chaplains have been involved, often with those who are not Christians, in seeking to develop a spirituality of work as an alternative perspective to an all-pervasive materialistic market-driven culture (see Mulligan, *IMA Agenda*, April 2004, pp. 12–13; Caton, *IMA Agenda*, November 2004, pp. 2–13).

Stance   Many sector ministers and industrial chaplains have sought to exercise their ministry as servants of the kingdom community. They have exemplified the power of redemptive love through standing alongside their colleagues in the workplace rather than replicating a coercive ecclesiastical (or secular) authority exercised from above. They have regarded themselves as being on a journey of spiritual discovery to learn more about the nature of the kingdom community. In the process, they have tried to gain a deeper understanding of organizations as learning communities, and to discover how such communities might be sustained in a society based on economic competition.

The laity   Industrial chaplains have repeatedly asserted that one of their major concerns is 'encouraging lay people who seek to express their faith at work' (*Industrial Mission*, 1988, p. xiv). In its early days, the Sheffield Industrial Mission (SIM) was very much engaged with lay-led groups that included many non-churchgoers (Reindorp, 2000, p. 8). In more recent years a number of those involved in the Industrial Mission have set up groups, usually on a diocesan basis and outside the workplace, to help lay people explore faith and work issues (see CIPL, Olwen Smith, R2, 1992; CIPL, Ann Leonard, G8, 1993; CIPL, David Welbourn, R12, 1994), though these have been occasional or one-off initiatives.

Of particular interest here has been the pioneering work of Peter Challen of the South London Industrial Mission in developing what he has called 'theological auditing' (Challen in Clark, 1997, pp. 115–16). This is a process whereby individuals or groups (by no means always Christians) are helped to reflect on their working lives in the light of 'themes of faith' such as 'creation', 'jubilee', 'shalom' and 'covenant'. They then explore how these themes might be applied to and expressed through their work.

However, SIM, as with most Industrial Missions, has always 'set [its] face against Christian groups [meeting] in the workplace' (Harold Clarke, *IMA Agenda*, June 2004, p. 3). The general feeling has been that the inclusive and open nature of the workplace has to be honoured and that if Christians employed there wish to come together as the gathered church, this should be off work premises and out of working hours. (For a different viewpoint see Chapter 13, pages 254–64.)

Hearings and communal groups The 'missionary approach [of Industrial Mission] has been "dialogical" – a willingness to listen and learn as well as to give and share' (*Industrial Mission*, 1988, p. 87). Industrial chaplains have also been proactive in the use of communal groups as mini learning communities to enable the laity to explore issues of faith and work in relation to the organizations they served. Thus the communal group and the hearing have been very much to the fore in Industrial Mission.

Networks Industrial Mission has increasingly used networking as a means of fostering mutual support among chaplains. A major development in this context was the setting up of the Industrial Mission Association (IMA) in 1969. IMA now publishes a lively quarterly magazine entitled *IMA Agenda* and holds a bi-annual conference as a means of linking teams of chaplains across the country. Sector ministers too have regarded networking as an important means of strengthening the links between them, as the history of the Methodist Sectors Group shows. The Anglican MSEs' association, CHRISM, also offers important networking opportunities to its members through its magazine *Ministers-at-Work*, its web site and an annual conference and retreat.

The communal institution   The only attempts at institution building have been SIM's abortive attempt at the end of the 1950s to set up a non-territorial diocese and, more recently, occasional calls for a similar kind of body to meet the needs of MSEs (see *Ministers-at-Work*, January 2004, p. 19).

Partnerships   Sector ministers and industrial chaplains have been at the forefront of promoting an ecumenical approach to mission in the work context. Both the Methodist Sectors Group and CHRISM (MSEs) have invited members of other denominations to join their networks or attend their conferences. In 1987 the two associations explored setting up a 'Ministers in Secular Work Ecumenical Network' (*Methodist Sectors Group Newsletter*, June 1987, No. 8), but the demise of the Sectors Group aborted this initiative. Despite a temporary setback for ecumenical relations in the mid 1960s, SIM also remained fully committed to working ecumenically, and in 1990 became an ecumenical body entitled Industrial Mission in South Yorkshire.

Leadership   The leadership role of sector ministers and industrial chaplains has frequently reflected our own understanding of the role of deacon. Many have operated in diaconal mode, working alongside lay people and non-Christians alike in trying to create secular organizations that reflect the nature of the kingdom community. 'The role of enabler or catalyst . . . is a key one for the MSE' (Eric Forshaw in Fuller and Vaughan, 1986, p. 71), as it is for the industrial chaplain. Many have acted as intermediaries, bridging the divides between management and workers, between occupations and between professions, as well as between church and world. Sector ministers and industrial chaplains have also seen themselves as resource persons for those, Christian or otherwise, involved in the world of work as well as for the institutional church. Though beginning very much as a male preserve, sector ministry and industrial chaplaincy have become fully open to women.

Nevertheless, despite the many features of the diaconal church, and especially of diaconal church leadership, displayed by sector ministers and industrial chaplains, there have been a number of factors that have prevented them helping the church to gain a clear and credible understand of the role of deacon. We explore these factors below.

The Christendom church

Ministry to the world of work 'has been done against a background in which for much of the time the Christendom model of society has been taken for granted' (Reindorp, 2000, p. 61). Despite the many diaconal features of the ministry of sector ministers and industrial chaplains, their ability to fufil the role of deacon has been severely circumscribed and sometimes negated by the dominance of a Christendom model of church.

The *sacralism* and *proselytism* inherent within the Christendom church have made it very difficult for sector ministers and industrial chaplains to find support for their conviction that they are 'ministers of the kingdom'. Within a church where there is so much emphasis on the gathered congregation, ministers who do not gather, and thus do not appear to contribute to the maintenance of the gathered congregation, are regarded as something of an anomaly.

Added to its restrictive understanding of mission, the *clericalism* of the Christendom church has led to considerable 'resistance thrown up by an entrenched parochial and stipendiary system' (Vaughan, 1990, p. vi). Ordained ministers who are engaged in the world of work are regarded by some as a threat to the 'real' ministry of the presbyter. Sector ministers and industrial chaplains are viewed as blurring the distinction between church and world and thus the 'apartness' of the ordained. Their Christian identity is felt to be compromised by overexposure to a secular and humanistic culture. It is felt, especially by parish clergy, that these ministries lead to a devaluing of the gathered church and of the difficult and sometimes onerous task of sustaining it.

At the same time, sector ministers are seen as benefiting from both the status (and the salary) of a secular occupation. Their independence enables them to question the authority and resist the control of the church with a freedom not available to those employed by the church itself. These are powerful criticisms for sector ministers and industrial chaplains to handle. As a result many of them have felt under considerable pressure to deflect these attacks by undertaking overtly presbyteral duties, over and above their work-related ministries.

Many lay people also feel uncomfortable with the idea of sector ministry and, to a lesser extent, that of industrial chaplaincy. For them, *parochialism* 'in geographical terms [can become] as restrictive as parochialism in terms of vision and understanding' (*Industrial Mission*, 1988, p. 105). This leads to a very limited understanding of what ordained ministers are doing in the world of work. *Conformism* has also led lay people to collude with the idea of the clerical profession as 'a holy order' that should restrict itself to things 'spiritual' and not get involved in the secular world of work, and the evils that are seen as an integral part of it.

The *institutionalism* of the Christendom model of church has reinforced these objections to the ministry of the ordained in the working world. Major reservations about sector ministry have been expressed in a number of reports to the Methodist Conference. Likewise, Industrial Mission 'remains deeply marked by the church's continuing failure to take real interest in it,' writes Mostyn Davies (1991, p. 10). Nor has much notice been taken of the many attempts made by sector ministers and industrial chaplains to feed back to the institutional church what they have discovered about the meaning of mission in the world of work. Because of these factors, the authority of both these forms of ministry has been considerably weakened

The *authoritarianism* and *unilateralism* of the Christendom church have dogged sector ministry and industrial chaplaincy. A Christendom church has more often stepped in to constrain initiatives in this field than to encourage them. A concern to control and constrict has been clearly demonstrated by such events as the termination of the worker-priest movement in France by the Roman Catholic hierarchy in 1954 (not discussed in this chapter), the undermining of Ted Wickham's influence over the future of SIM, described by Bagshaw as the 'revenge of the church hierarchy' (1994, p. 65) and the negative attitude of Methodism towards its sector ministers' contribution to *The Ministry of the People of God* report in 1988.

'English IM is still too dependent on relationships with individual bishops, with diocesan structures and boundaries,' writes Reindorp (2000, p. 62). Thus, industrial chaplaincies have remained 'peripheral to the church structures' (*Industrial Mission*, 1988, p. 95) and particularly vulnerable where the church has financed them in part or in whole. Over the years teams of industrial chaplains that were once vital in giving chaplains a peer group to support them in a demanding form of ministry have steadily declined in size and strength.

Other challenges

A secular society and a market-led economy

Sector ministers and industrial chaplains face not only ecclesiastical but also secular resistance to their role. A secular society, even when inclusive and open, does not speak religious language. 'When the church leaves its own place and enters worldly places . . . its language has a definite remoteness, and familiarity no longer serves to give it meaning' (Reindorp, 2000, p. 50). There is thus an increasing communication problem for Christians within the world of work, one becoming more acute as Western culture grows steadily away from its Christian roots. The coming of a multifaith society, with its diverse religious languages and symbols, also makes communicating the distinctiveness of Christian faith to a secular society more problematic.

Where the secular world does retain a picture of what is meant by 'the church', this is all too often an image of a Christendom church in which priest means parish. For this reason, some people continue to suspect that the only reason that sector ministers and industrial chaplains are found working outside the parish is to infiltrate the workplace and get people (back) to church. Thus it can take considerable time and tact for sector ministers and industrial chaplains to gain the trust and confidence of their fellow workers.

More recent changes in the culture and ethos of western society also call into question the ministries of sector ministers and industrial chaplains. *Industrial Mission – An Appraisal* commented (1988, p. 43) that 'a new, harsh "realism" had entered British political and economic life [with] the great theological themes which had so influenced IM, creation, incarnation, reconciliation, servanthood [now giving way to those of] crucifixion, judgment and apocalypse'. The Thatcher era as such may be over, but a market culture that is closed to many kingdom community values is now deeply entrenched. The communal needs of a market-driven, highly competitive and mobile world remain as urgent as ever, and many sector ministers and industrial chaplains are trying to respond to these as best they can. But it is a world that is often inhospitable if not hostile to the church they ostensibly represent.

Presbyters and 'laity' but not deacons

Despite the undoubted value of their ministry, however, there remains one major reason why sector ministers and industrial chaplains are not offering church and world a clear and credible understanding of the role of deacon, and demonstrating its vital importance for community building in a world facing chaos. All too many sector ministers and industrial chaplains collude with the expectations of the Christendom church, and of many secular organizations, by interpreting their role as that of presbyter (and, in the case of some sector ministers, as that of lay person). In the process, they devalue and undermine the role of deacon (see Figure 4, p. 112).

In the case of sector ministers, Vaughan (1990) suggests that they may be seeking to reduce 'the dissonance arising from their non-normative roles as "layman" on the parish staff, and "clergyman" in the workplace ... by playing down the "work" aspect of ministry, and by emphasizing the "parish" aspects' (p. 318). Thus sector ministers are tempted to justify their presence in the workplace by majoring on the presbyteral dimension of that role. On occasions, some sector ministers choose to wear a clerical collar at work to reaffirm their presbyteral identity. Many interpret their role as a pastoral one while others readily celebrate the Christian rites of passage for work colleagues.

On the other hand, where sector ministers refuse to assume a presbyteral role at work they are often seen as lay people who have chosen to act as presbyters at weekends. Yet if they attempt to adopt a higher profile by engaging in a more 'prophetic' style of ministry in the workplace, 'the likelihood is that such prophets will soon find themselves out of a job' (Fuller and Vaughan, 1986, p. 211). Expectations and pressures such as these hinder, if not prevent, many sector ministers developing the deacon's role of servant leader and community educator of the laity.

Industrial chaplains face similar role problems. 'Anglican led Industrial Mission [is] largely a clerical ministry,' states Reindorp (p. 11). Industrial chaplains, like sector ministers, are usually seen as presbyters exercising a ministry in the workplace, 'parish priests located in factories', as Bagshaw describes them (1994, p. 80). Thus their role is assumed to be largely that of pastor or counsellor. The dominance of the presbyteral role is even greater in the case of chaplains serving in schools and colleges, in hospitals or in the armed forces, where they regularly conduct services of worship and celebrate rites of passage as well as undertake pastoral duties.

Where industrial chaplains attempt to take a more critical or prophetic approach to the world of work, they often have to do so as 'lone mission-aries' (*Industrial Mission*, 1988, p. 88). As such, they risk being marginalized, not only by a Christendom church but also by the secular institutions with-in which they work, a dilemma that has constrained Industrial Mission since its inception. Here again external expectations and pressures have hindered chaplains acting as servant leaders and community educators of the laity.

While industrial chaplains (even when formally ordained as 'deacons') restrict themselves to a presbyteral role, and while sector ministers oscillate between the role of presbyter and lay person, the role of deacon is lost to the church. Furthermore, if industrial chaplains and sector ministers then seek to justify their presence in the world of work by claiming to be 'representa-tives of the church' in ways that lay people are not (a line that Crain and Seymour unfortunately take when considering the role of 'deacons' in the workplace: 2001, p. 105), they devalue the role of the laity as the diaconal church's primary representatives in the world.

The outcome of this role confusion is that, despite the occasional educa-tional initiatives taken by industrial chaplains, they and sector ministers are failing to fulfil the all-important diaconal role of equipping the laity for their ministry as community builders. The Church of England's appraisal of *Industrial Mission* in 1988 stated that 'IM has been noticeably unsuccessful in becoming a lay movement' (p. 81). Bagshaw, at the end of his survey of SIM from 1944 to 1994, concluded that 'apart from some aspects of its first phase, SIM has not effectively been a lay movement' (1994, p. 137). Nor have sector ministers and industrial chaplains been very successful within the gathered congregation in raising the awareness of laity to their community building responsibilities in the world. Bagshaw writes that SIM 'was unable to persuade clergy to integrate industrial issues into their worship and teaching, or to inspire the laity to more effective Christian witness at work through parish-based activity' (p. 79).

The failure of industrial chaplains and sector ministers to equip the laity for their ministry at work can be summed up as an inability to work across the boundary of church and world. When they act simply as presbyters, they import the culture of the gathered church into the workplace. If, as with some sector ministers, they refuse to adopt a presbyteral role, yet do not develop a diaconal role in its place, they are taken to be lay people with part-time presbyteral jobs.

Because the Christendom church assumes the role of industrial chaplains and sector ministers to be either presbyteral or 'lay' with presbyteral duties attached, it does not regard them as having any greater expertise in interpreting the world to the church than other presbyters or lay people. It is not surprising, therefore, that such ministers often complain that the church fails to take any notice of their contribution to its missionary endeavours. Anglican MSEs, for example, have recently protested that a major report on a 'mission-shaped church' (2004) pays no attention to the work of MSEs (*Ministers-at-Work*, July 2004, p. 7).

The Roman Catholic Church deals with the ambivalent role of industrial chaplains by insisting that the priest 'leaves his people at the factory gates' and that 'the relationship of clergy to industrial and economic mission must be through the enabling, formation and animation of the laity for this work' (*Industrial Mission*, 1988, p. 84). This is a genuinely diaconal perspective. The problem here, however, is that the Roman Catholic Church does very little to train its parish priests to educate and equip the laity for their ministry as the church in the world, even its permanent diaconate being largely confined to presbyteral duties.

One other factor weakens the authority and influence of sector ministers and industrial chaplains: their inability as professional groups to relate creatively to each another. Despite spasmodic attempts to forge ongoing links, there has been very limited contact between sector ministers and industrial chaplains over the years. This may be because industrial chaplains see themselves as operating with a more presbyteral, and sector ministers with a more lay, model of ministry. Whatever the reasons, it is a situation that negates the diaconal church's insistence on partnership as a key feature of its life and work.

Conclusion

The emergence first of industrial chaplains and then of sector ministers (including MSEs) was for many within the church motivated by a vision of diaconal ministry, a ministry that might bridge the massive gap that over centuries of industrialization and urbanization had opened up between the church and the world of work. Over recent years, such ministers have sought, often at considerable personal cost, to discover how Christian leadership might be exercised in a work-related context. In the process, many insights have been gained, many lessons learnt and, even more important, many of those with no previous interest in or understanding of Christian faith have been attracted to the kingdom community.

As ordained and thus visible representatives of the church, industrial chaplains and sector ministers have been in a position to witness to a Christian faith that affirms the world of work as an integral part of God's creation, and to the fact that all those engaged therein are stewards of that creation. They have been able to encourage and support both employer and employed, both those with considerable power and influence as well as those with very little. Where the worlds of business and commerce have been seen as denying the values of the kingdom community, they have been on the spot and, in principle at least, able to raise questions about the direction in which these worlds have been going.

Industrial chaplains and sector ministers have also been in a position to help the church acknowledge and appreciate the world of work. They have had an ongoing opportunity to identify and support Christians in the workplace, as well as to bring the affirmation of the ministry of the latter into the life and worship of the gathered church. They have been a constant reminder to the church that if Christians neglect the working lives of their members, a crucial aspect of mission is undermined. In all these respects, industrial chaplains and sector ministers have done much to challenge the Christendom model of church and to compel it to respond to new forms of Christian leadership.

However, the expectations of a Christendom church, as well as of a secular world still living with a Christendom image of church, have pushed many industrial chaplains into presbyteral mode, and many sector ministers into lay mode with their presbyteral duties seen as bolted on. Fulfilling a presbyteral role in a secular context, for example as a chaplain in education, health, the prison service, the armed forces and even industry, remains an important calling within the diaconal church as a whole. There are many contexts, other than that of the local church, where people, whether Christians or not, need to be given opportunities to gather together to pray and to worship, as well as to receive pastoral support. Likewise, it can be argued that for sector ministers to play a 'lay' role is important in demonstrating the church's solidarity with both Christians and non-Christians in their working lives.

Yet fundamental problems remain. One of these is that the very existence of such ministries has enabled a Christendom church to continue to devalue and neglect the primacy of the laity as the church in the world. Both sector ministers and chaplains can come to be seen, and can come to see themselves, as being the 'true' representatives of the church in the work-place, whereas the primary representatives of the church in the world are first and foremost the laity.

Another fundamental problem is that the existence of chaplains and sector ministers can mask the church's almost total failure to provide church leaders who operate in diaconal mode, and whose principal task it is to equip the laity, within the gathered church and beyond it, for their calling to be the people of God in the world. As a consequence, it has been no one's responsibility to prepare lay people to be community builders within their places of work. This has crucially undermined the mission of the church. This responsibility is at the heart of the deacon's role, a role that must now come to the fore if the mould of Christendom is to be broken, a diaconal church be brought into being and the laity liberated to be what God intended them to be.

Overview

The five case studies presented in Part 3 portray different features of the diaconal church in action, features previously identified in Part 2 (see particularly Figures 3 and 4). No single case study is able to encompass all these features, but each can provide some pieces of the jigsaw. Though many pieces are still missing, fitting together what we have can give us an idea of what the diaconal church in action might look like. If the mould of Christendom is to be broken, it is important for us to get this picture as clear as possible so that we know the nature and scale of the task facing us.

Mission   The Human City Initiative (Chapter 11) perhaps gives us the clearest understanding of the mission of the diaconal church: a kingdom community-centred mission focused on the creation of our world as a community of learning communities. The human city is a vision of such a world writ small. A vision of the kingdom community is also seen in many of the Christians in Public Life Programme's position papers (Chapter 10), and in the life and work of the Christian Community Movement (Chapter 9). Sector ministers and industrial chaplains (Chapter 12) claim to be 'ministers of the kingdom'.

Culture   Affirmation of a secular world as the locus of the kingdom community is seen in all the case studies, but comes to the fore in the work of the Human City Initiative, St Mark's ministry in West Greenwich (Chapter 8) and the role of sector ministers and industrial chaplains. A commitment to transformation not preservation is again present in all the case studies, but particularly strong within the Christian Community Movement and the Human City Initiative.

Stance   The attitude of servanthood is perhaps most striking in the often sacrificial acts of service and caring undertaking by those involved in the Christian Community Movement. It is also evident in the work of the many small local groups (sites), often based in disadvantaged neighbourhoods, linked to the Human City Initiative.

The laity   The Christians in Public Life Programme, in particular through its position papers, explicitly focused as much attention as any project on raising the profile of the laity as the people of God in the world. It also put into practice the ideas expressed in those papers through two projects: Selly Oak at Work (based on a local church) and the Human City Initiative (based on Birmingham). The Christian Community Movement also saw the ministry of lay people moving centre stage.

Social collectives

The hearing   Hearings, named as such, were an important feature of the public visioning process instigated by the Human City Initiative. In many respects, the exchange of insights and ideas facilitated by the Christians in Public Life Programme represented a 'virtual' hearing on a national scale. St Mark's, through its Operation Meeting-Point project, sought to use the hearing as a means of visioning and of mission on the local scene.

The communal group   The communal group was a social collective of fundamental importance for the life and work of the Christian Community Movement. It also lay at the heart of the concepts of 'human city sites' and 'human neighbourhood sites' developed by the Human City Initiative. It played a significant part in the life of St Mark's.

The network   The network was an important form of social collective for those involved in all the case studies (even though during this period the Internet was either non-existent or in the early stages of its development). However, for the widely scattered groups (as well as for those associations that were networks in their own right) involved in the Christian Community Movement, networking was an essential and communal process. It was a process in which the National Centre for Christian Communities and Networks played a key enabling role. The Christians in Public Life Programme was also a national networking endeavour. The Human City Initiative saw the connecting up of its sites, within and across the three cities involved, as vital in its approach to community development.

The communal institution   None of the case studies encompassed social collectives that would normally be described as institutions. The Human City Institute, set up by the Human City Initiative, was a communal institution of sorts. However, its life was too short-lived for very much to be learnt from the way it operated.

The partnership   St Mark's was a notable model of ecumenical partnership, both between the (then) Presbyterian Church and the Methodist Church at national level and the two congregations locally, as well as between St Mark's and the other churches in West Greenwich. On a citywide basis, the Human City Initiative was an important example of partnership between a wide range of Christian and secular agencies involved in the life of Birmingham. On a national and sometimes international level, the Christian Community Movement saw a host of informal partnerships develop across the denominations, across areas of engagement, as well as between Christians and those with no Christian affiliations.

Leadership and governance

Leadership   Other than my never having been an industrial chaplain, I was involved in a leadership role in all the case studies. In all these situations I was engaged in what I would now see as a diaconal form of leadership (Chapter 7). In the case of St Mark's, my Presbyterian colleague played the role of presbyter while I was able to develop the role of deacon. In the case of the Christian Community Movement and the Human City Initiative, my role was more explicitly that of a community educator, focusing especially on the functions of catalyst, enabler, intermediary and resource person. In the Christians in Public Life Programme, my role as a community educator took more the form of a catalyst and an intermediary.

A significant number of other people in leadership positions mentioned in the case studies, especially in connection with the Christian Community Movement, also exemplified the role of deacon. The case study on sector ministers and industrial chaplains majored on the diaconal features of those roles, features rather more clearly in evidence in the ministry of industrial chaplains. However, in both cases, there were expectations and pressures preventing the role of deacon emerging with any real clarity and credibility.

The case studies also portrayed a number of Christian collectives operating as intermediary agencies, an important aspect of the mission of the diaconal church. Especially noteworthy in this respect was the National Centre for Christian Communities and Networks and the Human City Institute.

Governance   The social collectives described in the case studies were not sufficiently institutional in nature to exemplify diaconal aspects of governance.

Part 4

The emergence of the diaconal church

13

The wider scene

Breaking the mould?

In Part 4 we first look at five Christian 'renewal' movements that have appeared on the world scene in recent years (Chapter 13). Our concern is to explore whether or not these are movements paving the way for the emergence of the diaconal church. Our exploration is necessarily brief, but it shows that the quest for the diaconal church must be set within a global context. In evaluating the diaconal character of each of these movements, we usually follow the order in which we described the distinctive features of the diaconal church in Part 2. In most of the evaluations we look first at where these movements converge with the model of the diaconal church and then suggest where they have more in common with the Christendom model of church.

In the final chapter of Part 4 (Chapter 14), we focus on 'a renewed diaconate', a form of church leadership that we see as the key to the liberation of the laity and thus to the emergence of the diaconal church to become the servant of the kingdom community.

Basic ecclesial communities

Basic ecclesial communities (or BECs as they have come to be widely known) first emerged on the Latin American scene, notably in Brazil, in the late 1950s (Clark, 1984, pp. 77–80). BECs are almost wholly a Roman Catholic phenomenon. They are parish-based, lay-led groups whose members are often related to one another. Each BEC gathers together regularly to worship, to strengthen its communal bonds and to find ways of addressing the economic hardships many of its members experience. Where it is feasible, BECs are linked together by an itinerant priest or member of a religious order, usually operating over a very wide area.

From a sociological and political vantage point, the main reasons for the emergence of BECs were an increase in population and its concentration in urban areas, endemic poverty and deprivation and, as a consequence, the growth of a political radicalism that 'condemned neo-colonialism, exploitation, and the institutionalized violence of capitalist society (Jenkins, 2003, p. 145). From the vantage point of ecclesiology, BECs also came into being because of a drastic shortage of Catholic priests, the steady growth of an educated lower class laity and people's desire that faith be more clearly related to the harsh realities of daily life.

Though BECs are diverse in character, they share a number of important characteristics (Clark, 1984, pp. 188–91). BECs were originally drawn from the poorest elements of Brazilian society and were located in both rural and, increasingly, urban areas. BECs varied considerably in size, but were often made up of 20 to 30 families associated with one or more parish. They gathered for worship and other activities at least weekly. Most BECs 'began as lay-led bible study groups, compensating for the shortage of priests'. From such religious beginnings, many BECs went on to discover a new political awareness and gain a new commitment to social justice. Out of the experience of the early BECs, a 'theology of liberation' developed as a way of reflecting theologically on radical political practice. This was given clarity and universal exposure by academic theologians such as Gustavo Gutiérrez (1973) and Leonardo Boff (1985) (cf. Torres and Eagleson, 1981).

In 1968 the Latin American bishops' meeting at Medellín gave recognition and encouragement to the emerging BECs. By 1974 there were some 40,000 and by 1985 some 100,000 BECs in Brazil alone, with another 80,000 in other Latin American countries (Hinton, 1995, p. 3). In 1975 the first congress of representatives of BECs was held at Vitoria in Brazil, from then onwards assemblies occurring at regular intervals. Elsewhere in the world, BECs appeared in greatest numbers in the Philippines (from the 1970s onwards). In the few other countries where they have emerged, for example in East Africa, they have tended to take on a character that is more pastoral than political.

The 1980s saw the high water mark of BECs. The Sandinista revolution had triumphed in Nicaragua in 1979, and the Latin American bishops' meeting at Pueblo in the same year had given further encouragement to BECs. However, with the appointment in 1978 of a Pope who was highly distrustful of left-wing political movements, theologians such as Leonardo Boff, who championed a theology of liberation, were gradually silenced. A series of episcopal appointments over the next 20 years created a much more 'conservative' ethos within the Latin American church (Jenkins, 2003, p. 146).

Although BECs have continued to play an important part on the Latin American scene (in 1989, for example, some 5,000 members attended the seventh BECs congress in Duque de Caxias), their initial impetus has diminished and their impact steadily declined. Their character has become gradually more pastoral and catechetical. They are now heralded by many Catholics as a force for parish renewal rather than for political awareness and change. For example, Margaret Hebblethwaite, writing in 1993, appears over-concerned to stress that the movement was never 'an underground church' or ever envisioned any break with Rome (1993, pp. 138–40, 31–3).

At the present time, the Catholic Church appears to be much more interested in the emergence of 'new ecclesial movements' as a whole (Ker, 2001) than with BECs as such. In 1998 the Pope convened a 'World Congress' of representatives of 200 new ecclesial movements in Rome, following more modest gatherings in 1981, 1987 and 1991 (Ker, 2001, p. 23). BECs were regarded as representing only one kind of new ecclesial movement. Now regarded as of equal significance, if not more important, were the l'Arche Communities, the Focolare Movement, Charismatic Renewal, the neo-Catechumenal Communities and Youth 2000, among many others (p. 4). The Pope, in his address to the 1998 Congress, spoke of 'the great need for living Christian communities', stating his conviction that 'the movements and the new ecclesial communities [are] one of the most significant fruits of that springtime in the church which was foretold by the Second Vatican Council' (pp. 51, 39–40). Thus, the contribution of BECs to the renewal of the Catholic Church, though still acknowledged, is now being set in a broader context.

Towards the diaconal church?

Jose Marins, commenting on documents issued by the Latin American bishops before 1982, offers his own vision of the 'new model' of church that BECs presented (Rossa, 1983, p. 69):

- from a church enclosed within the religious to a church open to the social.
- from a church with emphasis on sacramentalization to one with emphasis on evangelization and mission.

- from a church more allied with the privileged classes . . . to a church which is much more with the poor.
- from a church which expresses itself more through traditional parishes to a church lived as an experience of community and service . . .
- from a traditional and conservative church to a liberating church with a priority option for the poor.

Marins' words indicate that at this stage of their development, BECs encapsulated many of the hallmarks of the diaconal church. Their theology was kingdom community-centred not church-centred. BECs sought to live out faithfully their 'mission of establishing the kingdom of God in communion with the whole church' (Bishop of Ciudad Guzman, Mexico, in Rossa, 1983, p. 90). Many were actively engaged in tackling the injustices that kept their members poor and disadvantaged. They understood the church to be priests and people, the whole people of God. BECs were committed to building up mutually supportive mini communities founded on a deep commitment to Christian faith. They exploited the communal group to the full and frequently networked locally and well beyond, as witnessed by their regular national congresses. They were lay led and lay co-ordinated.

However, in spite of their many diaconal features, the potential of BECs for transforming church and world has so far not been realized. By the early 1980s the mould of Christendom was beginning to constrain their more political activities. It was also undermining the hopes that were being projected onto them by theologians and activists from all denominations and from well beyond Latin America. Rome was increasingly emphasizing that BECs were essentially 'ecclesial' communities (Hebblethwaite, 1993, pp. 138–40) under the authority of the hierarchy, and was stressing their potential for the renewal of the Catholic parish rather than the transformation of church and society. Though BECs were lay led, their lay 'co-ordinators' (usually male) were often trained and supervised by priests and religious (Clark, 1984, p. 191). The Latin American bishops were prominent in the early years in support of BECs but became much more cautious as Rome increasingly expressed reservations.

As noted, in more recent years other 'new ecclesial movements' have come to the fore within the Roman Catholic Church. Some of these movements also possess features akin to those of the diaconal church. Many are concerned to create community across parish boundaries, they have the ability to network with one another and are often lay-led. When he set up meetings of the representatives of such movements, the Pope was in fact fulfilling the diaconal role of intermediary. Some people, like Ian Ker, look to such movements to exercise a Christian ministry in a way that is more effective than that undertaken by the traditional parish, the latter described by him as a Christian collective that 'does not appear to be a community of the Holy Spirit' (2001, p. 49).

Nevertheless, it seems that once any new ecclesial movement, not least BECs, threatens even to dent the mould of Christendom, the forces of retrenchment immediately come into play. The cutting edge of such reformist endeavours is blunted, and their contribution to the life of the church only recognized where it does not challenge the status quo. It remains to be seen whether, over the long term, BECs, as well as other new ecclesial movements, are able to bring into being the diaconal church in a way that, as Ker hopes, will 'profoundly change the church of our time' (2001, p. 56).

Pentecostalism

Pentecostalism 'now appears more complex and enigmatic than could ever have been imagined a half century ago', writes Everett Wilson (in Dempster et al, 1999, p. 110). Little wonder, for we are now dealing with a 'movement' that Peter Brierley estimates (1999, p. 121) will have grown from 1 per cent (12 million) of the world's Christian population in 1960, to 8 per cent (150 million) in 2010. Others see this estimate as far too conservative and believe even the current figure, including the indigenous churches (largely found in Africa), to be 'some 400–500 million' (Dempster et al, 1999, pp. vii, 131).

Most commentators trace the origins of Pentecostalism to an inner-city mission in Azusa Street, Los Angeles, where in 1906 an extraordinary experience of 'baptism in the Spirit' sparked off what, during the ensuing century, was to become a global phenomenon. Over the next decade similar experiences occurred in churches across many continents. From the 1920s onwards, Pentecostal churches began to set up Bible institutes and colleges, notably in the United States, though they still remained very much a minority on the global Christian scene. Pentecostalism was reanimated in the late 1940s through 'the Latter Rain' movement, but 'the take-off point can be located in the mid 1960s' (Davie, 2002, p. 58) when it '[entered] mainstream Christianity through the charismatic movement' (Margaret Poloma in Dempster et al, 1999, p. 364).

Pentecostalism continued to flourish throughout the 1970s, but it was the so-called 'Third Wave' of the 1980s that became a watershed for Pentecostalism. Then, for the first time, 'Pentecostals surpassed all other groups of Protestants to become the largest Protestant family in the world' (Grant McLung in Dempster et al, 1999, p. 44). The 'Toronto Blessing' phenomenon that appeared among the Toronto Airport Christian Fellowship in 1994 sparked the most recent revival of international note within the movement. There is every indication that Pentecostalism will continue to grow. Jenkins believes that its numbers may even reach a billion by 2050 (2003, p. 8). However, other observers think that growth has reached a plateau (in Asia) and is showing some signs of 'aging' (in Latin America) (Dempster et al, 1999, pp. 185, 142).

Brierley (1998, p. 124) offers a map indicating the projected proportion of Pentecostals, in relation to other denominations, in each continent for the year 2010: 38 per cent in Latin America, 27 per cent in the United States, 20 per cent in Africa and 11 per cent in Asia. He states that 51 per cent of the world's Pentecostal population lives in Brazil and the United States, and if Nigeria, Indonesia, Zaire, South Africa and India are added in, 71 per cent of the world's Pentecostal population lives in those countries (p. 128). But he also notes that this concentration of Pentecostals in just seven countries could leave the future of the whole movement exposed to major economic, social and cultural changes there.

The reasons for the explosion in the number of Pentecostals in the latter part of the twentieth century are complex. David Martin (1990) believes that in Latin America at least and probably elsewhere, Pentecostals found within their churches the 'free space' they needed to liberate themselves from the stigma of social disadvantage, as well as from dependency on Roman Catholicism and especially the priesthood. Within these 'spaces' they were able to make a bid to control their own destiny. The timing of this explosion also suggests that it may have occurred as the result of many countries shedding colonial rule after World War Two and along with that the constraints of a Christendom model of church.

Pentecostalism today remains a highly diverse movement with 'thousands of small Pentecostal denominations worldwide' (Brierley, 1998, p. 122). Its largest denomination is the Assemblies of God, followed by the Church of God of Prophecy and the Church of God (Cleveland). The

Elim Pentecostal Church, that best known in Britain, is one of its smaller denominations.

Across all continents Pentecostalism has arisen, and continues to thrive very largely among poor and disadvantaged groups, notably black. There is, however, some indication, especially in Latin America, that a 'Protestant ethic' is coming into play and that Pentecostals are gradually 'creeping up the economic scale' (Davie, 2002, p. 71). Whether or not this begins to change the character of the movement, making it more 'respectable', and thus more at home in mainstream society, remains to be seen.

The hallmarks of the Pentecostal phenomenon are well known. They include ecstatic experiences, healing and other miracles, exorcisms, speaking in tongues, visions and prophesies. All spring from a personal and passionate experience of the work of the Spirit. It is these experiences, taken as a whole, that give Pentecostalism 'its excesses, its colourfulness ... its tangents, its pendulum swings, its creativity' (Wilson in Dempster et al, 1999, p. 100).

Towards the diaconal church?

At first glance Pentecostalism would seem to have well and truly broken the mould of Christendom, or at the very least provided us with an alternative that has, as Wilson puts it (in Dempster et al, 1999, p. 89), 'been a pain for the ecclesiastical establishment'. Because of this it is very important to consider the extent to which Pentecostalism offers us a model of the diaconal church.

Theologically, Pentecostalism has been associated with a 'unitarianism of the Spirit' and some neglect of a Trinitarian understanding of the faith. Its theology of the kingdom retains a strong apocalyptic and eschatological thrust, though Pentecostalists have moved somewhat away from the 'soon-coming kingdom' convictions of the movement's early years (Frank Macchia in Dempster et al, 1999, p. 8). Many academic theologians associated with the movement in recent decades are encouraging Pentecostals to set their experiences within a Trinitarian framework, as well as to associate the kingdom with the present as well as the future transformation of society. Until this happens, however, Pentecostalism cannot be said adequately to reflect the images of Trinity and kingdom community that underpin the diaconal church.

Like the diaconal church, Pentecostalism believes that building community is at the heart of its life and work. It is a church that 'provides a safe-haven, freely joined but firmly directed . . . in which disadvantaged people, if they so choose, can find both mutual support and a sense of worth (individually as well as collectively) as members of a redeemed community' (Davie, 2002, pp. 62–3). The sense of solidarity that many small (often familial and tribal) congregations offer their members is of the utmost importance as a way of surviving poverty and disadvantage. Such congregations also give their members a profound sense of significance, 'an open field for personal liberty', as Edward Cleary puts it (in Dempster et al, 1999, p. 144).

However, the very intensity of this communal experience can militate against the creation of communal bonds not only with other denominations, but also with other Pentecostal churches. This means that many Pentecostal churches are failing to address what we have called 'the communal dilemma'. They are afraid to widen their communal horizons in case such a development threatens the sense of community so precious to them as gathered congregations.

In recent years, the emergence of a network of Pentecostal theologians has begun to question the inherent anti-intellectualism of Pentecostalism and make attempts to open up a wider dialogue. Just one such example was a conference in Costa Rica in 1996, from which many of the quotations in this section are taken. However, most Pentecostal churches still take a literalist approach to the Bible, which leads to an inherent conservatism. It creates an ethic that is 'largely negative and often ascetic, sometimes giving rise to a naive cultural imperialism and . . . cultural escapism' (Ivan Satyavrata in Dempster et al, 1999, p. 214). Biblical fundamentalism that upholds Old as well as New Testaments as the uncontested 'word of God' can also entrench traditional gender and familial relationships. Such dogmatism does not make it easy for Pentecostal churches to become learning communities, the hallmark of the diaconal church.

For Pentecostal churches, mission is a top priority. Their approach to mission is essentially one of inviting non-Christians to enter into a personal experience of being born again in the Spirit, and as a consequence of that experience to become active members of a Pentecostal church. Proselytism, with respect to other Christian churches, such as Roman Catholicism in Latin America (Davie, 2002, p. 65), as well as other faiths, is regarded as not only legitimate but beholden on a movement that is calling the church back to its New Testament roots.

For Pentecostals, mission is often set in the context of 'spiritual warfare', a battle with massed forces of evil represented by a personalized Satan.

From the perspective of the diaconal church this gives rise to a number of problems. When combined with the fact that many small and poor Pentecostal congregations are oppressed people, such a 'spiritualized' approach to mission can lead to the neglect of issues of social justice. Jungja Ma (in Dempster et al, 1999, p. 197) states that Pentecostalism (in Asia) 'has not given much attention to the world outside the church', while Satyavarta adds that (in India) 'Pentecostals . . . have failed to overcome . . . deep cultural prejudices (caste and regionalism) despite their experience of the Spirit' (in Dempster et al, 1999, p. 209).

Pentecostalism's preoccupation with 'spiritual warfare' can also foster 'a crusade-like, militaristic spirit and shallow triumphalism' (Dempster et al, 1999, Satyavarta, p. 212) that smacks of the imperialistic spirit of colonial occupation that it has only recently overcome. Satyavarta (p. 213) suggests that, as missionaries, 'Pentecostals need to walk humbly in the footsteps of the Servant-King himself and put on the mantle of servanthood in their evangelistic and missionary engagement,' a truly diaconal perspective.

However, there are signs that Pentecostalism's neglect of the political arena is beginning to change, with 'its interracial impulse in North America, its growing political involvement in Latin America and its protest role in Africa' (Vinay Samuel in Dempster et al, 1999, p. 256). Many Pentecostals have also been prominent in the emergence of the Christian Right in the USA (Brown, 2002, pp. 192–3), though the kingdom theology of the diaconal church would lead to some important reservations in relation to that particular expression of their ethical convictions (see later in this chapter).

One of Pentecostalism's most important diaconal characteristics is that it is 'a church of the people'. In many situations, Pentecostal groups have sprung into being within a familial, neighbourhood or tribal context, without any one person as leader. Where individual leaders have emerged, they have usually come from the people and been given authority by the people. Breaking clear of the clericalism of the mainstream churches in this way (especially that of the Roman Catholic Church in Latin America) has contributed greatly to Pentecostalism's sense of liberation and self-worth.

Like the diaconal church, Pentecostalism recognizes the importance of the communal group. However, the concept of the church as a diaconal institution is relatively undeveloped within Pentecostalism. It is a movement that has grown by the dividing of existing congregations or the planting of new ones, not by the emergence of an overarching organization that strategically plans for mission. Denominational structures do exist on a national and international basis, but they carry little authority. Congregational autonomy rules the day. This makes it difficult for Pentecostalism to connect with secular institutions. Those heralding global Pentecostalism as the shape of the church to come, as in the case of Philip Jenkins in his book *The Next Christendom* (2003), are focusing our attention more on Pentecostalism's impressive numerical expansion than its ability to contribute in new and creative ways to a world facing a momentous choice between community and chaos. This lack of a corporate institutional identity also makes it difficult for Pentecostalism, even if it so wished, to enter into partnerships with institutions representing other denominations and other faiths.

We have noted that Pentecostalism is a church of the people. Its leaders are given authority by the people. However, such leadership is often 'firmly directed', as Davie puts it (2002, p. 62), or authoritarian, as we would describe it. Although many pastors have been visionaries and inspired leaders, others have been instrumental in bringing about the ongoing fragmentation of Pentecostalism, creating a plethora of personality cults that have led to the proliferation of a host of tiny 'denominations'.

Pentecostalism has also retained a good deal of paternalism. Women have always played a prominent role as members of Pentecostal congregations, and in the early days of the movement many were ordained as pastors. In more recent decades this practice has diminished and a more paternalistic culture that fails to reflect the nature of leadership within the diaconal model of church has taken over. However, this kind of authoritarian and paternalistic leadership may be difficult to sustain as more members of Pentecostal churches begin, in educational terms, to leave their leaders behind.

Is Pentecostalism destined to be a major player in any movement for the emergence of the diaconal church? Only if it can rid itself of the legacy of Christendom, many attributes of which it continues to reproduce, and more fully reflect the model of the diaconal church. In this context, we leave it to Wonsuk Ma, a Pentecostalist theologian, to suggest a number of ways forward (in Dempster et al, 1999, pp. 63–64):

A spirituality rooted in God's word found in Scripture and nurtured by the Holy Spirit is greatly needed if Pentecostals are going to successfully negotiate effective ministry in a post-modern world. Such biblically-based spirituality will empower Pentecostals to address the issues of the institutionalization of Pentecostalism, the engagement of Pentecostal social concern, the inclusion of women in Pentecostal ministry, the continued vibrancy of the church's global mission, the necessity of racial reconciliation, and the renewal of the vision held by early Pentecostal pioneers for a healthy ecumenical relationship with other Christians.

The Christian Right (USA)

The Christian (or Religious) Right in the United States has gained worldwide media coverage since George W. Bush was first elected President in 2000. Though its roots go back to the 1970s, it was not until the presidential elections of 2000 that the Christian Right decisively swung the vote in the Republican Party's favour. In 2004, 78 per cent of evangelicals (making up 23 per cent of the electorate) voted for Bush, giving him some 3.5 million extra votes ('The triumph of the religious right', November 2004, *The Economist* web site). It should also be noted that in 2004, 52 per cent of Catholics also voted for George Bush, from a church in which a majority usually votes Democrat.

The origins of the Christian Right lie in its negative reaction to the upheavals of the 1960s, a decade identified with protests against the Vietnam war, the civil rights movement and a cultural and sexual revolution especially among the young. However, the roots of the Christian Right lie much deeper within American history, reaching back to the framing of the American Constitution, the North–South divide in churchmanship and ethical outlook, and the many legal battles fought over the relationship of church and the state (Brown, 2002, pp. 17–21).

We use the term 'Christian Right' to describe a broad nationwide movement made up of a wide diversity of smaller movements, each having its own particular religious and ethical focus, each led by those with a strong personality and distinctive leadership style, and each rising and falling in its ability to catch the popular mood of the moment. Above all, it is a movement united around a literal interpretation of the Bible and a belief in the inerrancy of scripture, both Old and New Testaments. In this sense, the Christian Right, like Pentecostalism, is a 'fundamentalist' movement, though within the former there are widely differing forms of churchmanship.

Members of the Christian Right are convinced that personal salvation, not least being 'born again', is the hallmark of what it means to be Christian. They believe the Bible offers definitive directions as to how the Christian life should be lived out in daily life. They also see the United States as called by God to be a Christian nation and believe it to be their God-given duty to ensure that their nation is faithful to that call.

In the South of the USA, it is members of the Church of Christ, Baptists and a small number of Methodists who have been most prominent in the movement. Elsewhere the movement has been supported by Roman Catholics, Mormons and Jews (Brown, 2002, p. 69). Until the 1990s the Christian Right failed to attract the attention of many Pentecostals or charismatics as they did not see political activism as part of their faith commitment. From then on, however, an increasing number of charismatics have associated themselves with the movement.

Ruth Brown (2002) sees the emergence of the Christian Right as going through two main stages, with a transitional period in between. The first stage was focused almost entirely on family values and ran from the early 1970s to the early 1980s. This stage began in 1972, when Congress voted to submit the Equal Rights Amendment (ERA) to each state legislature for ratification. It was a move that brought together many hundreds of American women to fight what they saw as the federal government's attempt to 'modernize' family life, interfering in the biblically decreed roles of husband and wife and pressurizing women to go out to work and thus neglect their children.

The STOP-ERA campaign took a more structured form when in 1975, Phyllis Schlafly's Eagle Forum was established, and when in the late 1970s Beverly Findley set up Women Who Want to be Women. By 1982, the anti-ERA campaign had persuaded enough states to vote against the amendment to prevent it becoming law. At the same time, the anti-feminist movement was linking up with related organizations, including Focus on the Family led by James Dobson and Concerned Women for America led by Beverly LaHaye.

The 1980s was something of a transition stage in which the earlier focus on family values, though still much in evidence, gave way to a wider moral agenda. In the background a concern to restore the Christian vision of America's Founding Fathers was gaining momentum. An organization typical of this stage was Jerry Falwell's Moral Majority, set up in 1979. Its main concerns were ending abortion and a call for a return to the values of 'Christian America'. Meanwhile, other organizations were moving into the fray. These widened the moral platform to embrace such issues as abortion, homosexuality, pornography in the media and the interference of the state in Christian freedom of expression on the public scene.

In 1972 a Supreme Court decision had opened the way for the legalization of abortion. Although most of those initially opposing this ruling and involved in launching 'the pro-life campaign' were Roman Catholic, by the 1980s fundamentalist Protestants began to outnumber Catholics in that campaign. The issue of homosexuality surfaced somewhat later, in the early 1990s. Although a notable number of fundamentalists felt that homosexuals should have equal rights with other citizens, the vast majority was opposed to same-sex marriages.

A second stage in the development of the Christian Right began in the late 1980s. It was focused more explicitly on the theme of 'Christian America', the belief that God favoured America because of the 'faith of the forefathers' (Brown, 2002, pp. 234–51). This belief gave rise to two main objectives. One was to show, by appealing to history, that the legislation enacted by the Founding Fathers was intended to lay the foundations of America as a *Christian* nation. However, America was a nation now being destroyed by moral laxity and one that urgently needed to reclaim its Christian heritage.

The Christian Right's other objective was to win back religious liberties by a campaign to reverse legal rulings that, over many years, had prevented Christians being free to give expression to their faith in public life. Typical of this concern was a growing opposition to what was seen as the domination of 'humanism'. For the Christian Right, 'humanism' was regarded as an ideology that insisted that art, science, philosophy, and even theology, should be judged by their effect on human welfare rather than by reference to revealed truth as found in the Bible. Opposition to humanism spilled over into a wider agenda that opposed the way in which the state had made education a no-go area for Christian faith and had rejected fundamentalists' wishes to have their point of view taught in schools, for example on the creation of the world and with respect to sexual relationships.

During this second stage 'there was less railing against the evil empire of Babylon and more longing for the promised land of Zion' (Brown, 2002, p. 24). The Christian Right gradually became 'less like a social movement and more like other interest groups employing lobbyists and using letter-writing and telephone campaigns to influence legislators' (p. 24). Falwell's Moral Majority had collapsed in 1989, but in the same year Pat Robertson's Christian Coalition was founded with the ambitious agenda of radically changing the profile of American politics and restoring America as a Christian nation. Though the Coalition faltered in the mid 1990s, it helped to set the tone for the future: a cohort of more professionally run organizations, loosely linked but working together 'for however long it takes' to reaffirm and re-establish the nation's Christian heritage.

Though the Christian Right had always had greater affinity with the Republican Party than with the Democrats, it was not until President Carter's presidency in the mid 1970s that religious and political concerns began to converge and strengthen the Republican link. Ronald Reagan's administration greatly benefited from this growing alliance. But it was the reaction to the presidency of Bill Clinton, from 1992 to 2000, and the anger felt by many members of the movement as a result of his moral indiscretions as well as his political agenda that cemented the bond with Republicanism. The results of this development were witnessed in the voting patterns evident in the presidential elections of 2000 and, crucially, of 2004.

Towards the diaconal church?

It may, at first sight, seem absurd to consider the Christian Right in the United States as having anything to offer to the freeing of the diaconal church from the legacy of Christendom. Yet the Christian Right represents one of the most formidable political Christian movements of our time. We cannot, therefore, dismiss it out of hand as a movement from which there is nothing to learn.

The Christian Right does, in fact, reflect a number of features associated with our diaconal model. It is a movement that confronts secularism – a philosophy that seeks to impose its belief that we live in a godless universe. We may not go as far as accepting the Christian Right's view that we are now engaged in a 'culture war', but many Christians in western society believe that a creeping secularism is creating no-go areas in public life where any expression of religious faith is denigrated, if not forbidden. The diaconal church, too, challenges the assumption that, for human rights to be protected, cultural secularism must take precedence over cultural pluralism. Nor does it believe that action by the state can ever be value-free.

The Christian Right includes people who, like the diaconal church, are committed to kingdom concerns. In 2004 *The Economist* stated that many members of the Christian Right were campaigning for increasing anti-poverty programmes, stricter environmental regulation and America giving a high priority to fighting HIV/AIDS abroad (*The Economist* web site, 2004). The problem, however, is that the Christian Right's overriding aim seems to be that of replacing secularism with sacralism. It seeks a Christian society espousing an ethic founded on biblical fundamentalism and regards any view deviating from that ideal as 'against God's plan' (Brown, 2002, p. 43). Such an attitude reveals a Christian Right that is neither communally inclusive nor educationally open, and thus unable to further the diaconal concept of the church as a learning community.

In more recent years, the mission of the Christian Right has been to reclaim what they believe to be America's Christian heritage. In this sense it is a mission more concerned with Christian values than with religious conversion, though the latter remains a related agenda. However, this belief in America as God's chosen people has an all too familiar imperialistic ring, raising the spectre of America as a new form of Christendom. It is also a mission that is being undertaken not in the diaconal spirit of servanthood, but through the power of material wealth and of the media.

The Christian Right has certainly raised the awareness of Christian lay people, within and beyond that movement, to their responsibilities as the people of God in the world. The liberation of the laity is a key aspect of a diaconal agenda. For much of the twentieth century, lay people in the States were as apathetic as the general population about national politics. From the 1970s onwards, however, the Christian Right has stirred a whole generation, and notably women, not only to recognize that there are vital ethical issues that Christians need to address, but that they have the responsibility as well as the means to shape the future of their country. The problem is that the Christian Right defines that future in terms of a narrow and definitive theological and ethical package, rather than an ongoing journey of discovery to which they should be contributing in partnership with others.

The Christian Right has made use of social collectives, especially that of the network, that are likewise important to the diaconal church. However, because most of its supporters come from well-established denominations of a fundamentalist kind, the Christian Right has not been concerned with building new communal institutions. There is something of a paradox here in that the issues pursued by the Christian Right have enabled denominations, previously anathema to one another, such as the ultra conservative Southern Baptist Convention and the Roman Catholic Church, to work more closely together than ever before. This might be interpreted as heralding an ecumenical breakthrough; it is more like a coalition representing a new form of Christendom.

The nature of leadership evident within the Christian Right has changed over the years. In the early days, women were very much to the fore, often taking the political initiative in a way that would never normally have occurred to them (and, incidentally, de facto, denying their rallying cry that 'a woman's place is in the home'). From then on, more ministers of religion have taken up the cause, some of them high-profile figures such as Jerry Falwell and Pat Robertson, both Baptists. As the concerns of the movement have widened, campaigning become more demanding, and a closer link been forged with the Republican Party, paid lay leadership has come to the fore, with people such as James Dobson, Gary Bauer and David Barton gaining increasing prominence. At the same time the number of influential women leaders has steadily declined. Thus the movement might be said to have perpetuated a culture of clericalism and, in its more recent years, of paternalism. Only in the early years, in the largely voluntary role played by a significant number of women, could the leadership of the movement be said to have been anything like diaconal in character.

Like the diaconal church, the Christian Right opposes centralism and statism. However, it appears to hold the contradictory view that the federal government has the responsibility to legislate for the whole of America where that legislation accords with the Right's own moral position.

Because of its unique role on the political scene, the Christian Right in the United States offers a fascinating example of one kind of movement of 'renewal'. It has far more in common with a Christendom than a diaconal form of church. Nevertheless, it has some important things to teach us, not least about the intimate relationship between religion and politics, and the ability of lay people having the courage of their convictions to call to account the power structures of a secular society.

Evangelical workplace associations and agencies (UK)

(Note: The web site addresses of the main evangelical workplace collectives mentioned below, and from which many quotations are taken, can be found under 'Evangelical workplace collectives' in the Bibliography.)

We direct our attention to evangelical workplace collectives for one main reason. Since the 1940s, apart from the creation of workplace groups associated with the ministry of a number of industrial chaplains in the UK (Chapter 12), there have been relatively few Christian associations and agencies, other than those from the evangelical wing of the church, that have deliberately set out to support and equip lay people for their ministry in the workplace. The reasons for the failure of other wings of the church to pay much attention to lay ministry in the workplace are complex. They may include the growing divide between church and world in the UK since the William Temple era, the coming of a secular society in which the leaders of industry, business and the trades unions have steadily lost their links with the church, the decline in a sense of lay Christian vocation, especially outside the helping professions, the coming of the welfare state and an ostensible decline in deprivation and poverty.

Though the emergence of evangelical workplace associations and agencies is not a particularly recent phenomenon, the past couple of decades have seen the founding (or refounding) of a number of such evangelical initiatives. And since the turn of the millennium, there has been a considerable quickening of interest in so-called 'workplace ministry' within the evangelical wing of the church. It is, therefore, important to explore whether or not the growing number of evangelical workplace associations and agencies are helping to break the mould of Christendom and helping bring the diaconal church into being. The UK will be the main focus of our attention in this section, though there is something of an explosion of interest occurring in this field among evangelical Christians in North America, and across the western world as a whole. Many of the groups and associations mentioned below are part of, or closely related to, what are now international associations.

We define evangelical collectives in the way they often define themselves. That is, collectives whose theology embraces the supreme authority of the Bible (both Old and New Testaments) as the inspired and infallible Word of God, the sinful state of the whole of humankind caused by 'the fall', redemption through the propitiatory sacrifice of Christ on the cross, Christ's return to judge the world, the necessity of the work of the Spirit to impart and sustain the spiritual life and faithful obedience to Christ's call 'to make disciples of all nations'. This said, it is recognized that the term 'evangelical' covers a very wide spectrum of churchmanship, spiritualities, lifestyles, attitudes to issues of justice and peace, to relationships with other faiths and, not least, to the nature of mission. These are differences that often lead to as deep divisions among evangelicals as exist within any other wing of the church.

'Christians at Work'

One evangelical workplace association with an explicit brief to support and connect Christian groups in a wide diversity of workplace situations is Christians at Work, now based in Rugby. In 1942 a War Time Christian Union was set up by a Miss 'Daisy' Wright to enable Christians 'engaged in different kinds of work associated with the war effort to gather together for fellowship and prayer'. After the war, the agency changed its name to the Workers' Christian Fellowship. By 1953 it had some 85 Christian Fellowships affiliated to it. A number of full-time staff were employed and the association steadily grew. By 1959 the number of affiliated groups was 230. In 1985 the name Christians at Work was adopted.

By 2005 there were over 300 affiliated groups 'representing a wide variety of professions and sectors of industry such as banking, retail, engineering, education, petrochemical, passenger transport, research, manufacturing and local government'. Groups meet for prayer, mutual support, to explore ways in which they can live out their faith in the workplace and to discuss how they can 'make disciples' of those with whom they come into contact there. The groups vary considerably in strength and size, though membership generally ranges from 6 to 12. Members are drawn from an evangelical constituency representing all denominations. Because the groups are inevitably at the mercy of the fortunes of the firms and businesses with which they are linked, the appearance and disappearance of groups is ongoing. Christians at Work also has over 300 individual Associates. It holds an annual conference and publishes a regular *Newsletter*. Its current (2005) National Director is Brian Allenby.

Christians at Work has set itself three main priorities for the future: to enable its groups to develop a more effective workplace ministry and for this purpose to produce resources for them, to develop its Associates' scheme further, and to persuade local churches to give greater support to their lay people in their working lives.

Professional associations

The other Christian workplace collectives of major note in the UK are the wide range of evangelical associations that draw together Christians working in different professions for prayer, mutual support, discussion of ethical issues and evangelism in their places of work. Members come from all denominations, though there is a strong Anglican presence. Many of these associations have a very long history; the Lawyers' Christian Fellowship, for example, traces its origins to 1852, and the Christian Medical Fellowship began in 1949. Among the most active of these associations are the Christian Medical Fellowship, with 4,500 doctors and 1,000 medical students on its books, the Association of Christian Teachers with around 2,500 members, and Christians in Science with some 600 members. Other associations include the Christian Engineers Association, Christians in Architecture and Planning, Christians in Sport, the Social Workers' Christian Fellowship and the Agricultural Christian Fellowship. The Universities and Colleges Christian Fellowship seeks to introduce members to these professional associations while they are students, as does Youth With A Mission, though the latter attracts a somewhat different constituency.

Most of these professional associations are independent but some are affiliated to the Evangelical Alliance. Additionally, a Workplace Forum was set up in 2004 to help such associations to link up and share their experiences, skills and resources more easily.

Business associations

The evangelical wing of the church has given birth to a number of Christian business associations. These seek to bring together businessmen, and sometimes women, for fellowship and prayer, and to raise the awareness of Christian businessmen to the need to be true to the faith they hold as they undertake their daily responsibilities. The participants are in general from middle management. Two of the best known of these associations are the Business Men's Fellowship and the International Christian Chamber of Commerce.

The Business Men's Fellowship began in the 1950s in the United States, but following the death of its founder in 1993 it was relaunched two years later in a somewhat different form. In the same year, 1995, this reformed association was launched in the UK where it has local chapters up and down the country. Its declared aim is 'to reach men for Christ'. Its main mode of operating is through breakfast, lunch or dinner meetings usually held in secular venues. The International Christian Chamber of Commerce was the vision of a Swedish businessman and came into being in 1985. Members state their purpose as being to put 'the kingdom of God as the first priority in our business lives and to teach and train men and women to respond to the biblical challenge of a walk with Christ in the market-place'.

In the UK the Chamber has a network of some 30 groups that meet regularly for meals, also in secular venues.

In addition to these two international associations, there is a diverse range of independent and more locally based businessmen's associations, usually located in major cities, especially London. These meet for a similar purpose and in a similar way. The networking between these associations is informal and usually on a personal basis.

It is hard to assess the overall numerical strength of these associations. Some meetings are very large, attracting hundreds of people for an early morning breakfast or evening dinner. Others take the form of small groups of only a dozen or so. Participation is often fluid with the constituency changing considerably from meeting to meeting.

Agencies focusing on workplace ministry

Over recent years many Christian agencies from the evangelical wing of the church have moved the ministry of lay people at work a long way up their agendas. The London Institute for Contemporary Christianity, founded by John Stott in 1982, has been a lead agency in this field, currently through the creative energies of its Executive Director, Mark Greene. A major part of its programme is concerned with helping Christians to relate more effectively to the world of work, and is undertaken through conferences, courses, workshops, consultancy and a range of videos and publications, including its magazine *Workwise*. One of these publications, entitled *Supporting Christians at Work* (Greene, 2001), addressed mainly to clergy, has so far been distributed to 34,000 people across all denominations.

In 2004 the London Institute for Contemporary Christianity, in conjunction with Christian Viewpoint for Men, launched a portal web site entitled 'getting God to work' (gg2w) to offer a location where those concerned with ministry in the workplace could gain information about workplace fellowships, events, books and resources.

Another agency well known for its workplace resources is WorkNet, set up by Geoff Shattock in 1997. This offers a 'Wake up call' (an email service with a Christian message each morning) and WorkTalk, a course for churches focusing on 'how to work well by working spiritually'. The Agape Workplace Initiative works with businessmen and women, particularly those in the City and advertising industry, offering courses, workshops and a consultancy service. Alpha, based on Holy Trinity Brompton (see 'Emerging church' below), offers a course called Alpha in the Workplace.

The Transformational Business Network (TBN) is a very different kind of agency using the expertise of business people and professionals from the UK to assist the economic development of poor areas in the developing world.

A number of evangelical theological colleges are active in supporting workplace ministries. Prominent here are the London Bible College, Oak Hill and Ridley Hall, Cambridge. In 1989 Ridley Hall set up the 'God on Monday' project, led by Richard Higginson, later changing its name to 'Faith in Business'. This undertakes research into faith and business issues, holds seminars and conferences, and publishes books, resources and a magazine, *Faith in Business*.

A number of evangelical city centre churches provide opportunities for Christians to find support for their workplace ministries. Notable here are All Souls, Langham Place, London and, established in 2002, OASIS, an initiative of St Cuthbert's and other West End churches in Edinburgh. OASIS aims to 'offer a supportive Christian presence to individuals, groups and companies' in the area.

One other significant development in this field is that major conferences and conventions of evangelical Christians are increasingly introducing themes related to workplace ministry into their programmes. The Spring Harvest organization has now held three major conferences, in 1998, 1999 and 2002, entitled 'At Work Together', focusing on 'what it means to be faithful to Christ in the workplace'. Other bodies that have introduced the workplace theme into their programmes are the annual Keswick Convention, the London and Northern Men's Conventions and the UK New Wine Network.

Towards the diaconal church?

Convergence

Evangelical workplace associations are now taking the ministry of the laity in daily life more seriously than any other wing of the church, even though the numbers involved are still very small compared with those of the laity worshipping in church every Sunday. Many evangelical agencies, theological colleges and conventions are also integrating workplace ministry permanently into their programmes. Resources produced by them to assist Christians at work are proliferating.

In tune with the mission of the diaconal church, there is a focus on community building among a number of these bodies. For example, there has been a recent move to set up so-called 'bands' – groups, existing or new, that commit themselves to 'purposeful community among Christians at work' and, alongside other concerns, strive for a kingdom 'where there is justice, righteousness and peace' (*If you want to make a difference at work join a band*, 2005, pp. 4, 5). OASIS, in Edinburgh, is particularly outward-looking and aims 'to foster a sense of community in the often hectic, pressured world that is the business and office environment'. Some evangelical bodies seek to operate as learning communities. Open discussion of ethical issues is fostered by such associations as the Christian Medical Fellowship and Christians in Science. Agencies such as Faith in Business, at Ridley Hall, and the London Institute for Contemporary Christianity, undertake research.

Evangelical associations and agencies take their engagement with a secular society very seriously. As noted, many are actively concerned about the ethical issues that arise within their sectors. Others take it upon themselves to confront injustice and to work for the transformation of a market-driven culture. An outstanding example here is the Transformational Business Network (TBN). As noted, this employs 'the skills and resources of business people and professionals . . . to bring about [physical and spiritual] transformation in the lives of the poor in the developing world by generating long-term business employment and wealth for a local community'. This task is achieved through Transformational Business Groups of '6 to 12 business people and professionals' who use their skills to assist local businesses or potential enterprises in the developing world to succeed.

Some associations make explicit reference to 'a servant ministry', a key feature of the life of the diaconal church. They are concerned that, as Christians at Work puts it, 'Christians will be seen, by their attitude to others, to be a people who genuinely love and care for those around them.' Some, such as WorkNet and OASIS, are addressing the increasing problem of stress at work and seeking to use their professional skills to offer counselling and support.

Evangelical associations and agencies engaging with the workplace have made good use of groups, networks, and sometimes hearings, social collectives that the diaconal church also regards as important in giving expression to its own mission. Christians at Work has an explicit brief to work with small groups located within firms and businesses, and the professional associations and some of the business associations meet in small groups.

The development of Christian 'bands' over the past four years constitutes an interesting move to give a stronger communal basis to workplace groups. The hope here is that evangelical workplace groups can be 'a place where people can be real with one another' and 'work together for a purpose' (*If you want to make a difference*, 2005, p. 4).

Networking is of increasing importance for these associations and agencies, as seen in the growing number of web sites. Portal sites, such as 'getting God to work' (gg2w), with the purpose of providing a way in for people wanting to access different aspects of the faith and work movement, are also multiplying. Networking through the Internet has undoubtedly given a huge boost to the vitality and growth of organizations seeking to support Christians in the workplace.

Hearings are also used by a number of these associations and agencies. The London Institute for Contemporary Christianity has set up a number of study programmes on capitalism and society, the media and communication, as well as on work-related issues, which involve people in visioning and dialogue. The Agape Workplace Initiative has set up 'dialogue suppers' described as 'a free open forum' in which listening without interrupting is seen as an important principle.

Evangelical associations and agencies are very ready to enter into partnership with one another, the 'links' button on their web sites indicating the informal but close connections between many of the bodies described above. Some also express a commitment to work in partnership with other organizations, Christian or not. For example, an aim of OASIS is 'to be of personal assistance to people of all faiths and none, by offering a listening ear'. The Transformational Business Network likewise works with its clients 'regardless of race, creed or religion'. It is actively involved in 'partnering local people' and seeks to enter into 'strategic partnerships with local organizations' on local people's behalf. Their groups of experts operate as teams on the principle that 'Together Everyone Achieves More'.

In all the many ways described above, evangelical workplace associations and agencies are taking on the characteristics of the diaconal church and, as such, are lending their weight to those challenging the legacy of Christendom. However, there are unfortunately other areas where their approach remains more akin to that of a Christendom, than a diaconal, model of church.

Divergence

Although its field of operations is well beyond the local church, the mission of many workplace evangelical associations and agencies appears to be more church-centred than kingdom community-centred. With a few notable exceptions (for example, *If you want to make a difference*, 2005), the concept of 'the kingdom' does not loom very large in their mission statements. In the few places where the concept is given prominence, for example on the web site of the Christian Chamber of Commerce, 'the kingdom' appears to be equated with a gathered 'church' that people enter once they have been rescued from 'an arena of darkness'. The transition is from an evil world into a religious sanctuary. This is an understanding of mission far removed from that of the diaconal church that calls the laity to be servants of the kingdom community omnipresent in the world, and to build communities rooted in and transformed by God's gifts of life, liberation, love and learning throughout the whole of society.

A top priority for many workplace evangelical associations and agencies is to 'make disciples', with the focus on personal conversion (see the web sites of Fusion, an organization working among students, or Christian Viewpoint for Men). Attention is focused on the redemption of the individual who then joins a Christian community in order that he or she, in turn, can bring others to Christ. In contrast, the priority for the diaconal church and its laity is on building communities that manifest the gifts of the kingdom community. It is as people respond to that process that they come to discern, comprehend and are able to claim God's gifts of life, liberation, love and learning.

For many evangelical workplace associations and agencies, Christian faith is largely defined by a view of the Bible that believes it to be a sacred but closed book that unambiguously and definitively marks out the boundaries of belief (see the web sites of Christians at Work, the Christian Medical Fellowship and the Business Men's Fellowship). The Christian faith is communicated as a set of propositions, often through a process of instruction such as Alpha in the Workplace, that its recipients must accept if they are to be counted among the faithful.

For the diaconal church, however, Christian faith is a journey of spiritual discovery and growth. It is a journey that cannot be undertaken with permanent boundaries placed around a definitive set of beliefs about that journey's destination. Convictions will still be held with some passion, but the journey is open to learning in response to every new challenge. It is a journey that will also be different for every person as they seek to find out what it means for them to be servants of the kingdom community. What is certain is that God will bestow his gifts of life, liberation, love and learning on all who commit themselves to that journey.

In relation to the theme of culture (Chapter 5), some evangelical associations, particularly those associated with the world of business, appear not to question the social and economic status quo, let alone wish to transform it. The language used, though often of a lurid nature when referring to the spiritual 'principalities of darkness' at work in the world, makes little reference to the destructive effects of a market-driven global economy or to the many issues of social justice to which it gives rise. The ethics of wealth creation and distribution appear to be disassociated from ill-defined forces of evil 'rampant in the world'.

It is not entirely surprising, therefore, that the understanding of 'servant ministry' by a number of evangelical business associations, where there is a focus on such a ministry being about meeting the needs of the customer or client, can take on very different connotations from those we have identified as characteristic of servanthood within the diaconal church (Chapter 5).

In the case of some associations, again notably connected within the business world, the attitudes and language of imperialism permeate the literature and web sites. For the Christian Chamber of Commerce, for example, 'being a genuine kingdom ambassador requires the obedience that is needed to receive the authority to actively and consistently direct God's power and exercise dominion here on earth'. This is the language of Christendom, not of the diaconal church.

All these factors mean that a good number of evangelical associations and agencies are in danger of being collectives that are far from communal. Thus hearings, groups and even networks can become 'closed' and unable to assist the associations and agencies employing them to grow as learning communities. Partnership can also suffer where, as seems to be beginning to happen, web sites set up to facilitate the sharing of experience, skills and resources among evangelical workplace bodies start to compete in their attempts to shape, if not control, this sphere of ministry.

The leadership of evangelical workplace associations and agencies draws predominantly on the commitment of lay people, though a small number of ordained ministers is working full-time in this field. Such leadership is, in contrast to the leadership of the diaconal church, dominantly male and often openly entrepreneurial.

In summary, from a diaconal church perspective, evangelical workplace associations and agencies have both strengths and weaknesses. Overall, they are putting the workplace ministry of the laity on the map with impressive commitment and energy. Many individuals and groups are blazing a trail that could help the church to realize that it is a matter of the utmost urgency that its laity are liberated to be its representatives in the world. On the other hand, there are many other evangelical workplace bodies that are operating in a way that simply perpetuates the attributes of a Christendom church.

It is important to note, however, that few evangelical workplace associations and agencies of any kind are getting the active support of an institutional church itself still shaped by the legacy of Christendom. Where the church does take an interest in this field, there remains the danger, as Mark Greene of the London Institute for Contemporary Christianity puts it, that workplace ministry will come to be regarded as simply one more 'niche' for mission. The institutional church responds to this niche by providing short courses on faith and work, optional modules in an already crowded theological college curriculum, or the occasional 'slot' on workplace ministry at conferences or conventions. This means that the visions, insights and experiences of those evangelical workplace bodies that are trying to take the model of the diaconal church into their system, are shunted into a lay-by along with all the rest. Thus the ministry of the laity in the world, as a fundamental paradigm of how the church should engage with the whole of life, is again relegated to the sidelines.

'Emerging church' (UK)

'Emerging church' is a phrase that has appeared over recent years to describe a plethora of diverse initiatives currently exploring what it means to be Christian in a 'postmodern' world. Most are small-scale, innovative, youthful and self-generated initiatives born out of a deep dissatisfaction with the ability of the mainstream churches to worship and to communicate the gospel in a way that has any relevance for a new millennium.

Numerous other terms, such as 'new ways of being church', 'fresh expressions of church' and 'shapes of future church', have been used to describe the same phenomenon. However, the concept of 'emerging church' has become an increasingly popular phrase as it speaks of what is acknowledged to be a gradual and often messy process (Ward, 2002), 'hard to track, classify and evaluate' (Murray, 2004a, p. 253), and one that frequently fights shy even of the word 'church'. Michael Moynagh (2004, p. 25) talks of emerging church as a 'mindset' or even a 'mood' rather than a 'movement'. In the literature, the 'e' of 'emerging' is often kept in lower case, even at the beginning of sentences, to indicate its non-institutional nature. Some writers contrast emerging church with 'inherited church', indicating churches associated with the mainstream denominations. In this section, we follow this practice and use the term 'inherited church' in a similar way.

'Emerging churches' are in evidence in many countries across the globe but especially in the United States, Canada, Australia and New Zealand. They are also found in Asia (Korea's cell churches) and Africa (though there they are more indigenous in nature). However, our focus here will be on the United Kingdom.

In the UK, the rapid decline in churchgoing over recent decades has made the search for alternative forms of church a powerful driving force. Emerging church is the most recent of a succession of earlier endeavours to create alternative expressions of church: for example, the Christian Community Movement (Chapter 9), the charismatic movement (Clark, 1984, pp. 49–53), the 'house church' movement (pp. 87–91) and 'the Decade of Evangelism' called for by the British churches in the 1990s. The Decade of Evangelism witnessed three significant renewal initiatives: Alpha groups, 'church planting' and 'alternative worship'. These initiatives have influenced a good number of emerging churches.

The first initiative, Alpha, is a course in Christian discipleship that originated in 1977 at the parish church of Holy Trinity Brompton in Knightsbridge, London (Booker and Ireland, 2003, pp. 12–32). In the 1990s Alpha suddenly took off. Though in recent years its growth has slowed, over 7,000 churches in the UK have used the Alpha course and it is currently running in nearly 150 countries around the world. The second initiative, 'church planting', the establishment of new congregations either as an off-shoot of a 'sponsoring' church or as independent initiatives, also gathered momentum in the 1990s. Of late, many church plants are looking less like 'clones' of the inherited church (Booker and Ireland, 2003, pp. 155–170). Even so, the high hopes that church planting would herald a wave of Christian renewal have not yet been fulfilled. The third initiative, 'alternative worship', was initially given impetus by such ventures as the Nine O'Clock Service in Sheffield, the Late Late Service in Glasgow and the Third Sunday Service in Bristol.

Though emerging churches began to appear around the mid 1990s, they have proliferated since the turn of the millennium. They are usually evangelical (Moynagh, 2004, p. 27), with Anglican and Baptist initiatives to the fore. Their members are mainly in the 20 to 30 age bracket, though their leaders may be somewhat older. Those involved are mostly 'white, educated [and] middle class' (Murray, 2004a, p. 260). However, excluding the black and ethnic churches (which we are not considering in this section), the emerging church scenario represents only a 'tiny proportion' of church life in Britain (Murray, 2005).

Emerging churches are very diverse. Thus attempting to categorize them is not only hazardous but runs the danger of making the whole scenario appear more definitive and coherent than it is. Stuart Murray has addressed this task as thoroughly as anyone and offers a comprehensive list of references and web sites for those wishing to follow up the categories he identifies (2004b, pp. 67–98). He also offers a 'tentative classification' by means of which he divides emerging churches into three main types: 'mission-oriented (a refocusing of inherited church); community-oriented (reconfiguring); and worship-oriented (re-imagining) (Murray in a lecture in 2005). Within these categories, he distinguishes some 40 'new expressions' of church. On the other hand, *mission-shaped church* (2004), a report from a working group of the Church of England's Mission and Public Affairs Council, settles for a dozen categories in all (p. 44). These include alternative worship communities, basic ecclesial communities, café church, cell church, churches arising out of community initiatives, multiple and midweek congregations, network-focused churches, school-linked congregations, seeker churches and youth congregations.

In comparing emerging churches with our model of the diaconal church, it may help to highlight four fields of Christian renewal on which emerging churches are currently concentrating their endeavours. The first field is new expressions of church that relate to specific age and/or culture groups. For example, the Legacy Youth Congregation in Benfleet and the Red Cafe in Swansea focus on young people, while the Church of the Glorious Undead in London relates to the underground music scene. A second field of renewal covers groups interested in alternative forms of worship, such as Visions in York, Grace in Ealing and Sanctus 1 in Manchester. Some of these groups are also engaged in exploring a contemporary spirituality.

A third field of renewal is facilitating discussion about the meaning of Christian faith for today's world. Moot in Westminster and Bar None in Cardiff make explicit mention of this activity. A fourth field is engaging as

Christians in some form of social service or community development project, as in the case of the Youth Project in Bargoed or the Eden Project in Manchester.

The emerging church scenario comprises groups ranged on a broad continuum, from those working within inherited churches or in close partnership with them to those going it alone. However, even the latter appear to need the inherited church from time to time to assist with personnel, resources, meeting places and even clerical support.

More information about most of the groups named above can be found on the web site www.emergingchurch.info/stories, sponsored by a number of evangelical agencies in partnership with Churches Together in England, one of an increasing number of such portal web sites. In February 2005, for example, 'Fresh Expressions', a new national initiative of the Archbishops of Canterbury and York, supported by the Methodist Church, was formally launched. This aims to help to 'establish many different expressions of church life in the next decade to carry the gospel to every part of our society'. Its current web site is www.freshexpressions.org.uk.

Towards the diaconal church?

Convergence

The emerging church scenario in the United Kingdom possesses a number of characteristics associated with our model of the diaconal church. First, many emerging churches put the creation and development of a sense of community at the heart of their understanding of the nature of the church and of its mission. Booker and Ireland assert that 'evangelism is about creating a community' (2003, p. 3); while Moynagh states that 'emerging church is a catch-all for a wide range of attempts to re-imagine Christian community' (2004, p. 37). 'Community-oriented' emerging churches are one of Murray's three major categories (2004b, pp. 83–7). Many emerging churches also display the diaconal characteristics of 'learning' communities. Observers comment on such churches' 'humility, vulnerability and openness [that] contrasts markedly with the "this-is-the-answer" strategies in later Christendom' (Murray, 2004a, p. 256), the 'provisional' nature of their endeavours (Moynagh, 2004, p. 14), and a time ahead of 'watching, waiting and learning' (p. 227). The language of 'the journey' is also conspicuous, as in the case of The Mass (Derbyshire) and Third (Worthing).

Second, emerging churches take the changing nature of society very seriously and the 'Atlantic Ocean [that now] exists between the church and the surrounding culture' (Moynagh, 2004, p. 16). Moynagh identifies two of the emerging churches' key words as 'contextual' and 'customized' (p. 11). Many expressions of emerging church seek to 'go with the flow', affirming the cosmopolitan nature of contemporary society, 'taking seriously the culture of choice' (p. 66) and acknowledging the differing layers of generational identity that have developed over recent decades.

Emerging churches raise doubts about the ideal of 'all-age worship' that characterized the 1970s and 1980s. They offer separate acts of worship for those with differing lifestyles and cultural tastes, often from different age groups, on a Sunday or midweek. The forms and location of worship developed for these different cultural groups also diverge from the norm, with 'multi-voiced participation' in 'accessible venues' such as homes, pubs, cafés, clubs, schools and places of work, increasingly used as meeting places (Murray, 2004a, p. 258; 2004b, pp. 78–80).

The diaconal stance of servanthood is most clearly seen within those emerging churches involved in social work and community development, not least in areas of urban deprivation, such as the Eden Project in Manchester and Urban Expression in the East End of London.

Emerging church and diaconal church are closely aligned in their use of communally important social collectives. Emerging church places particular emphasis on what Murray terms 'nimble structures' as a key factor in Christian renewal (2004a, p. 285), in particular the use of small groups and networks. The concept of 'cell church' here comes to the fore (Booker and Ireland, 2003, pp. 139–54). Cell churches emerged first on the Asian scene (Korea). Variations of it were then incorporated into the life of emerging churches in Britain. 'At its most basic [cell church] means recognizing the small group as being the central unit of church life.' Cell church is not so much 'a church *with* small groups' as 'a church *of* small groups'.

Emerging churches recognize that many people now relate more frequently and at greater depth through networks focused on similar occupations, leisure interests or social and political concerns, than because of where they live. It is again noteworthy that such connections have dramatically increased through the rapid development of the Internet. Ward gives particular attention to new expressions of a networking church in his book *Liquid Church* (2002).

Divergence

Despite the affinity of emerging church with these features of the diaconal church, there are other ways in which it more closely resembles a Christendom model of church.

Many emerging churches retain a church-centred understanding of mission. They have a clear concern to engage with 'non-members' and 'non-believers' (Moynagh, 2004, p. 30); to meet people where they are and to introduce people to Christ. They also recognize that mission will require greater sensitivity and patience than in previous eras. However, they are primarily focused on reinventing or replanting the gathered church (albeit in new locations such as the workplace, the café or the pub). The gathered form of church also dominates the agenda of emerging churches instigating multi-congregational initiatives or developing alternative forms of worship.

It is not surprising, therefore, that in the literature and on web sites concerned with emerging churches, the word 'kingdom' once again hardly gets a mention (*mission-shaped church* spends only a couple of sentences on the concept of the kingdom). Nor are kingdom issues such as 'justice, peace and the integrity of creation' very much in evidence. A commendably frank 'Afterword' to Michael Moynagh's book on emerging church, written by his colleague Howard Worsley, raises the pertinent question, 'What's in it for the poor?' (2004, pp. 243–50). Emerging churches will only be able to help free the diaconal church when their mission is more clearly identified with serving the kingdom-community in the world and building communities transformed by its gifts of life, liberation, love and learning.

In relation to culture, emerging churches are caught on the horns of a dilemma. On the one hand they often employ the language of a counter-culture movement, especially when occupying a position on the margins of church or society. On the other hand a significant number of emerging churches seek to go with the cultural flow by offering potential 'consumers' a wide diversity of choice, accepting the growing cultural divides between generations and even toying with the 'branding' of different expressions of church (Moynagh, 2004, p. 80). There is little evidence here of a radical critique of a competitive and divisive consumer-oriented market society and many of the ethical issues it presents. Emerging churches could address the question of 'How "counter" is the counter-culture of emerging churches?' with greater awareness of the ambiguities of the position they espouse.

The preoccupation of emerging churches with new expressions of gathered church also shapes their understanding of the ministry to which the laity are called. Within the diaconal church, lay people are seen as the servants of the kingdom community, wherever and whenever it manifests itself. Few emerging churches appear to understand lay vocation in this way. Instead, the message that comes across is that the real calling of the laity is to give 'out of work' time to engage in diverse forms of evangelism. For example, a leader from the Eden Project in Manchester, speaking at a conference on 'Shapes of Future Church' in 2005, commended the commitment of an accountant and a bank employee as members of the project's community development team, yet made no mention of their responsibility to discover what God was calling them to do within their places of work every day of the week.

A few local congregations within the inherited church have taken the experience of the emerging church to heart by trying out new times and forms of meeting together for worship and for Christian education, for example, at St Thomas' in Sheffield and the Maybridge Community Church in Worthing. However, resistance to this kind of experimentation remains strong. Within the Church of England, with which many emerging churches are associated, an attitude of parochialism means that many clergy are unwilling to accommodate expressions of emerging church within their parish boundaries, especially if such initiatives are sponsored by neighbouring parishes (*mission-shaped church*, 2004, pp. 123–4). In the longer term, there is also a danger that an ongoing institutionalism will allow, or even encourage, emerging churches to do their own thing 'on the margins', while the Christendom church continues on its way unchanged.

There is some ambiguity in the attitude of emerging churches towards partnership. On the one hand its advocates have a vision of 'evangelical, Catholic and liberal approaches to mission enrich[ing] each other' (Moynagh, 2004, p. 29); on the other some activists feel that working with those of other denominations can slow down and complicate new initiatives. This may be true. But unless emerging churches can address the problem of denominational separatism, the boundaries of Christendom will remain unchanged and continue to undermine ecumenical missionary endeavours.

Emerging churches are dominantly lay and collectively led. In this they have a diaconal ethos. However, many of them, especially Anglican initiatives, retain close links with their local parish or diocesan staff. As a result, few questions appear to be asked by the emerging church about the appropriateness of inherited church expressions of leadership. The result is that the Christendom model of church leadership is perpetuated in two ways.

First, even those church leaders who do support emerging churches are largely concerned with how these churches can create and sustain new expressions of gathered church. This may be commendable. However, it leaves the deacon's role of catalysing and enabling the laity to build community beyond the church neglected and undeveloped. Thus the church remains deprived of leaders with the responsibility of preparing and equipping the laity to fulfil their calling as the church dispersed in the world.

Second, few emerging churches seem to be challenging forms of church leadership that perpetuate élitism and authoritarianism and, in some cases, paternalism. As far as Anglican emerging churches are concerned, a situation in which deacon, priest and bishop retain their places in a hierarchical order of ministry remains securely in place. For example, the bishop is still seen as 'the broker . . . with the ability to authorize a new venture or to deny it permission to proceed' (*mission-shaped church*, 2005, p. 138). He remains the person to whom innovators are 'accountable' (Moynagh, 2004, p. 226), rather than being a servant leader whose task it is to help the laity become better community builders. Within other denominations too, the controlling and monitoring role of church leaders typical of Christendom contributes nothing towards the emergence of the diaconal church.

Emerging churches possess many hallmarks of the diaconal church. They bear witness to an impressive endeavour to explore radically different expressions of church. Many are visionary and invigorating projects driven by a genuine Christian concern to reach a 'postmodern' culture with which inherited forms of church are increasingly out of touch.

Emerging churches offer a host of new ways of being church, some of which are highly creative and very exciting. In this task, communal groups and networks are well to the fore. Above all, emerging churches are demonstrating to the inherited church that it is often the church, not the gospel, that is alienating non-Christians, and that things can and must change if people are again to take Christian faith seriously.

Nevertheless, many emerging churches remain tied to the Christendom model of church in ways that call into question their ability to free the diaconal church. For this to happen, emerging churches not only need to become more diaconal in nature, but to show that they can come together to form a critical mass coherent and sustainable enough to transform a diverse and fragmented 'movement' into a dynamic communal whole.

14

'A renewed diaconate'

Liberating the laity

Our five British case studies (Part 3) and our reflections on five movements of Christian 'renewal' on the wider scene (Chapter 13) present a number of notable features of the diaconal church in action. Nevertheless, the Christendom model of church remains firmly entrenched. There would seem to be two main reasons for this. On the one hand, those attempting to break the mould of Christendom make some headway but then succumb to countervailing forces of considerable strength. On the other, they are drawn into replicating the Christendom model of church, albeit in a new guise, without realizing that this is what is happening.

Nevertheless, we believe that freeing the diaconal church from the mould of Christendom remains a divine imperative. In this chapter our concern is how such a process might gather momentum. Before we address that question, we remind ourselves as to why we see the diaconal church as vital to the future of world and church alike.

The world, the kingdom community and the diaconal church

In Chapter 1 we argued that it was of the utmost importance that all discussions about the future of the church should take place against the background of the needs of the world. We contended that our world now faces a momentous choice between community and chaos. Our only hope of avoiding chaos is a commitment by humankind to creating a global community of learning communities: 'communities', because it is essential that all of us come to experience a strong and inclusive sense of community (Chapter 2); and 'learning', because it is essential that all of us are open to learning how to live together communally (Chapter 3). For learning communities to emerge, a new form of leadership, that of the community educator, is now required (Chapter 4).

Second, we argued that for a world striving to become a global community of learning communities, it is the Christian vision of the kingdom community as the ultimate learning community that gives meaning and direction to that quest (Chapters 2–4). We described the gifts of the kingdom community as life, liberation, love and learning.

Third, we argued that the mission of the church is to build communities that are transformed by the gifts of the kingdom community, and to invite all people to discern, comprehend and receive those gifts (Chapter 5).

Fourth, we argued that such a mission cannot be accomplished unless the church becomes a 'diaconal' church: that is, a church that is the servant of the kingdom community. We contended that because the diaconal church is the servant of the kingdom community, it is servanthood, not coercion or control, that must exemplify the way in which the church engages with the world (Chapter 5).

Fifth, we argued that it is through the ministry of the laity that the diaconal church accomplishes its mission in the world. As members of the diaconal church, lay people are called to be community builders empowered by and offering to others the gifts of the kingdom community (Chapter 5).

Sixth, we discussed the types of social collective that we saw as most conducive for developing the ministry and mission of the diaconal church (Chapter 6).

Seventh, we argued that the task of the leadership of the diaconal church is to be servant leaders and community educators of the laity. We contended that a new leadership role for presbyter, bishop and above all deacon must be developed if the church is to address its failure to challenge, assist and equip lay people to be the servants of the kingdom community in the world (Chapter 7).

Finally, throughout this book, our thesis has been that for the diaconal church to be able to fulfil its mission as the servant of the kingdom community, the mould of Christendom that still holds it captive must be broken.

The diaconate as change agents

This chapter explores how the diaconal church might begin to take on a rich and creative life of its own.

It is our belief that this process must start with the liberation of the laity, the primary resource that the church has for the fulfilment of its mission in the world. It is also our conviction that the liberation of the laity will only be achieved if, from within the leadership of the church, someone is given the explicit responsibility of enabling lay people to fulfil their servant ministry in the world. We shall argue that a renewed diaconate is in 'pole position' to assume that role.

It seems highly unlikely that any attempt to transform the Christendom model of church will be initiated from what is currently 'the top down'. In all churches, hierarchical forms of church leadership continue to dominate the scene, with the laity located firmly at the base of the pyramid. It would be a totally unexpected development if those at the top of the church's hierarchy set about turning that pyramid on its head. Nor are presbyters likely to bring about radical change of the kind we are suggesting. Their time and energy are increasingly consumed in striving to ensure that the gathered church survives. Even those sector ministers and chaplains attempting to help the church re-engage with a secular world find it very difficult to break clear of their presbyteral role (Chapter 12).

Nor does it seem likely that the liberation of the laity can be brought about by the laity themselves from 'the bottom up'. The legacy of Christendom has for centuries conditioned the laity to acknowledge their lowly place in the ecclesiastical order of things and accept their dependency on clerical leadership, even within the post-Reformation churches. Where lay people, not least women, are questioning that legacy, lack of time, energy and resources and, increasingly, a falling off of personal commitment militate against their ability to alter the status quo. Where then can we find the catalysts needed to bring the diaconal church into being?

We believe that the group of people ideally placed to undertake this task is the diaconate. In Chapter 7 we set out an overview of the role of the deacon as one of three forms of leadership within the diaconal church (see Figure 4, p. 112). In what follows, we argue that if a renewed diaconate of the kind we have already described (and expand on more fully below) were to come into being, a 'chain reaction' would occur that would open the way for the liberation of the laity to be the church in the world and thus for the emergence of the diaconal church. This might happen as follows:

A renewed diaconate would make its prime task that of catalysing and enabling the laity to recognize and reclaim their vocation as *the church dispersed* to serve the kingdom community in the world.

As a consequence presbyters, through their ministry to *the gathered church*, would be inspired to give greater attention to their part in nurturing and resourcing the laity for their ministry in daily life. As Crain and Seymour put it (2001, p. 35), a renewed diaconate 'has the potential to redefine the ministry of the laity and reinvigorate and refocus the ministry of the elder [presbyter]'.

These shifts in the ministries of deacon and presbyter would, in turn, enable bishops, or their namesakes, to reclaim their role, notably as intermediaries, of connecting and co-ordinating these refocused ministries of deacon and presbyter throughout *the whole church*.

Why the diaconate?

Current literature on a renewed diaconate

Our vision of deacons as change agents is reflected in some of the recent reports on a renewed diaconate.

The ministry of the deacon as intimately associated with the image of the kingdom is prominent in a number of commentaries. *For such a time as this* (2001), the Church of England's report on the future of the diaconate, states unequivocally that, 'The deacon is an instrument of God's purpose, of the Kingdom of God' (pp. 35–6). The Methodist Church states that 'the Good News of God's Kingdom . . . is the foundation of, and template for, diaconal ministry' (*What is a Deacon?*, 2004, para. 4.4).

However, it is by equipping the laity to be the servants of the kingdom community in the world that a renewed diaconate would make a key contribution to the emergence of the diaconal church. Some commentaries echo this point.

In 1996, in a report to commemorate the 50 years since DIAKONIA, the World Federation of Diaconal Associations and Communities, was founded (*DIAKONIA – Challenge and Response*, 1996, p. 59), Reinhard Neubauer writes: 'The diaconate . . . is the group of people in the church committed to support and co-ordinate the diakonia of all Christians. If only that were clear!' The Hanover Report of the Anglican–Lutheran Commission, also of 1996, states that the diaconate should ' "have a multiplying effect, leading others to their own specific tasks of service", showing the way, enabling and resourcing the ministry of the laity' (quoted in *For such a time as this*, p. 18).

The Church of England's own report, *For such a time as this*, argues that 'deacons are to be found playing a vital role in enabling the people of God to exercise their personal and corporate discipleship' (p. vii). It goes on to state that 'the touchstone of a renewed diaconate is whether it builds up the diverse gifts and callings of the members of the Body of Christ' (p. 46). The Roman Catholic Church, though much more cautious, acknowledges that the permanent diaconate could 'be a sign of the Church's vocation to be the servant of Christ and of God' and that 'the presence of the deacon, consequently, could renew the Church in the evangelical spirit of humility and service' (*From the Diakonia of Christ*, 2003, p. 57). The Methodist Church is as forthright and wholehearted as any church, stating that 'The primary purpose in focusing diaconal ministry is to help all Christians discover, develop and express their own servant ministry. Deacons therefore engage in educational and nurturing activities to enable people to see God's activity in daily life and world, and to encourage them in expressing their faith in relevant ways' (*What is a Deacon?*, para. 5.4).

Assets of the diaconate as change agents

The diaconate has a number of assets that suggest that deacons would be ideally placed to become agents of change in the transformation of a Christendom model of church.

All churches recognize the diaconate as an authentic form of ministry that goes back to the days of the early church. In this sense, the diaconate is already well 'embedded in the system', so to speak, and cannot be dismissed lightly either as an intruder or as the latest fad of ecclesiastical management. The fact that after centuries of neglect we are now talking about the importance of a renewed diaconate bears witness to this 'embeddedness'.

Because of the fact that it is an order of ministry that has been neglected over the centuries, the diaconate has not been tainted by the élitism and authoritarianism so often associated with the offices of priest and bishop.

Their adaptability, flexibility and mobility mean that deacons are able to serve the dispersed church as and where its needs are greatest. 'The deacon . . . has the freedom and flexibilty to nurture the growth of the faithful' (Atkinson, 2005).

The work and witness of deacons is supported and sustained by the communal nature of the diaconate in what is often an exposed and isolated role. For deacons, their life as a learning community 'is a way of belonging where differences are accepted, where broken relationships can be restored, where skills are developed and where companionship can be found. It is a place of reconciliation and forgiveness where individuals are respected . . . . This sense of community exists even when members are separated by great distances' (*Diaconal Reflections*, 1998, p. 3).

[The Methodist Diaconal Order offers one of the most notable examples of the diaconate as both an order of ministry and 'a dispersed religious order' (*What is a Deacon?*, paras 6.1. to 6.5). With reference to being a religious order, *What is a Deacon?* states that 'Methodist deacons make a public, life-long commitment to following [a] Rule of Life and living as members of a religious community' (para. 6.2). This Rule of Life speaks of deacons as 'careful stewards of God's gifts, faithful in all relationships and willing servants' (p. 27). It covers a commitment to worship, personal devotions and reflection, as well as to praying daily for members of the Order, participating in area groups and attending an annual Convocation' (p. 28). 'Following the Rule of Life is one key way in which deacons commit themselves to nurturing a sense of identity, belonging and responsibility' (para. 6.4).

'Being a religious order, however, has much wider significance than simply supporting fellow deacons' (para. 6.7). It also contributes to 'encouraging and enabling other Methodists – through representing and modelling a way of discipleship, [and through] . . . reminding the whole Methodist Church of its calling to be an open and welcoming learning community that reaches out beyond itself: a learning community where disciples share what they have and are, and lovingly watch over, build up and encourage one another in order to serve God in the world' (paras 6.7.1 and 6.7.2).]

One further asset of the diaconate as change agents is their collective commitment to servanthood, a concept that also lies at the heart of the diaconal church and of the ministry of the laity. The diaconate calls the church 'to come to new understandings of servanthood' (*Diaconal Reflections*, p. 4); an approach to mission that is not about coercive power but redemptive love. Thus the diaconate 'will be a prophetic voice to call the church to exercise its servant nature' (p. 4).

A diaconate for the future

Stages of development

Though the diaconate might be the form of church leadership that is ideally suited to renew and re-energize the laity for their ministry in daily life, is the diaconate as we know it today in a position to undertake such a demanding task?

In Chapter 5 we offered an overview of how and why new interest in diaconal ministry began to surface in the mid-nineteenth century and has continued to the present day. It is our view that during that time the renewal of the diaconate has moved through three stages. We believe that only the third of these, a stage that has barely begun, positions deacons to become liberators of the laity. Thus the emergence of the diaconal church depends to a great extent on the progress of the diaconate into this third stage.

Stage 1: The deacon as carer – 'works of mercy'

The first stage in the renewal of the diaconate ran from the middle of the nineteenth century to the 1960s or even 1970s. It was the era of sisterhoods and mother houses within the Lutheran tradition, and of deaconess orders in the case of churches such as Methodism. Though the former tradition was much less closely connected to the institutional church than was the latter, the dominant role of the deaconess in both cases was undertaking what were known as 'works of mercy' – nursing, social work, pastoral care and some teaching – often in impoverished areas of towns and cities.

This stage saw a diaconate that was formally structured and regulated. It was largely restricted to single women, many of whom had a role subservient to the presbyter or priest.

The later years of this stage of development witnessed growing uncertainty within the church about the role of deacon. On the one hand, as a result of Vatican II the permanent diaconate was reinstated within the Roman Catholic Church, though only for men. On the other hand, in 1974 the Advisory Committee for Church of England's Ministry recommended abolishing the diaconate altogether (though its General Synod declined this), while British Methodism closed its Wesley Deaconess Order in 1978.

Stage 2: The deacon as activist – a diversity of works

Stage 2, running from the 1980s up to the present time, has seen major changes in how the diaconate was viewed in principle and its ministry expressed in practice. A new understanding of the diaconate had been surfacing for some time but did not make real headway until this period. Thinking about the nature of a renewed diaconate was triggered by the publication in 1982 of the Lima document of the Faith and Order Commission of the World Council of Churches, *Baptism, Eucharist and Ministry*. That document stresses that the diaconate is an integral and essential part of the threefold order of ministry of (many) churches, but heralded 'a move away from a dominantly structural and hierarchical approach to ordained ministry towards a more integrated ecclesiological approach, grounding ordained ministry in the nature and mission of the church' (*For such a time as this*, p. 16). The Lima document set the stage for a proliferation of articles, books and reports, especially from the early 1990s onwards, on the theme of a renewed diaconate.

The outpouring of publications on a renewed diaconate during Stage 2 has been matched by major changes in the way in which the role of the deacon has developed in practice. The view of the diaconate as a body of women offering sacrificial yet sometimes menial service to church and world was seen as a relic of the past. Many have come to see the diaconate as not only making a unique contribution to the leadership of the church, but also having a proactive role to play in the transformation of society.

'Works of mercy' have remained an important part of diaconal ministry. Indeed, this aspect of diaconal ministry has continued to make a vital contribution to meeting the acute material, physical and social needs of desperately disadvantaged countries, especially in Africa and parts of Asia and Latin America. In the western world, too, pastoral care is still an important facet of the deacon's role, especially pastoral care associated with the local church. Nevertheless, worldwide deacons have been taking up an ever greater diversity of ministries. They are engaged, often with professional qualifications to match, not only in fields such as counselling and social work but in youth work, community work (Aitchison, 2003), the health service, the probation service, the prison service, teaching, the media and so on. An increasing number of deacons are also occupying chaplaincy roles relating to a wide variety of fields such as education, health, the prison service, industry, commerce and the retail trade (*Chaplaincy*, 2004).

Accompanying this move into an increasing diversity of ministries, many deacons have begun to take a more active role in the pursuit of such issues as justice, peace, the environment and human rights, including women's rights. This proactive stance has been reflected in a number of commentaries on the role of the deacon. For example, in 1997 the *Windsor Statement*, produced by an ecumenical consultation of all the diaconal bodies in the United Kingdom, included the following:

> We increasingly perceive our role to be pioneering and prophetic ... *proactive* [our italics] in opportunity through commitment to mission and pastoral care within and beyond the church. Opening doors of opportunity, encouraging others to take risks, the contemporary diaconate acting in its capacity as 'agent of change', engages imaginatively and collaboratively with issues of justice, poverty, social and environmental concerns.

A number of other diaconal associations have also adopted a proactive approach to their ministries, such as deacons in the Uniting Church of Australia where issues of race and immigration have been to the fore. This group of deacons describe themselves as ministers 'ordained to work primarily in the non church community, dealing with issues of social justice, empowering the marginalized to regain a measure of power in the community' (DIAKONIA web page, 2004).

One further important feature of Stage 2 has been the opening of many diaconal associations and communities to women and men. In 1986 British Methodism reopened its diaconal order, this time to men as well as to women. However, many exceptions remain, with the Roman Catholic Church continuing to restrict the permanent diaconate to men, and a number of other bodies, such as the Lutheran Deaconess Association of the Evangelical Lutheran Church in America, still only admitting women.

[Our description of Stages 1 and 2 has been undertaken with broad brushstrokes. In practice, the development of the diaconate in relation to these two stages has been different within different churches. For example, in the case of the Roman Catholic Church, the (all male) role of the permanent deacon remains largely liturgical and pastoral. He is still seen as belonging 'to the lowest degree of hierarchy' (*From the Diakonia of Christ*, p. 60). In the Church of England, the roles stressed are still pastoral, liturgical and catechetical, in that order (*For such a time as this*, pp. 53–7), even though other expressions of diaconal ministry are not ruled out. In that church, too, deacons are largely viewed as a 'lower order' of ministry than that of priest or bishop. In these and other respects, attitudes towards the diaconate within the Roman Catholic and Anglican Churches still seem more closely aligned with the practice and ethos of Stage 1 than with those of Stage 2.]

A diaconate diverted and a laity neglected

Deacons as carers (Stage 1) and activists (Stage 2) have made and are likely to continue to make a genuine contribution to the life of church and society. However, if deacons are to be agents for the liberation of the laity, and thereby for the emergence of the diaconal church, it is imperative that the nature of their leadership role develops beyond Stage 2.

Relative to other forms of church leadership, the diaconate is not strong on the ground. Thus deacons will have precious little time and energy left to give to a long-neglected laity if they continue to move into an increasingly wide diversity of proactive ministries. This problem will be exacerbated if deacons continue to take up chaplaincies that are presbyteral in nature, or if they are required to fill presbyteral 'vacancies'. However creative and dynamic the endeavours of such deacons may be, this fragmentation of their role means that they will no longer be in a position to act as catalysts for the liberation of the infinitely more numerous cohort of lay people who are already uniquely placed to represent the church in the world.

It is, therefore, a vital matter that the diaconate begins to move into Stage 3, as we describe it below.

Stage 3: The deacon as community educator – liberating the laity

Stage 3 would be one that brings into being a 'renewed diaconate' as we have described this in Chapter 7.

In this stage, deacons would, along with other church leaders, assume the role of community educators. This means that, following the Lima document, their ministry would be 'grounded in the ... mission of the church'. That mission is one undertaken primarily by the laity, called to build communities that are transformed by the gifts of the kingdom community. The task of a renewed diaconate would be, first and foremost, to educate the laity to build such communities.

This would involve the diaconate in rousing lay people from their dependency on the clergy, raising their awareness to their calling to be servants of the kingdom community in the world, preparing and equipping them for this task, and working alongside them in responding to the needs of a constantly changing society. To liberate the laity from the legacy of Christendom, the diaconate would need to fulfil two particular aspects of the role of community educator, that of catalyst and that of enabler.

Deacons would need to become catalysts because the laity still remain *God's Frozen People* (Gibbs and Morton, 1964), some 40 years on from when that book was written. The task of liberation would require a Copernican shift in attitudes and practices, from the passive acceptance of the Christendom model of church to a wholehearted commitment to the diaconal model of church. Nevertheless, we believe that, offered a vision and given a lead by a renewed diaconate, the laity can and would respond to this challenge. The Christendom church is often seen as irrelevant because its leaders have taken such a low view of lay people's readiness to revisit the issue of their Christian vocation, and as a result have denied them the tools for the job. The diaconal church is founded on the conviction that all lay people have the capacity to fulfil their community-building ministries in a deeply committed, informed and credible way.

As liberators of the laity, deacons would also need to be enablers. More is required than simply bringing lay people to an awareness of their calling as community builders. Christian vocation is also about discipleship, and discipleship is a lifelong learning process. Thus deacons would need to equip lay people to fulfil their high calling. This would entail offering them the means of acquiring the knowledge, skills and resources for their ministry as community builders and, in accord with the nature of any learning community, providing them with the opportunities of sharing their experience and insights with one another.

The move into Stage 3 would not be an easy transition for deacons themselves. In many ways, to be carers, to be pastors, to be active within a range of 'secular' occupations, and to be proactive in the pursuit of justice and peace, are more clear-cut forms of diaconal ministry. These forms of ministry often bring the rewards of face-to-face encounter, or the excitement of occupying a hands-on pioneering role. But if the laity are to be liberated to serve the kingdom community in the world, and the diaconal church set free from the legacy of Christendom, it is now imperative that a renewed diaconate of the sort that we have described comes into being.

To fulfil the roles of catalyst and enabler, deacons would need to be up to date in their understanding of the communal needs of the world and how these might be addressed. This means that their experience and training would need to embrace knowledge and skills relevant to an era in which building learning communities is an all-important task (see the Appendix on the training of deacons).

To fulfil their ministry in Stage 3, a renewed diaconate would need to progress further towards becoming an international and ecumenical 'religious order', though always shaped by the indigenous cultures within which diaconal ministry is exercised. Such an international religious order would be inclusive and open, and marked out by the minimum number of rules needed to give it a coherent and sustainable communal identity. It would be a means both of support and of mutual accountability. Because deacons are as yet relatively few in number and because they come from many different denominations and countries, belonging to such an order would offer the diaconate a new communal synergy. It would offer a deeper understanding of what it means to be a worldwide learning community, an experience that would be of benefit not only to the diaconate as such but to church and world.

This stage would also see a diaconate fully open to women and men working together as partners to fulfil their common calling.

In Stage 3, some deacons would still be called upon to undertake works of mercy, as well as to be activists or pioneers, especially in places where poverty, disease, or oppression dominate the scene. However, these roles would increasingly be expressed in a way that would catalyse and enable the laity to fill the roles that such deacons were occupying. They should not be allowed to divert energy and resources from the diaconate's primary task of liberating the laity to represent the church in the world.

The deacon as community educator in practice

In this section we explore the deacon's responsibilities as a community educator, and in particular the pivotal tasks of being a catalyst and an enabler. Our thesis is that where the deacon is committed to this role, the liberation of the laity and the emergence of the diaconal church will follow.

In exploring the practice of the deacon as community educator, we draw on examples of this role as it is being played out in a number of places on the British scene, sometimes by those who do not at present bear the title 'deacon'. In this section we also draw on our case studies of the diaconal church in action (Part 3) and on our vision for a renewed diaconate (set out in this chapter, and in Chapter 7).

The local church

Raising awareness

Because they are so wedded to the legacy of Christendom, few local churches have any awareness of the need to liberate their lay people to fulfil their calling to be community builders, empowered by and offering to others the gifts of the kingdom community.

A renewed diaconate's first task, therefore, would be to raise the laity's awareness of their calling by affirming what they are already doing to build community in daily life. One way of the deacon doing this is to ensure that the whole congregation is aware of the kind of work, paid or voluntary, in which its members are engaged during the week, and of the everyday responsibilities they carry. Another is to enable lay people to share stories, orally, in print or visually, of their experiences as the church in the world, and the opportunities and challenges that they encounter in that capacity.

The following are a few examples of things that deacons could do to affirm the ministry of lay people as the church dispersed in the world. At first sight these might seem modest initiatives but, multiplied throughout every local congregation, they could make an enormous contribution towards harnessing the lay resources of the church for the mission.

- Publishing a 'directory' of the work, paid or voluntary, in which members of the congregation are involved. In one Methodist church, the reasons given for such a directory were as follows:

  > To help us to be more in touch with the impressive range of work in which those attending our church are involved in during the week.
  >
  > To enable those with related interests and concerns to exchange experiences and ideas more easily.
  >
  > To assist us to reflect through worship, class meetings and other gatherings on how our faith influences our work, and our work impinges on our faith.
  >
  > To help us to support one another in prayer and pastoral care in a more informed way.

- Displaying photographs of church members to enable them to come to know one another by name. Under each photo providing some information about the person's family, daily work, and a short CV.
- Publishing short articles in newsletters about how people are trying

to link their faith and their work, either written by lay people or put together from interviews with them.

- Making the congregation aware of where their children and young people are being educated and the subjects they are studying.
- Setting up a 'charities forum' where lay people are invited to display literature about the charities for which they work and to talk to others about them.
- Displaying posters or collages, perhaps using logos, depicting the organizations for which people work.
- Displaying a map indicating where lay people work, including the schools and colleges where children and young people study.

In taking initiatives such as these, deacons would be attempting to raise the awareness of lay people to their collective calling as servants of the kingdom community. Deacons would also be seeking to inspire and excite the laity with a vision of a world transformed by the kingdom community's gifts into a global community of learning communities and of a diaconal church whose calling it is to make this vision a reality.

Through the kind of initiatives suggested above, deacons would be trying to catalyse the laity to throw off the legacy of Christendom and collectively commit themselves to their ministry of community building within the world beyond the church. As an integral part of the liberation process, deacons would also be helping lay people to understand what it means for the church to be a learning community and for the Christian faith to be an ongoing journey of spiritual discovery and growth.

Equipping the laity

A Christians in Public Life's enquiry into the experiences of nearly 400 lay 'Christians at work', conducted across the UK in 1993 (Clark, 1993), found that 'worship', 'pastoral care' and 'Christian education' in most churches did 'very little' to support the large majority of lay people in their working lives. Thus a renewed diaconate faces a formidable task in equipping the laity for their community building vocation. We set out below a few ways in which deacons could begin to tackle this task.

Using the experiences and concerns of lay people as a starting point, deacons would help them to create a biblical and theological framework through which they could find meaning and direction for their community-building ministries. In this process deacons would seek to develop lay people's understand of the nature of the kingdom community and its gifts of life, liberation, love and learning. This would involve lay people exploring the concept of the learning community, using the resources of theology, sociology and education.

Deacons would work with lay people to reflect on ways in which their faith might enrich their experience of community, and how their experiences of community might inform their faith. This would mean helping lay people to acquire the skills of the 'reflective practitioner', skills that for some could include social and ethical analysis of the everyday situations in which they found themselves.

An educational tool of real value to deacons in this context is the 'theological audit' (Chapter 12). This is a way of enabling lay people to 'check out' how some of the great communal themes found in the Bible (such as creation, exodus, jubilee, shalom and covenant) are being or might be expressed in their working lives. It is a tool that has been used in the context of industrial mission, but so far not in local churches. A form of audit more concerned with daily life as a whole was produced by the Christians in Public Life Programme (Clark, S. in Clark, 1997, pp. 130–3). With careful development and application, such audits could be a valuable asset in stimulating learning within the local church context.

An important aspect of equipping lay people for ministry in daily life would be developing their practical community-building skills. Of particular importance would be deacons assisting lay people to enhance communication skills that could help them to translate their experience of the gifts of the kingdom community into language that has meaning within a secular society.

Deacons would need to have access to a range of resource materials, including what is now available on the Internet, which could help lay people prepare themselves for their community-building ministries.

[A growing quantity of materials relating to lay ministry is now being produced. However, quantity does not mean quality. On the world scene, the Internet provides a vast array of resources (see, for example, the Bibliography under 'Faith and work programmes in the USA') though these still fail to address the community-building vocation of the laity as we have described it in this book. Nevertheless, two British publications with a wider remit have proved their worth: Mark Greene's *Supporting Christians at Work* (2001) and John Ellis' *Let Your Light Shine* (2003), the latter produced with the Methodist Church in mind. For the Scottish Episcopal Church, Anne Tomlinson, a deacon and Provincial Collaborative Ministry Officer, a pioneer in this field, working with congregations across Scotland to develop the vocation of lay people in the world (*Diakoneo*, 2003), has produced some excellent materials for this task (see Bibliography). However, she would be the first to argue that by far the best way to develop such work is for deacons to prepare their own courses, or to adapt existing materials, so that these are as relevant as possible to the needs of each local church.]

As community educators, deacons would work with lay people in exploring the spirituality of the kingdom community and its gifts, and how meditation, prayer and worship might assist their journey of spiritual discovery.

The types of social collective that deacons would use in their catalysing and enabling roles would be as communally enriching as possible. One such collective could be the hearing (Chapter 6). This could be used to bring lay people together to share their visions of the kingdom community and of ways in which they might put their visions into practice. Deacons would use the communal group to encourage members of the congregation to share experiences of ways in which they were seeking to link their faith and daily life and how they had tackled the difficulties encountered. Where churches were large enough, or more than one church was involved, deacons could bring together lay people who work in similar fields, such as education, health or business, to share their occupational concerns. In some churches lay people might undertake structured courses to explore community building in daily life.

Deacons would be on the lookout for how reflection on faith and life issues could be integrated into existing church programmes. For example, in cases where discussion groups gather on a regular basis (as with Methodist class meetings), a clear opportunity presents itself to invite group leaders to use some of their meetings to explore lay vocation. Many other existing church groups and meetings could be employed to explore lay vocation.

Bringing life to worship

Deacons have a special responsibility to connect worship with daily life. They would strive to see that worship challenges, inspires and empowers lay people to fulfil their vocation as community builders. Deacons would ensure that the vocation of the laity as the dispersed church is affirmed in every act of worship, and that lay people leave worship with a sense that their ministry is of the utmost importance to God, the world and the church. In playing their distinctive part in the worshipping life of the congregation, deacons would work closely with presbyters.

As part of their task of affirming, supporting and empowering the laity through worship, deacons might make use of some of the following suggestions. Again these might appear to be modest initiatives, but if undertaken within every church they could transform how lay people saw their place in the mission of the diaconal church.

- Encouraging lay people to write prayers about their work that could be used in worship, and perhaps printed out for church members to use during the week.
- Ensuring that intercessions do not neglect the everyday concerns of lay people.
- Preparing lay people to speak about their faith and their work during normal Sunday services.
- Interviewing a panel of lay people about their faith and work during worship.
- Encouraging lay readers and local preachers to draw on their personal experience of the world of work (past or present) much more often than they currently do to inform and enrich their leading of worship or their preaching.
- Using work-related visual aids to remind the congregation that the whole of life belongs to God (for example, placing the tools of people's trades on the altar or communion table).
- Ensuring that family or 'all-age worship' does not neglect the themes stemming from living out one's faith in daily life, including the ministry of children and young people at school and college.
- Refocusing some special services, such as Harvest Festivals, to reflect issues raised within today's world of work, urban as well as rural.
- Practising the art of communal living Benedictine style as a church – work (indoors or outdoors), eat, study and pray together – for a day retreat.
- Arranging an annual 'commissioning' service to affirm the ministry of the whole church as servants of the kingdom community in the world.

In these ways deacons would be working alongside their presbyteral colleagues to hold daily life and worship together so that all that happens in worship has meaning for the daily lives of the laity and all that happens in the daily lives of the laity has a place within worship.

Caring for the dispersed church

The main focus of the caring role of deacons within the diaconal church would be on supporting the laity as the church dispersed in the world, a role complementary to the presbyter's role of serving the needs of the gathered church (Chapter 7). Because deacons need to avoid replicating the role of the presbyter, the importance of team ministry here comes to the fore.

This caring ministry would require deacons to be as well acquainted as possible with the working lives of lay people. It would benefit greatly if time were given to learning 'on the spot' about the situations in which church members worked, and not simply by hearing about their experiences at home or at church. In this context a process such as work-shadowing might be extremely helpful to lay people and deacons alike.

Linking church and society

In some situations, those in diaconal roles have been instrumental in encouraging the local church as a body to affiliate to organizations such as Habitat for Humanity, Amnesty International, the United Nations Association, Jubilee 2000 or the Make Poverty History campaign, organizations that are engaged in community building on the national or international scene. These sorts of connections, which raise issues of an ethical and political nature, offer an important means whereby the local church can both serve the wider world and, in the process, discover more about its role as a servant of the kingdom community.

Cross-church ministry

The ministry of a renewed diaconate could be exercised across a number of churches, rather than focused on a single church. For example, if congregations were small in size, it might be more realistic, as well as more effective, if the deacon's ministry were to be carried out across the whole of a deanery (Anglican) or a circuit (Methodism). Though it would be important not to spread the work of the deacon so thinly that the human factor was lost, a limited form of itinerancy of this kind could be helpful in catalysing and supporting the ministries of lay people who were members of these small or isolated churches. One way of testing this model of diaconal leadership would be for a number of churches to invite a deacon to work with them, to monitor what helped or hindered such a ministry and to suggest ways in which such a ministry might be developed more fully in the future.

Beyond the local church

In Stage 3, some members of a renewed diaconate would continue to be engaged with and sometimes employed by secular agencies. In this context, their role as community educators would be likely to be played out in two main ways.

As sector ministers or chaplains, a key aspect of their daily work would be as 'reflective practitioners'. Alongside the laity, they would be the ears and eyes of the church in the world, discerning, learning about and making known the work of the kingdom community. They would have a special responsibility to hone their skills of social analysis (see for example, Healy and Reynolds, 1983, and Holland and Henriot, 1983) and employ these to assist church and society to engage more effectively in the task of community building. It would be their responsibility to feed back their insights to the whole church so that its worship, learning and caring could become more effective in supporting lay people in their ministry in the world. In this way a renewed diaconate could become an invaluable educational resource for the church, as well as for the secular institutions with which they were associated, a role that would neither clone nor ignore the ministry of the laity.

The other responsibility of deacons actively engaged with society would be that of pioneering ways in which the diaconal church could serve the kingdom community more effectively. This would mean some deacons being directly involved in situations of acute human need, or with social and political issues of public concern. As we have argued earlier, however, the role of deacons as carers and activists must still be seen as secondary to that of enabling lay people themselves to become carers and activists. Nor must it allow the diaconate as a whole to take their eye off their primary responsibility of equipping the laity for their ministry as community builders.

As one aspect of their role as pioneers, some deacons might themselves be directly involved in community building. My own role as Director of the Human City Initiative could be seen as one such example (Chapter 12). In that project (as a presbyter in name, but a deacon in practice), my concern was not only to encourage individuals and organizations to be involved in building Birmingham as a human and thus communal city, but in so doing to develop a new model of mission to assist an emerging diaconal church to engage more creatively with urban life.

The way ahead

The growth of a renewed diaconate

The responsibilities we are placing on the shoulders of a renewed diaconate are formidable. We are asking that deacons act as change agents and community educators to liberate the laity and free the diaconal church from captivity to the Christendom church. Where would the human resources come from for this undertaking? We suggest that they would come from two main quarters, from the worldwide diaconate and from 'deacons' beyond the diaconate.

The worldwide diaconate

As we have already noted, the diaconate worldwide is small. It is estimated that some 23,000 diaconal workers, deacons and deaconesses are associated with DIAKONIA, the World Federation, though this number excludes Roman Catholics and most Orthodox deacons. Nevertheless, it is with the diaconate that we believe the task of liberating the laity must begin. It is the quality not the quantity of the diaconal models of church that emerge that will help people to catch the vision of what such a movement of liberation is all about, and encourage them to make that vision a reality in their own situation.

Though the diaconate worldwide is small, it has the synergy of a group of people who share a deep commitment to the God of the kingdom community, to one another and to the wider church. If that synergy, produced by the whole becoming greater then the sum of the parts, can lead to the creation of a renewed diaconate which dedicates itself to the task of the liberation of the laity, then 'the God of surprises' (Hughes, 1985) will have a lot of surprises in store for us.

In the creation of this synergy, DIAKONIA has an important part to play. It currently consists of some 80 member associations and communities from across the globe. It is playing an increasingly active role in enabling deacons and deaconesses across every continent and many denominations to connect, to share visions, to tell stories, to worship together and to shape the diaconate to come. In 1979, DIAKONIA's thirteenth international assembly gathered for the first time in the Third World (Manila). In 2005 its nineteenth assembly met in Durham, England, and some 400 delegates from 50 different countries attended.

DIAKONIA is thus in a unique position to stimulate and encourage deacons on both an ecumenical and an international basis, to develop their ministry as servant leaders of the laity and to free the diaconal church to help build a global community of learning communities that manifest the gifts of the kingdom community.

'Deacons' beyond the diaconate

Nevertheless, a renewed diaconate faced with the great responsibility of bringing a diaconal church into being needs more human resources than the worldwide diaconate can offer. Where will these additional human resources come from?

Our response is that the church is filled with 'deacons'. There is a multitude of priests and presbyters, in particular those working as sector ministers, chaplains or as leaders of centres and organizations concerned with lay ministry, who are, in reality, engaged in a diaconal rather than a presbyteral ministry. Their vision, their skills, their passion to serve the dispersed church, are essential if the biggest revolution in the life of the church since Christendom came into existence is to be brought about.

The emergence of this hidden 'diaconate' beyond the diaconate will depend on such priests and presbyters becoming aware that their ministries are in reality diaconal, and committing themselves to develop their work even further in this direction. However, the importance of their contribution to the birth of the diaconal church will depend even more on such leaders recognizing themselves as leaders of the church as a learning community, and being ready to connect with those in a similar position across all churches to share insights, experiences, expertise and resources. This cohort of 'deacons' beyond the diaconate will need to connect with the existing diaconate in ways that would create more synergy than the existing diaconate on its own can produce.

There is one other group of people who might be described as 'deacons' beyond the diaconate. This group is made up of the many lay people occupying leadership roles in the life of the church, on a paid or voluntary basis, who are currently exercising a diaconal ministry. This group of lay people often operates in the back rooms of a Christendom church in which clericalism is still rampant. Nevertheless, they too could make an invaluable contribution towards liberating the laity to be the church in the world. Such lay people may not be in a position to offer the amount of time that the ordained leadership of the diaconal church could offer to the dispersed church, but they would be another vital source of experience and expertise.

It may well be, as we have already noted in Chapter 7, that in future, to help identify such 'diaconal' groups currently operating beyond the diaconate, the title of 'deacon' might need to be adapted, or a different title altogether chosen. However, what is now important is that the diaconate as we know it, and all those working as 'deacons' beyond the diaconate, ordained and lay, recognize that they are being called to play a vital catalytic role in the life of the church and that the process of their inclusion within a global ecumenical diaconal 'order' begins.

However, there is a caveat. The role of the deacon as a community educator supporting the ministry of the laity is a very demanding one. Whether those fulfilling that role be ordained or lay, they would need to be well prepared and equipped for the task in hand. The role of servant leader and community educator is one that can only be adequately fulfilled by those who have the commitment, knowledge, skills and experience needed. In the Appendix, we have outlined a model of the kind of curriculum that all deacons might study. It would be essential that, in future, those wishing to undertake the role of deacon, whether or not they wished to assume that title, would have undertaken some such preparation for their ministry.

Where next?

We see three immediate steps that could be taken to begin the task of liberating the laity and bringing the diaconal church into being. One would be to seek out actual examples of how lay people are being challenged and equipped to become community builders, to affirm and support these initiatives and to disseminate their stories. DIAKONIA, among other associations, could play a major role in this process. New beginnings are often small and vulnerable, undertaken against the odds and frequently neglected because they do not 'fit' the established patterns of a Christendom model of church. But small is not only 'beautiful', it can also be 'powerful'. Such micro examples of the diaconal church in action could be of value far beyond their size or immediate achievements in enabling the church to discover how the task of building community might be undertaken in today's world.

A second immediate step that could be taken to get the liberation of the laity under way is by Christians engaging in a worldwide debate about the mission of the diaconal church and their place in that mission. Such a debate might take the form of a global series of hearings, with the active participation of lay people across all churches. These hearings would have the express purpose of visioning the future of the diaconal church, the ministry of the laity and the role of a renewed diaconate. Here DIAKONIA could once again have a notable part to play.

A third immediate step would be a radical change in the way in which men and women are trained for the diaconate (see Appendix). The common practice of training deacons as presbyters, and then expecting the 'diaconal' bit to be added in or added on when time and circumstances permit, has to cease. Church and world now need the ministry of the deacon as never before. The task required of deacons needs a range of competences. It is thus beholden on those with responsibility for the training of church leaders within every denomination to equip deacons fully for the ministry to which God has called them.

Conclusion

The growth of the diaconal church will be slow and, in many situations, unobserved and unacknowledged. It will not be a sledgehammer that breaks the mould of Christendom. It will be a host of tiny shoots revealing the nature of the diaconal church for those with eyes to see and ears to hear. The new grand narrative, 'the story that God would tell if God could tell a story' (Cox, in McLeod and Ustorf, 2003, p. 206) that must now replace the tired narrative of Christendom and the increasingly hedonistic narrative of secularization, is about a kingdom community quietly at work through 'a thousand tiny empowerments' (Sandercock, 1998, p. 6).

This book is written in the conviction that in this new era God is willing a new kind of church, the diaconal church, to come into being to fulfil his purposes for humankind. When this happens we shall be witnessing the most fundamental change in the life of the church since Christendom began. What matters now is our commitment to free the diaconal church to become the servant of the kingdom community and to engage in building a global community of communities that manifests God's gifts of life, liberation, love and learning.

Appendix

Education for a renewed diaconate

If the liberation of the laity and the emergence of the diaconal church are to come about, a great deal of work needs to be done on the creation of a curriculum that will equip deacons for their responsibilities as community educators, and not least as catalysts and enablers.

In Chapter 7 we outlined some key components of a course for future leaders of the diaconal church, be they deacons, presbyters or bishops. Here we focus on curriculum material that would need to be added to equip deacons as such to fulfil their role as community educators. At the same time we recognize that, as all church leaders of the diaconal church exercise the role of community educator in some shape or form, parts of the curriculum described below could well be of use to presbyters and bishops too.

A course for deacons

Overview

A prerequisite for those training for a renewed diaconate would be a faith commitment to the mission and ministry of the diaconal church.

Before being accepted for training, diaconal students would need to have had considerable experience of working life so that they could appreciate the situations that lay people face in their own ministry in the world. They would also need to demonstrate that they were 'reflective practitioners', with the ability and willingness to learn from past experience in order to apply theological and practical insights to their understanding of diaconal ministry. The ability to reflect in this way would normally be demonstrated by the possession of a recognized academic qualification.

Part 1 of a course for the education of deacons would be concerned with the biblical and theological basis of diaconal ministry, knowledge of the history of diaconal ministry across different denominations, and current experience of diaconal ministry. An important task would be evaluating different models of diaconal ministry, from its commencement to the present day. An exploration of more recent models of diaconal ministry, such as that set out in this book, would also be part of such a course.

Part 2 of the course would be related to the deacon as a community educator, particularly as a catalyst and enabler, but also as an intermediary and resource person. As the Christendom model of church is still very much with us, the curriculum would focus on the deacon as a change agent. This part of the course would also offer the practical skills of the community educator (see below).

Part 3 of the course would be concerned with the spiritual formation of the deacon, and what it means to be part of a religious order: its corporate life, rule of life, the nature of mutual support and accountability, and being members of a worldwide learning community.

Below we look at a possible way of approaching the second part of the course, that dealing with the role of the deacon as community educator.

A model for Part 2 of the course

[Some of the key elements of this part of the diaconal course were designed and developed as a higher degree course in community education for which I was responsible during my time as a lecturer at Westhill College, Birmingham. Those who undertook the Westhill course included teachers, college lecturers, youth workers, social workers, community workers, health workers, police officers, a number of ministers of religion and those training to be church-related community workers (in the United Reformed Church). Here the course is adapted to the requirements of a renewed diaconate.]

Unit 1: *Models of the learning community (theory)*

The first unit would look at current models of the learning community. It would explore models developed within the world of business and commerce, where the concept of the learning 'organization' (but note, not yet that of the learning 'community') has produced a considerable literature, and at models of the learning community to be found in other faiths. Student deacons would study the nature of 'community' from both a sociological and a theological perspective, making explicit use of the images of the Trinity and the kingdom. Likewise they would study the nature of 'learning' from an educational as well as a theological perspective.

[An illustration of the way in which secular and religious approaches to an understanding of the learning community can be brought together is provided by a curriculum designed by the William Temple College when it was based in Rugby (see Chapter 10). The course, which I attended as an ordinand, was divided into three terms, and followed a Trinitarian model of community focused on the themes of life, liberation and love.

Term 1 dealt with the physical world, and the work of God as Creator and Life-giver. It included both religious and scientific interpretations of 'creation', seeking to bring these two perspectives together into a holistic world-view.

Term 2 focused on the individual, and the work of Christ as Liberator. It included theological as well as psychological and anthropological approaches to understanding the nature of 'man'. The curriculum then sought to link theological and secular insights to help students gain a deeper understanding of the human being as a person.

Term 3 focused on society, and the work of the Holy Spirit as Unifier. It included both theological and sociological perspectives on the nature of social collectives (including the church). Once again an attempt was made to integrate both religious and secular insights related to this field of study.

Throughout the William Temple College course, learning was undertaken as an educational process, not as a process of instruction or training.]

Unit 2: The role of the community educator (theory)

The second unit of the course would deal with the role of the deacon as a community educator. It would explore the deacon's responsibilities in equipping lay people to become community builders.

A key part of this unit would be to enable the student to gain an understanding of the deacon's role as change agent in the emergence of the diaconal church, particularly as a catalyst and enabler. This would involve exploring those forms and stages of intervention likely to be of use in bringing about change within organizations (Clark, 1996, pp. 99–114).

Unit 3: Social collectives as learning communities (practice)

This unit of the course would involve the student deacon observing the practice of organizations that identified themselves as learning communities. Such organizations could be drawn from any sector of society. One form of learning community investigated would be the local church. A particular task would be observing the role of a community educator (who could well be a deacon) working in such an organization.

Unit 4: Building partnerships (theory and practice)

This unit would focus on the role of the deacon as intermediary. It would explore the nature of partnership and how this is best developed and sustained. It would explore the practical skills required to build partnerships between the church and other bodies, secular as well as those of other faiths, and to equip lay people to be able to do likewise.

Unit 5: Field-work

This unit would involve student deacons testing out their skills in 'real-life' situations. Students would undertake one placement with a secular organization and one with a local church. It would be important for students to be placed with experienced deacons who were aware of the responsibilities of a renewed diaconate and who were involved in developing their own role in that context.

Shared education for deacons and presbyters – better together?

Should deacons be educated alongside presbyters? We have spent much of this book exploring the role of the deacon. However, our argument throughout is that presbyters as well as deacons are servants of the kingdom community, servant leaders of the laity and community educators. We have argued that the key difference is that the skills, time and energy of presbyters are focused on building up the gathered congregation as a learning community, while the deacon's responsibilities lie primarily with the mission and ministry of the dispersed church. We have also argued that keeping this distinction in mind is vital if lay people are not only to be nurtured as members of a gathered church but also equipped to be the church in the world.

Because the roles of presbyter and deacon have much in common, though exercising complementary ministries, it makes sense that they be educated together. However, in the UK, where this is the norm, the Christendom model of training dominates many courses. It is a model that perpetuates the assumption that deacons are presbyters-in-waiting, pseudo presbyters, or that the specific requirements of their role differ so little from that of presbyters that these can be picked up on the job.

Present practice needs to be turned on its head. It is presbyters that now need to study a diaconal curriculum, alongside deacons, as both require an understanding of the mission and ministry of the diaconal church in its gathered and dispersed forms. This would form a common core curriculum (see Chapter 7). From this shared induction into the nature of the diaconal church, presbyters would then go on to train for a ministry focused on the gathered church, and deacons for a ministry focused on the dispersed church.

Bibliography

Adair, J. (2000) *How to Find Your Vocation*. Norwich: Canterbury Press.

Adair, J. (2001) *The Leadership of Jesus and its Legacy Today*. Norwich: Canterbury Press.

Adair, J. and Nelson, J. (eds) (2004) *Creative Church Leadership*. Norwich: Canterbury Press.

Aitchison, R. (2003) *The Ministry of a Deacon*. London: Epworth Press.

All are Called – Towards a Theology of the Laity (1985) London: Church Information Office.

Arias, M. (1984) *Announcing the Reign of God*. Philadelphia: Fortress.

Argyris, C. (1990) *Overcoming Organizational Defenses*. Boston, MA: Allyn and Bacon.

Armytage, W. H. G. (1961) *Heavens Below*. London: Routledge and Kegan Paul.

Atkinson, C. G. (2005) *The Place of the Deacon within the Methodist Church*. Paper presented to the Methodist Diaconal Order.

Baelz, P. and Jacob, W. (eds) (1985) *Ministers of the Kingdom. Exploration in Non-Stipendiary Ministry*. London: CIO Publishing.

Bagshaw, P. (1994) *The Church Beyond the Church – Sheffield Industrial Mission 1944–1994*. Sheffield: Industrial Mission in South Yorkshire.

Banks, R. (1987) *All the Business of Life*. Sutherland, Australia: Albatross Books. Reprinted (1993) as *Redeeming the Routines*. Wheaton: Victor Books.

Baptism, Eucharist and Ministry (1982). Geneva: World Council of Churches, Faith and Order.

Barnett, J. M. (1981) *The Diaconate: A Full and Equal Order*. New York: Harper and Row.

Bauman, Z. (2001) *Community*. Cambridge: Polity.

Beck, U. (trans. M. Ritter) (1992) *Risk Society*. London: Sage.

Berger, P. (1980) *The Heretical Imperative*. New York: Anchor Press/Doubleday.

Berger, P. L., Berger, B. and Kellner, H. (1974) *The Homeless Mind*. Harmondsworth: Penguin.

Berger, P. and Luckmann, T. (1984) *The Social Construction of Reality*. Harmondsworth: Penguin.

Bethge, E. (1979) *Bonhoeffer*. London: Collins.

Bevans, S. B. (1992) *Models of Contextual Theology*. Maryknoll, NY: Orbis Books.

Blakebrough, E. (ed.) (1995) *Church for the City*. London: Darton, Longman and Todd.

Bloom, A. (1988) *The Closing of the American Mind*. Harmondsworth: Penguin.

Boff, L. (1985) *Church, Charism and Power: Liberation Theology and the Institutional Church*.

New York: Crossroad. (Originally published in Portuguese in 1981.)

Booker, M. and Ireland, M. (2003) *Evangelism – Which Way Now?* London: Church House Publishing.

Borgegard, G. and Hall, C. (eds) (1999) *The Ministry of the Deacon, 1: Anglican–Lutheran Perspectives.* Uppsala: Nordic Ecumenical Council.

Borgegard, G., Fanuelsen, O. and Hall, C. (eds) (2000) *The Ministry of the Deacon, 2: Ecclesiological Explorations.* Uppsala: Nordic Ecumenical Council.

Bosch, D. (1991) *Transforming Mission.* Maryknoll, NY: Orbis Books.

Boswell, J. (1990) *Community and the Economy: the Theory of Public Co-operation.* London: Routledge.

Brierley, P. (1998) *Future Church.* Crowborough: Monarch Books.

Brown, R. (2005) *The Ministry of the Deacon.* Norwich: Canterbury Press.

Brown, R. M. (2002) *For a 'Christian America' – A History of the Religious Right.* Amherst, NY: Prometheus Books.

Called to be Adult Disciples (1987) London: Church of England Board of Education.

Capra, F. (1983) *The Turning Point.* London: Fontana.

Catholic Bishops of England and Wales (1996) *The Common Good.* Manchester: Gabriel.

Chaplaincy (2004) Birmingham: Methodist Diaconal Order.

CHRISM (Christians in Secular Ministry). Web site: www.chrism.org.uk

Christifideles Laici (simplified version) (1989) Pinner, Middlesex: The Grail.

CIPL (Christians in Public Life Programme). For current information about CIPL contact David Clark: email dclark@fish.co.uk

CIPL Position papers (January 1992 to December 2001). Birmingham: Christians in Public Life Programme, Westhill College.

The Cities. A Methodist Report (1997) London: NCH Action for Children.

Clark, D. (1968) *A Memorandum on the East End of the South Bank* (South-East London Mission Circuit). Unpublished report: Methodist Home Missions Department.

Clark, D. (1969) 'Community and a Suburban Village'. Unpublished PhD thesis. University of Sheffield.

Clark, D. (1970) 'Local and Cosmopolitan Aspects of Religious Activity in a Northern Suburb', in Martin, D. and Hill, M. (eds), *A Sociological Yearbook of Religion in Britain* 3. London: SCM Press.

Clark, D. (1971) 'Local and Cosmopolitan Aspects of Religious Activity in a Northern Suburb: Processes of Change', in Hill, M. (ed.), *A Sociological Yearbook of Religion in Britain* 4. London: SCM Press.

Clark, D. (1974) 'The Church as Symbolic Place', *Epworth Review* 1.2, London: Methodist Publishing House.

Clark, D. (1977) *Basic Communities.* London: SPCK.

Clark, D. (1981) 'Sector Ministry – A Re-appraisal'. Unpublished paper.

Clark, D. (1984) *The Liberation of the Church.* Westhill College, Birmingham: NACCCAN.

Clark, D. (1985) *On the Frontiers: From the beginning to 1985.* Westhill College,

Birmingham: NACCCAN.

Clark, D. (1986) 'An Examination of Sector Ordained Ministry'. Unpublished paper.

Clark, D. (1987) *Yes to Life*. London: Collins.

Clark, D. (1988) *What Future for Methodism?* Birmingham: Harborne Group.

Clark, D. (1993) *A survey of Christians at Work*. Westhill College,Birmingham: CIPL.

Clark, D. (1996) *Schools as Learning Communities*. London: Cassell.

Clark, D. (1997) *Changing World, Unchanging Church?* London: Mowbray.

Clark, D. (1998) 'The Political Community as a Learning Community', in Ranson, S. (ed.) *Inside the Learning Society*. London: Cassell.

Clark, D. (1999) 'The Human City', in Burgess, S. J. (ed.) *Coming of Age: Challenges and Opportunities in the 21st Century*. Boston Spa: Outset Services.

Clark, D. (2004) 'Mission in a Society without God' in *Crucible* (April–July). Lowestoft: Tyndale Press.

Coalition for Ministry in Daily Life. Contact PO Box 239, South Orleans, MA 02662, USA. Web site: www.dailylifeministry.org

Cohen, A. P. (1985) *The Symbolic Construction of Community*. London: Ellis Harwood and Tavistock.

Collins, J. N. (1990) *Diakonia: Re-interpreting the Ancient Sources*. Oxford: Oxford University Press.

Collins, J. N. (1992) *Are All Christian Ministers?* Newtown, Australia: E. J. Dwyer.

Collins, J. N. (2002) *Deacons and the Church*. Leominster: Gracewing.

The Commission on the Church's Ministries in the Modern World (1968 and 1970). Methodist Conference.

Congar, Y. M. J. (trans. D. Attwater) (1957) *Lay People in the Church: A Study for the Theology of the Laity*. Westminster, MD: Newman Press.

Cox, H. (1965) *The Secular City*. London: SCM Press.

Crain, M. A. and Seymour, J. L. (2001) *A Deacon's Heart*. Nashville: Abingdon Press.

Crockett, B. (2003) *Deacons Calling!* Buxton: Church in the Market Place Publications.

Croft, S. (1999) *Ministry in Three Dimensions*. London: Darton, Longman and Todd.

Davey, A. (2001) *Urban Christianity and Global Order*. London: SPCK.

Davie, G. (1994) *Religion in Britain since 1945: Believing without Belonging*. Oxford: Blackwell.

Davie, G. (2002) *Europe: The Exceptional Case*. London: Darton, Longman and Todd.

Davies, M. (1991) *Industrial Mission – The Anatomy of a Crisis*. Manchester. William Temple Foundation.

Davis, C. (1994) *Religion and the Making of Society*. Cambridge: Cambridge University Press.

Dawson, P. (1981) *Making a Comprehensive Work*. Oxford: Blackwell.

Deacons in the Ministry of the Church (1988). London: Church House Publishing.

Dempster, M. W., Klaus, B. D. and Petersen, D. (eds) (1999) *The Globalization of Pentecostalism*. Oxford: Regnum.

Diaconal Reflections: How we experience our diaconal calling in our diversity (1998). A paper produced for DIAKONIA (see below) and later (2005) reproduced as *DIAKONIA's Diaconal Theology*.

DIAKONIA. The World Federation of Diaconal Associations and Communities. For legal purposes domiciled in the Netherlands. Web site: www.diakonia-world.org

DIAKONIA – Challenge and Response (1996) The Netherlands: World Federation of Diaconal Associations and Communities.

The Distinctive Diaconate (2003) Diocese of Salisbury.

Drucker, P. F. (1993) *Post-Capitalist Society*. Oxford: Butterworth-Heinemann.

Dulles, A. (1976) *Models of the Church*. London: Gill and Macmillan.

Durkheim, E. (trans. J. A. Spaulding and G. Simpson) (1951) *Suicide: A Study in Sociology*. New York: The Free Press.

Ecclestone, A. (1975) *Yes to God*, London: Darton, Longman and Todd.

Echlin, P. E. (1971) *The Deacon in the Church: Past and Future*. New York: Alba House. *Epworth Review* 24.2.

The Economist (2004) 'The triumph of the religious right' (November) Web site: www.economist.com

Ellis, J. (2003) *Let Your Light Shine*. London: Trustees for Methodist Church Purposes.

Evangelical workplace collectives: Web sites

    Agape Workplace Initiative: www.agape.org.uk/workplace

    Alpha in the Workplace: www.alphacourse.org/workplace

    Association of Christian Teachers: www.christian-teachers.org.uk

    Business Men's Fellowship: www.bmf-uk.com

    Christian Medical Fellowship: www.cmf.org.uk

    Christian Viewpoint for Men: www.CVMen.org.uk

    Christians at Work: www.christiansatwork.org.uk

    Christians in Science: www.cis.org.uk

    Fusion: www.fusion.uk.com

    Getting God to Work: www.gg2w.org.uk

    International Christian Chamber of Commerce: www.uk.iccc.net

    Langham Place: www.allsouls.org

    Lawyers' Christian Fellowship: www.lawcf.org

    London Institute for Contemporary Christianity: www.licc.org.uk

    OASIS: www.oasisedinburgh.com

    Ridley Hall Foundation: www.ridley.cam.ac.uk

    Spring Harvest: www.springharvest.org

    Transformational Business Network: www.tbnetwork.org

    Universities and Colleges Christian Fellowship: www.uccf.org.uk

    WorkNet: www.worknet.org

    Youth With a Mission: www.ywam.uk.com

Faith and work programmes in the USA: Web sites

    The Alban Institute: www.alban.org

Coalition for Ministry in Daily Life: www.dailylifeministry.org

Episcopal Church in the USA: www.episcopalchurch.org.

Faith @ Work USA: www.faithatwork.org.com

Intervarsity Ministry in Daily Life: www.ivmdl.org

National Centre for the Laity (Roman Catholic): 1 E. Superior Street, Chicago, IL 60611, USA.

Faith in the City (1985) London: Church House.

Faith in the City of Birmingham (1988) Exeter: The Paternoster Press.

Farnell, R., Lund, S., Furbey, R., Lawless, P., Wishart, B. and Else, P. (1994) *Hope in the City?* Sheffield: Sheffield Hallam University.

FitzGerald, K. K. (1999) *Women Deacons in the Orthodox Church: Called to Holiness and Ministry.* Brookline, MA: Holy Cross Orthodox Press.

For such a time as this. A renewed diaconate in the Church of England (2001) London: Church House Publishing.

Fowler, J. W. (1984) *Becoming Adult, Becoming Christian.* San Francisco: Harper and Row.

Fraser, I. M. (1975) *Fire Runs.* London: SCM Press.

Fresh Expressions. Web site: www.freshexpressions.org.uk

From the Diakonia of Christ to the Diakonia of the Apostles (2003) International Theological Commission. London: Catholic Truth Society.

Frost, M. and Hirsch, A. (2003) *The Shaping of Things to Come.* Peabody, MA: Hendrickson.

Fuller, J. and Vaughan, P. (eds) (1986) *Working for the Kingdom: The Story of Ministers in Secular Employment.* London: SPCK.

Galbraith, J. K. (1992) *The Culture of Contentment.* Harmondsworth: Penguin.

Garner, R. (2004) *Facing the City. Urban Mission in the 21st Century.* Peterborough: Epworth Press.

Garratt, B. (2001) *The Learning Organization.* London: HarperCollins.

Gibbs, M. and Morton, T. R. (1964) *God's Frozen People.* London: Fontana/Collins.

Gibbs, M. and Morton, T. R. (1971) *God's Lively People.* London: Fontana/Collins.

Gilbert, A. D. (1976) *Religion and Society in Industrial England.* London: Longman.

Gilbert, A. D. (1980) *The Making of Post-Christian Britain.* London: Longman.

Gilding the Ghetto. The State and the Poverty Experiments (1976) Birmingham: CDP.

Glasner, P. E. (1977) *The Sociology of Secularisation.* London: Routledge and Kegan Paul.

Glover, J. (1999) *Humanity.* London: Jonathan Cape.

Goffman, E. (1961) *Asylums.* New York: Doubleday.

Graham, E. D. (2002) *Saved to Serve: The Story of the Wesley Deaconess Order 1890–1978.* Peterborough: Methodist Publishing House.

Green, L. (2003) *Urban Ministry and the Kingdom of God.* London: SPCK.

Greene, M. (2001) *Supporting Christians at Work.* London: London Institute for Contemporary Christianity.

Greene, M. (2003) *Imagine How We Can Reach the UK.* London: London Institute for Contemporary Christianity.

Grey, M. (1989) *Redeeming the Dream*. London: SPCK.

Grey, M. (1993) *The Wisdom of Fools?* London: SPCK.

Gunton, C. E. (1993) *The One, the Three and the Many*. Cambridge: Cambridge University Press.

Gutiérrez, G. (1973) *A Theology of Liberation*. Maryknoll, NY: Orbis Books.

Hall, C. (ed.) (1992) *The Deacon's Ministry*. Leominster: Gracewing.

Hammond, P., InterVarsity Ministry in Daily Life, Madison, WI, USA. www.ivmdl.org/reflections

Handy, C. (1990) *The Age of Unreason*. London: Arrow Books.

Handy, C. (1994) *The Empty Raincoat*. London: Hutchinson.

Hanover Report (1996) *The Diaconate as Ecumenical Opportunity*. Report of the Anglican–Lutheran International Commission. London: Anglican Communion Publications.

Hardwicke, O. (2001) *Living beyond Conformity*. Blackrock, Co. Dublin: The Columba Press.

Harvey, A. (ed.) (1989) *Theology in the City*. London: SPCK.

Hastings, A. (1991) *A History of English Christianity 1920–1990*. London: SCM Press.

Hauerwas, S. (1986) *The Peaceable Kingdom: A Primer in Christian Ethics* (3rd edn). Notre Dame and London: University of Notre Dame Press.

Haughton, R. (1981) *The Passionate God*. London: Darton, Longman and Todd.

Havel, V. (1990) *Guardian*, 20 September.

Hawkins, P. (1991) 'The Spiritual Dimension of the Learning Organization', *Management Education and Development* (22 (3)).

HCI (Human City Initiative). For current information about HCI contact David Clark: email dclark@fish.co.uk. Web site (in abeyance): www.humancity.org

HCI *Human City Bulletin* (from September 1995). Birmingham: HCI.

HCI (1997a) *Building the Human City: A Challenge for the Next Millennium Beginning with Us Now!* Birmingham: HCI (June).

HCI (1997b) *The Human City. A Global Project – Beginning with Birmingham. Towards a strategy for the Human City Institute*. Birmingham: HCI (September).

HCI (1997c) *The Human City Journey. Our Dream is For Real!* Birmingham: HCI (November).

HCI (1997d) *Generations Together: The Report of the Human City Youth Project*. Birmingham: HCI (December).

HCI (1998) *From Hearings to Happenings. 'Imagine Birmingham': Ten Public Hearings on Visions for Birmingham, Autumn 1997*. Birmingham: HCI.

HCI (1999) *Generations Together: The Human City Youth Project Phase II (1997–1998)*. Birmingham: HCI.

HCI (1999–2001) *Futures Papers*. Birmingham: HCI.

HCI (2001) *Hearings 2000* (ed. D. Clark). Birmingham: HCI.

Healy, S. J. and Reynolds, B. (1983) *Social Analysis in the Light of the Gospel*. Dublin: Folens.

Hebblethwaite, M. (1993) *Base Communities*. London: Geoffrey Chapman.

Hinton, J. (1995) *Walking in the Same Direction*. Geneva: WCC Publications.

Hobson, T. (2003) *Against Establishment*. London: Darton, Longman and Todd.

Holland, J. and Henriot, P. (1983) *Social Analysis – Linking Faith and Justice*. Maryknoll, NY: Orbis Books.

Holloway, R. (1990) *The Divine Risk*. London: Darton, Longman and Todd.

Howe, S. (2002) *Empire*. Oxford: Oxford University Press.

Hughes, G. (1985) *The God of Surprises*. London: Darton, Longman and Todd.

Hull, J. M. (1975) *School Worship – an Obituary*. London: SCM Press.

Hull, J. M. (1985) *What Prevents Christian Adults from Learning?* London: SCM Press.

Hull, J. M. (1993) *The Hockerill Lecture, 1993*. London: Hockerill Educational Foundation.

If you want to make a difference at work join a band (2005) London: London Institute for Contemporary Christianity.

Ignatieff, M. (1993) *Blood and Belonging*. London: Chatto and Windus.

IMA (Industrial Mission Association) Agenda. Editor (2005): Heather Pencavel, 9 Cross Hands Road, Pilning, Bristol BS35 4JB.

Industrial Mission (I.M.) – An Appraisal (1988). London: Board for Social Responsibility, Church House.

Isin, E. F. and Wood, P. F. (1999) *Citizenship and Identity*. London: Sage.

Jenkins, D. E. (1976) *The Contradiction of Christianity*. London: SCM Press.

Jenkins. P. (2003) *The Next Christendom*. Oxford: Oxford University Press.

Keeble, R. W. J. (1981) *Community and Education*. Leicester: National Youth Bureau.

Ker, I. (2001) *The New Movements*. London: Catholic Truth Society.

Klein, J. (1963) *Working with Groups* (2nd edn). London: Hutchinson.

Kraemer, H. (1958) *A Theology of the Laity*. Philadelphia: Westminster Press.

Kuhrt, G. and Nappin, P. (eds) (2002) *Bridging the Gap*. London: Church House Publishing (about readers).

Lakeland, P. (2003) *The Liberation of the Laity*. London: Continuum.

Lambert, L. (1999) *Called to Serve*. Manual for the Diaconate. Evangelical Lutheran Church in America, 8765 West Higgins Road, Chicago, IL 60631, USA.

Landry, C. (2000) *The Creative City*. London: Earthspan.

Landry, C. and Bianchini, F. (1995) *The Creative City*. London: Demos.

Lay ministry organizations: Web sites

    Christian Association of Business Executives: www.cabe-online.org

    European Association of Academies and Laity Centres: www.eaalce.org

    Industrial Christian Fellowship: www.icf-online.org

    London Institute for Contemporary Christianity: www.licc.org.uk

    MODEM: www.modem.uk.com

    Quakers and Business Group: www.quakerbusiness.org

    Ridley Hall Foundation: www.ridley.cam.ac.uk

BIBLIOGRAPHY

St Paul's Institute: www.stpauls.co.uk/institute
St George's House, Windsor: www.stgeorgeshouse-windsor.org
Von Hugel Institute: www.st-edmunds.cam.ac.uk/vhi
William Temple Foundation: www.wtf.org.uk

Learning City in Europe 2001 (2001) Birmingham City Council.

Lecture (Murray, S.) given at a conference on *Future Shapes of Church*, January 2005. Cliff College, Derbyshire.

Lewis, C. S. (1959) *Surprised by Joy*. London: Fontana.

Look to Christ: Methodist Prayer Handbook (2004–2005). Peterborough: Methodist Publishing House.

Lovell, G., Middleton, J. and Smith, H. (1996) *A Process Model for the Development of Individual and Collective Vocations*. Methodist Diaconal Order. Peterborough: Methodist Publishing House.

MacIver, R. M. (1924) *Community*. London: Macmillan.

MacIver, R. M. and Page, C. H. (1950) *Society*. London: Macmillan.

McLeod, H. and Ustorf, W. (eds) (2003) *The Decline of Christendom in Western Europe, 1750–2000*. Cambridge: Cambridge University Press.

Mcluhan, M. (1973) *Understanding Media*. London: Abacus.

McManners, J. (ed.) (1990) *The Oxford Illustrated History of Christianity*. Oxford: Oxford University Press.

Martin, D. (1990) *Tongues of Fire: The Explosion of Protestantism in Latin America*. Oxford: Blackwell.

Martin, I. (1987) 'Community Education: Towards a Theoretical Analysis', in Allen, G., Bastiani, J., Martin, I. and Richards, K. (eds), *Community Education: An Agenda for Educational Reform*. Milton Keynes: Open University Press.

Mason, D., Ainger, G. and Denny, N. (1967) *News from Notting Hill: The Formation of a Group Ministry*. London: Epworth Press.

Mead, L. B. (1991) *The One and Future Church*. New York: Alban Institute.

Methodist Sectors Group Newsletter (1985–1988).

Merton, R. K. (1957) 'Patterns of Influence: Local and Cosmopolitan Influentials', in *Social Theory and Social Structure*, rev. edn. New York: Free Press.

Ministers-at-Work – The Journal for Christians in Secular Ministry (CHRISM), Editor (2005): Rob Fox, 36 Norman Road, Stalybridge, Cheshire SK15 1LY.

The Ministry of the People of God (1988). Report to the Methodist Conference.

The Ministry of the People of God in the World (1990). Report to the Methodist Conference.

mission-shaped church (2004). London: Church House Publishing.

Moltmann, J. (1981) *The Trinity and the Kingdom of God*. London: SCM Press.

Morgan, G. (1986) *Images of Organisation*. London: Sage.

Moynagh, M. (2004) *emergingchurch.intro*. Oxford: Monarch Books.

Munson, J. (1991) *The Nonconformists: In Search of a Lost Culture*. London: SPCK.

Murray, S. (2004a) *Post-Christendom*. Carlisle: Paternoster Press.

Murray, S. (2004b) *Church after Christendom*. Milton Keynes: Paternoster Press.

NACCCAN's Archives. These are lodged in the Special Collection section of the University of Birmingham Library, Edgbaston, Birmingham B15 2TT and are available there for research purposes. Tel: 0121 414 3344.

NACCCAN (later NACCAN) Westhill College (1981–88), Woodbrooke College, Birmingham (1988–98), and Community House, Eton Road, Newport, Gwent NP19 0BL (1998–2003).

NACCCAN (1971–2003) *Community* (1971–93) and *Christian Community* (1993–2003). Birmingham: Westhill College.

NACCCAN (1980 and later editions) *Directory of Christian Groups, Communities and Networks.* Birmingham: Westhill College.

NACCCAN (1981) *1980 Community Congress Report.* Birmingham: Westhill College.

NACCCAN (1982–85) *New Christian Initiatives Series, Nos 1 to 7.* Birmingham: Westhill College.

NACCCAN (1985) *On the Frontiers.* Birmingham: Westhill College.

NACCCAN (1986) *Towards a New Vision of Church. A Report to the Inter-church Process.* Birmingham: Westhill College.

NACCCAN (1987) *Sharing the Vision* (D. O'Murchu). Birmingham: Westhill College.

Newbigin, L. (1980) *Your Kingdom Come.* Leeds: John Paul The Preacher's Press.

Newbigin, L. (1983) *The Other Side of 1984.* Geneva: WCC.

Newbigin, L. (1989) *The Gospel in a Pluralist Society.* London: SPCK.

The New Dictionary of Pastoral Studies (2002) London: SPCK.

'New Way of Being Church': Wells, Somerset BA5 2PD. Web site: www.newway.org.uk

Nichols, A. (1999) *Christendom Awake*, Edinburgh: T. and T. Clark.

Northcott, M. (ed.) *Urban Theology. A Reader.* (1998) London: Cassell.

On Being Ordained in Full Connexion (2002) Methodist Conference.

Palmer, P. (1987) *A Place Called Community.* Pennsylvania: Pendle Hill.

Pattison, S. (1997) *The Faith of the Managers.* London: Cassell.

Pedler, M., Burgoyne, J. and Boydell, T. (1991) *The Learning Company.* Maidenhead: McGraw-Hill.

Perham, M. (2000) *New Handbook of Pastoral Liturgy.* London: SPCK.

Plant, R. (1974) *Community and Ideology.* London: Routledge and Kegan Paul.

Plater, O. (1991) *Many Servants – An Introduction to Deacons.* Boston, MA: Cowley Publications.

Poole, R. (1991) *Morality and Modernity.* London: Routledge.

Porter, A. (2004) *Religion versus Empire: British Protestant Missionaries and Overseas Expansion, 1700–1914.* Manchester: Manchester University Press.

Pravera, K. (1981) 'The United States' in *Christianity and Crisis* (on Basic Christian Communities), vol. 41 no. 14 (September).

Reindorp, J. (2000) *Equipping Christians at Work.* London: Industrial Christian Fellowship.

Rice, A. K. (1965) *Learning for Leadership*. London: Tavistock.

Riesman, D. (1950) *The Lonely Crowd*. New York: Doubleday Anchor.

Rigby, A. (1974) *Alternative Realities*. London: Routlege and Kegan Paul.

Rockefeller Foundation (1994) *Communications as Engagement*. Washington DC: Millennium Communications Group.

Rossa, A. (1983) *Basic Ecclesial Communities – The Stand of Third-World Bishops*. Makati, Metro Manila: Society of St Paul.

Rowe, T. (1997) 'The Reformation of the Diaconal Order' in *Epworth Review* 24.2.

Rudge, P. F. (1968) *Ministry and Management*. London: Tavistock Publications.

Russell, H. (2001) *Local Strategic Partnerships*. Bristol: The Policy Press.

Sandercock, L. (1998) *Towards Cosmopolis*. Chichester: John Wiley and Sons.

Sarum College, 19 The Close, Salisbury SP1 2EB. Web site: www.sarum.ac.uk

Schon, D. A. (1983) *The Reflective Practitioner*. New York: Basic Books.

Schumacher, E. F. (1974) *Small is Beautiful*. London: Abacus.

Sedgwick, P. (ed.) (1995) *God in the City*. London: Mowbray.

Senge, P. M. (1990) *The Fifth Discipline*. New York: Currency and Doubleday.

Sherlock, C. (1996) *The Doctrine of Humanity*. Downers Grove, IL: InterVarsity Press.

Shreeve, E. and Luscombe, P. (2002) *What is a Minister?* Peterborough: Epworth Press.

Simpson, G. (1937) *Conflict and Community*. New York: Liberal Press.

SOM (1983) 'Four Personal Impressions of the Weekend Conference for Ministers in Other Appointments'. Unpublished paper. Cliff College, Derbyshire.

Stainback, S. and Stainback, W. (1992) *Curriculum Considerations in Inclusive Classrooms*. Baltimore: Pouch Books.

Staton, M. W. (2000) 'Biblical and Early Church Sources for Diaconal Ministry'. Unpublished paper.

Staton, M. W. (2001) 'The Development of the Diaconal Ministry in the Methodist Church: A Historical and Theological Study'. Unpublished PhD thesis. University of Leeds.

Staying in the City: Faith in the City Ten Years On (1995) London: Church House Publishing.

Stephenson, T. B. (1890) *Concerning Sisterhoods*. London: Charles H. Kelly.

Stevens, R. P. (1999) *The Abolition of the Laity*. Carlisle: Paternoster Press.

Taylor, J. (1979) *The Go-Between God*. Oxford: Oxford University Press.

'Theological and Biblical Reflection on *Diakonia*: A Survey of Discussions within the WCC' (1994), *The Ecumenical Review*, 46.

Thwaites, J. (2000) *The Church Beyond the Congregation*. Carlisle: Paternoster Press.

Tillich, P. (1962) *The Courage to Be*. London: Fontana.

Tolle, E. (2001) *The Power of Now*. London: Hodder and Stoughton.

Tomlinson, A. 'Encouraging the ministry of the baptized – a truly diaconal role' in *Diakoneo* (Easter 2003), Newsletter for the Center for the North American Association for the Diaconate (Episcopal) Providence, USA. For more information on 'local collaborative ministry', contact Anne Tomlinson at anniet@talk21.com.

Torres, S. and Eagleson, J. (eds) (1981) *The Challenge of Basic Christian Communities*. Maryknoll, NY: Orbis Books.

Touching Place: The Neighbours Community, 140–148 Ardington Road, Northampton NN1 5LT. Web site: www.touchingplace.co.uk.

Turner, J. M. (1998) *Modern Methodism in England 1932–1998*. Peterborough: Epworth Press.

Vaughan, P. H. (1990) *Non-stipendiary Ministry in the Church of England*. San Francisco: Mellen Research University Press.

Vicinus, M. (1985) *Independent Women: Work and Community for Single Women 1850–1920*. London: Virago Press.

Voices from the Margins (2005) Birmingham: Methodist Diaconal Order.

Walters, C. (1996) 'To the Circuits: the Methodist Diaconal Order', *Epworth Review* 23.1.

Ward, P. (2002) *Liquid Church*. Carlisle: Paternoster Press.

Warren, R. (1995) *Being Human, Being Church*. London: Marshall Pickering.

Wenger, E. (1998) *Communities of Practice*. Cambridge: Cambridge University Press.

Wenger, E. (2002) *Cultivating Communities of Practice*. Boston, MA: Harvard Business School Press.

What is a Deacon? (2004) Methodist Conference Report.

White, A. and Williams, D. (1987) *Deacons at Your Service*. Grove Pastoral Series, No. 33.

Whyte, W. H. (1956) *The Organization Man*. Harmondsworth: Penguin.

Wickham, E. R. (1957) *Church and People in an Industrial City*. London: Lutterworth Press.

Willie, E. and Hodgson, P. (1991) *Making Change Work*. London: Mercury Books.

The Windsor Statement (1997) United Kingdom Ecumenical Diaconal Consultation (1–3 October). Birmingham: Methodist Diaconal Order. Issued following a consultation between the Church of Scotland, the Scottish Episcopal Church, the British Methodist Church, the Roman Catholic Church and the Church of England. The consultation included conversations with a United Reformed Church CRCW and a Deacon in training in the Orthodox Church.

Winter, G. (1961) *The Suburban Captivity of the Churches*. New York: Doubleday.

Wuthnow, R. (1994) *Sharing the Journey – Support Groups and America's New Quest for Community*. New York: The Free Press.

Zanago, P. (2000) *Holy Saturday: An Argument for the Restoration of the Female Diaconate in the Catholic Church*. New York: Crossroad.

Subject Index

Names Index

Organizations Index